Sabine Raschhofer was born and
Following graduation from college, she set out to travel the world on a quest to find her calling. Seeking a life of freedom and fulfillment, and driven by a strong sense of adventure, Sabine moved between the various continents, taking on an eclectic range of jobs along the way. She eventually hit her stride as an entrepreneur in Australia but nine years down the track lost it all through an act of betrayal. Setting out to fight for justice, an intense legal battle and further international adventures ensued. Sabine returned to Australia in 2017 and now calls Sydney home.

Screw the Rules

Follow your heart and do your thing

Sabine Raschhofer

First published by Sabine Raschhofer in 2019
This edition published in 2019 by Sabine Raschhofer

Copyright © Sabine Raschhofer 2019
http://www.the-plan.com.au/
The moral right of the author has been asserted.

Screw the Rules

EPUB: 9781925786491
POD: 9781925786507

Cover design by Red Tally Studios

Publishing services provided by Critical Mass
www.critmassconsulting.com

Acknowledgements

Writing a book about your life is a surreal process, confronting at times but highly rewarding – more than I could have ever imagined. None of this would have been possible without the amazing support of my family. Mum, Dad, Heiner, Evelyn and Bettina, thank you so much for having always been so caring and encouraging in letting me walk my path and be who I am. Thank you for your unconditional support (in every respect) during tough times when you kept believing in me, rather than showering me with advice on what you thought was best for me or how I should be living my life. Above all, thank you for always being there for me. I couldn't have wished for a better family.

Inge Scheck, Doris Scheck and Christoph Scheck, Elfi Schmelzle, Andrew Piggott and family (including my very special goddaughter Stella) and Otto Wiesenthal from the Altstadt Vienna Hotel; thank you for sponsoring the publishing process of my book. I'm forever grateful for your support and your help in bringing my story to life.

To my editors, Ann Bolch, Jo Scanlan and Ariane Durkin (who each came onboard at various stages of the writing process); a heartfelt thank you for your efforts, inspiring insights and, above all, for taking 'my little project' so seriously.

And, finally, to Joel Naoum of Critical Mass Publishing; thank you for your patience and professionalism; it's a big world out there and it was very comforting to know that my years of work were in the best hands.

'Sometimes people don't understand the path you take. They don't have to. It's not theirs'
– Unknown

PART I

'I don't know where I'm going but I'm on my way'
– Carl Sagan

Chapter 1

An all-too-familiar bliss

It seems like madness to some that although I grew up in the spectacular beauty of the Austrian Alps, I was longing for more. I loved them – absolutely – but I was always aware of the world outside my ski-resort town of Bad Gastein, where, even though each season offered a different aspect of natural bliss, it was all too familiar. I was actually born in Salzburg, Austria, on 1 April 1970, the third of four children, all born within four years of each other. My parents had bought a hotel in the mountains a year and a half prior to my arrival, and that's where our family lived, in a congenial section of the hotel that provided us with plenty of private space (while at the same time we kids had access to various 'hide-outs' over six floors). I loved living in the hotel and, from when we were little, my siblings and I always made sure we did our part to contribute to the operations, be it by picking fresh flowers for the guest rooms in exchange for a scoop of ice cream, playing the flute for the guests in front of the Christmas tree on Christmas Eve, performing ballet (with my brother stepping in as the announcer) or acting as the head waiter's little helpers.

We learned to ski almost before we learned to walk, having the luxury of the perfect beginners' hill right on the doorstep. We spent most of our time outdoors, if not in the snow, then in trees, playing around the waterfall in town or making our first few schillings (the Austrian currency at the time) by selling bunches of fresh flowers to passersby on the promenade in front of the hotel. We only ever went home when we were hungry or when it got dark. As we grew older, the helping-out-in-the-hotel-part naturally grew less and less attractive and, by our mid-teens, during school holidays we had to decide between morning or afternoon shifts in reception, the restaurant, the kitchen or the laundry. We had to choose carefully as some shifts meant less or no time on the mountain skiing or missing out on the après-ski – dancing to live music with a beer in the hand and ski boots still on.

Testing times with Mrs G

In Austria, after primary school one either attends secondary school for four years, followed by an apprenticeship or another form of higher education, or moves on to high school, graduating with a High School Certificate (HSC). With no high school in Bad Gastein, once we each turned 13 we changed to a Catholic boarding school in Salzburg, 100 kilometres away. While one would usually enter high school at the age of ten, our parents were against sending us to boarding school at such young age so they decided to hold off until third grade when the subjects between secondary school and high school began to be markedly different.

During secondary schooling in my hometown, I never had to study much, always finishing the year among the top three. In high school, however, I was in for a surprise. I failed my first English test and I cried my eyes out on my mum's lap when she came to visit. Failing a test was completely new to me and, although my grades started to improve quickly, other than in mathematics the days of excelling were gone. This was most noticeable in German class where I seemed to have the rare talent of misinterpreting every poem or prose. And my essays, too, never quite managed to match the expectations of my German teacher, Mrs G, who quickly proceeded to postmark me *dumb*, a seal that she never removed.

Once I had reached the final year of high school and it was time to choose subjects for the HSC, I selected German as one of my three required oral exams. (If one failed a written exam, one would automatically have to take it orally. Considering I was bound to misinterpret what was going to be put in front of me

4

for my written exam, I had to be smart enough to make German one of my three oral exams from the onset to avoid ending up with a fourth subject.) Mrs G was not pleased. She wanted only her brightest students to take the oral exam, as their performance would reflect well on her teaching. As expected, I failed the written exam. Mrs G had made it clear she wanted me to fall at the next step. When it was time for the orals, I faced the challenge extremely well prepared, having studied German literature back to front for weeks, barely bothering with the other subjects that I had to pass at the HSC. Considering that the oral examination was going to take place in front of an internal committee as well as other students, I felt pretty confident that I would pass.

Mrs G, however, was a step ahead of me and had decided to test me on a subject that we had never touched on during class. I was rather confused when I was presented with the questions but figured it must have been covered on one of my days off. Thankfully, a couple of my classmates were present during my exam and, once I had been told that I had failed, approached me, confirming that they also didn't know what Mrs G had been talking about and that we had never gone over that specific subject matter in class. What followed was a meeting with the school's principal, my year's head teacher and the school's psychology teacher. I was given the option to either re-take the exam in front of an external committee or to report back after summer – in three months' time along with all the other students who had failed the first time round – after which I would be guaranteed a pass. (Obviously option two was the preferred option for the school considering the effect on the school's reputation if an external committee had to get involved.) I chose option two.

My German teacher's attitude towards my abilities left a significant emotional scar in regards to my confidence and self-esteem. Her degrading comments instilled over time ensured that – in certain areas in my life – I would feel inadequate for years to come. It was only in my mid-thirties that I started to look at it all from a different perspective, when someone for whom I had the utmost respect expressed his admiration of my communication skills.

The odd one out

Overall, my mid-teens were a challenge in the sense that I often felt like the odd one out, that I didn't quite fit in. Two years my senior, my brother Heiner was this naturally cool guy who, from a young age, had the ability to gather a squad of people around him; he was forever the leader of the pack and someone I invariably looked up to. My sister Evelyn, less than a year older than me, was also extremely popular and always part of the in-group. She was very pretty with a great sense of style and it seemed like every boy in town was after her. The number of letters, flowers and other presents that were delivered to her in boarding school was simply ridiculous. And Bettina, my younger sister by a year and a half, was this gorgeous girl everyone loved, the cute 'little one'. She had a lively and charming personality as well as a sense for fashion that was always ahead of her time. And then there was me – the one with the odd haircut, who always tried to copy her sisters but never quite succeeded. I remember that when Evelyn got a cool green pair of pants, I too wanted green pants; but my pants turned out to be a very uncool version – wrong material, wrong cut, wrong green. I was trying so hard, but I simply didn't have the style. I was also quite envious of my sisters' friends. They seemed to have a much more exciting and trendier group of girls in their year; they were always on the go and in general appeared to have a good deal more fun than me and my classmates.

When I was about 15, after a day of skiing with a few friends during Christmas break, I overheard one of my brother's cool friends say to another male friend '… Evelyn and Bettina are so pretty and so much fun, but Sabine doesn't really have anything to pride herself on'. I had always been rather shy and insecure and I was very much aware that I wasn't as popular as my sisters (not that I was ugly, I was just trying too hard to be someone I wasn't) but that comment stabbed me in the chest. The situation then got even worse when my brother's friend turned around and saw me standing right behind him.

Following that incident my sisters kept trying to push me to have more fun and join them on their nights out, but for quite a while I convinced myself more often than not that I would be better off staying at home, rather than having to change clothes, face the cold and not get much sleep. Although my brother's friend's comment at the time was a tough one to take, it was certainly character building. It taught me to fend for myself early on, igniting a 'just you wait!' kind of attitude. In school I gradually turned into a rebel, going against the rules when they didn't make sense and standing up for myself when I didn't believe in the status quo.

Envisioning my future

What I had always wanted from my mid-teens on was to travel and by the time I reached my final year of high school my main focus was on finding a way to live overseas for a while. The solution seemed to be a program through Rotary International that would give me the opportunity to study in the United States for a year. To qualify, I had to go to quite some effort, which included completing a set of forms, acquiring doctors' certificates and writing essays to prove a certain standard of the English language. It took me weeks to get it all done. When I proudly presented the completed file to my dad to get his seal of approval before submitting it, he readily put his signature on the first couple of pages that had to be signed off by a parent. But when it came to the final autograph, he paused, looked up at me and eventually stated, rather firmly, that I ought to have a higher education certificate before going overseas. I tried to argue my way out of it but to no avail. All those weeks of excitement and focus on gathering the information to qualify for my year abroad turned out to have been a waste of time and energy.

Although I had always known – or these days I prefer to say I believed I knew – that my future wasn't going to be in the hospitality industry, once I had passed my HSC at the end of the summer holidays, I ended up getting a Diploma in Hotel and Tourism Management. I had come to the conclusion that this would be the quickest and easiest way to get me travelling, rather than moving on to university and being stuck in one place for years to come. (Not to mention that I had never been the studious type to begin with. I had liked the idea of being a scientist but with the emphasis on *being*, rather than becoming.)

By the age of 18 I had found my own style and was starting to feel more confident in my skin. My two years at college turned out to be a time that I would cherish forever. My brother as well as my sisters had attended the same school. At the age of 14, my younger sister had started the trend with enrolling in the hotel school, which was located on the same grounds, then my brother and older sister followed suit by gaining the equivalent education at college. Over four years, each year there was an intake of yet another Raschhofer. By the time it was my turn, it appeared that every teacher had already put me into the 'love' or 'hate' basket – there didn't seem to be much in between – without having met me. Most of the students in my year were several years older than I and had come from all walks of life and all corners of the world, making for an interesting mix. With a certain reputation preceding my arrival, I quickly managed to join the cool gang, which was a very welcome change.

Within my family it was agreed that once we finished college, my siblings and I would take turns working at home – a year at a time each. Considering that I had envisioned my future elsewhere and certainly not in hospitality (not that I had a clue about the specifics of this 'elsewhere'), I couldn't quite call myself the originator of that idea; yet it seemed like a fair deal to start off with. My brother Heiner and my younger sister Bettina were going to be placed at the Hotel Auersperg in Salzburg, my maternal grandma's hotel that my parents had taken over years earlier. My older sister Evelyn and I were to rotate at Haus Hirt, the hotel in the mountains.

Dad was a 'born' old-school hotelier (although he was actually from an age-old beer-brewing family) who lived his profession with a heart and passion rarely seen these days. While Dad had always held the fort on the frontline, Mum was mostly behind the scenes, at least during the day. At night Mum would join Dad behind the bar to entertain the guests, while at the same time bringing up four children and trying to instil in us the high values that they both exemplified. And while Evelyn was the creative type and all about innovation and the comfort of the guests, I felt most at ease behind the desk, putting my efficiency and organisational skills to work. To my surprise, I ended up rather enjoying my full-time position at the hotel, but once I had served my first year working at home, I could hardly wait for Evelyn to return from overseas to take over my spot and open the gate for me.

Chapter 2

On the road

So here I was, finally on the road. My first stop was Sardinia, a stunning island off the coast of Italy where I was going to work as a receptionist at a hotel on the Costa Smeralda for the summer season. Having been given my grandma's old car, I drove off to Zucchero, one of my favourite Italian singers, blasting from the speakers and over the next nine hours only stopped for petrol and 'lap-food'.

At 3am and still rather awake, I arrived in Livorno, the port from which I was to take the ferry to Sardinia in the morning. After parking in a public car park in town, I wound back the seat and went to sleep. Shortly after I was woken by a knock on my window from the police. I told them I would be catching the ferry in a few hours' time, but they wouldn't have it. Instead they gave me a firm talk about the dangers of a young girl sleeping in a car and suggested I follow them in my car to find a hotel. As kind a gesture as this was, on no account was I prepared to spend any money on a hotel room, especially considering there were only a few hours left. The first hotel the *poliziotti* stopped at was fully booked. And when they got out of their car to knock on the second door, I quickly drove off. Once I was sure I had lost them I parked the car at a hidden car park in front of a large hotel close to the harbour. Proud of my successful escape, I couldn't wait for the real adventure to begin.

What a fabulous summer it was. There were days when I lay on the beach but couldn't relax due to the immense feeling of happiness that made my heart race. This was the first time I'd been away on my own and I loved every bit of it. I loved the island, the Italian way of life, the crystal clear ocean and the beautiful beaches; I loved working at the hotel and dealing with the mostly Italian clientele. Above all I loved the feeling of freedom.

Yet, it hadn't been easy to start off with. During a couple of months of a previous summer I had studied the Italian language at the Universita per gli Stranieri in Perugia, Italy, and although I was doing pretty well when it came to structuring sentences, I was lacking experience in communication. When I had first arrived at the hotel in Sardinia that I was going to work at for the season and Stephano, the hotel's director, flooded me with questions, I barely understood a word. This was embarrassing enough, but not as bad as the time when the maintenance guy – I think his name was Giovanni – who was based at the partner hotel Abi d'Oru at nearby Golfo di Marinella, stormed in one day and asked who the idiot was who couldn't understand Italian. *Well, that would be me*, I responded, with a bright red face. He had called several times over the previous couple of days and I always had to ask him at least three times to please repeat what he had just said. I simply couldn't understand him; mind you, he never considered adjusting his dialect or slowing down his speech. Being forced to speak and listen to the Italian language full-time, I didn't take long to get the hang of it. When Giovanni came by just a few weeks later, he looked at me and announced, '*Cazzo come parli bene adesso!*' (F..., you speak well now!). I couldn't have been more excited to hear these words.

My boyfriend at the time, Stephan, came to visit one day and ended up getting a job as a night auditor/bar-man/pool attendant. On our days off we drove around the island, slept on the beach or in the car and sneaked into the pool areas of exclusive five-star hotels for our morning showers. Having grown up in a hotel I was a bit more inhibited than Stephan when it came to certain behaviours that our lifestyle forced us into. We weren't quite in backpacker territory but rather the Costa Smeralda, one of the most expensive locations in Europe, well known for drawing the rich and famous. So when, one day, Stephan stripped down to his boxer shorts at a petrol station, took the water hose that he had spotted not far from the petrol pumps, hosed himself down and brushed his teeth right there in front of everyone, it hit my limit of bearable embarrassment. However, it wasn't long before I found myself at home in such situations.

My dad thought alternating between working at home and going overseas would be great for gaining work experience in various corners of the world. This was based on his own very successful career, which had started with the graduation from hotel school at the age of 18 and took him on a journey that, over 13 years, had seen him work in top positions at some of the most exclusive hotels around the world. I always loved listening to my dad's stories. In 1962 he drove a VW Beetle from Berlin in Germany to Jordan in the Middle East (and later on to Baghdad in Iraq) to be part of the pre-opening team of the Al Urdon Hotel in Amman. While Dad held the position of assistant manager, the hotel was later officially opened by His Majesty, King Hussein. Twenty-five years later, on a trip to Jordan with my mum in 1987, Dad returned to the Al-Urdon Hotel where he was excitedly greeted by a former employee still working there. With a huge smile on his face the employee pulled out his wallet and proudly presented a business card that Dad had given him all those years ago. He humbly told Dad that he was the best manager he had ever had.

So Dad's were big shoes to fill. But at that stage in my life, I had other priorities, especially considering that I was yet to find my real calling. And what better way to do that than to go backpacking around the world for a year – a plan that Stephan and I had forged while in Italy. Nervous about how to break the news to my parents, I thought it best to tell them while they were visiting in Sardinia for a week. In order to ease my parents into the idea of our backpacking trip, I told them that we would be gone for half a year. I figured that six months down the track, when we had only covered half the itinerary, they would get the idea that the whole trip might take a little longer. Expecting to be faced with having to defend and justify my plans, I was stunned – to say the least – to be met with not much of a reaction from either of my parents. Dad didn't show the slightest bit of disappointment in me. It couldn't have been easy to hold back words of worry and to not hand out well-meant advice as to what was best for me and my future. With the one 'hurdle' jumped, all that was now left to do was to strike a deal with my older sister to extend my absence from the family hotel by half a year, giving me a year and a half all up (including my summer in Italy). I would then do the same for her upon my return.

From when I was a young girl I had proclaimed that one day I was going to emigrate to Australia. I still don't have a clue where that idea came from, considering that, at the time, I didn't even know where Australia was. I can only assume that I heard someone talk about it or had seen a documentary on TV at some stage. When I told Stephan that I wanted to go to Australia and asked if he would be interested in joining me, he suggested we spend time in Asia along the way. This is how our idea of the round-the-world trip was born. Among my friends there had always been a sentiment that growing up in a nice hotel would be a free pass to a spoilt life and that every step I was going to take would be funded by my parents. Yet this couldn't have been further from the truth. From when we were little, Mum and Dad had always been careful not to 'spoil' us. For example, desserts, soft drinks and the like were out of the question. Only on Sunday were we allowed the occasional piece of cake and orange juice; any additional treat had to be earned. And an around-the-world airline ticket now certainly wouldn't be subsidised either. Working at home – followed by a season in a resort town – had the added benefit of saving money. With food and accommodation provided, I had been doing rather well in filling up the piggy bank over the previous year. While our trip was going to require significant investment, with the help of the occasional job along the way, we were positive we would manage.

As soon as we returned to Austria from our summer in Italy we organised our visas, got the required vaccinations and off we went. I can still see my parents waving me good-bye at the train station in Salzburg. I was 21 and, having grown up in a privileged and protected environment, this was going to be a very different experience. It was hard to imagine that I would be gone for a year, living a very exciting but comparably unpredictable and – considering our budget – most likely quite rough life. Stephan was a cool, fun guy, but from when I had first met him, he'd had the tendency to be rather hard – on me, and in general. There was never much room for being unwell, let alone for any moaning or groaning. He had travelled to Asia with his family twice before over the previous couple of years and, based on his experience and prior to getting onto the plane in Vienna, my backpack now had to go through his meticulous inspection. I wasn't 'allowed' much more than a rain jacket, jeans and shorts – a pair each – one jumper, a few t-shirts, a cap and a hand towel (we were going to get a thin and light sarong in Thailand, in lieu of a larger towel) and very basic toiletries. The rest of the backpack had to be filled with books and practical things like a torch and first aid kit.

Upon arrival in Bangkok, our first stop, Stephan assured me that in view of our plans and the fact that we were going to rough it over the following 12 months, I would be much better off with short hair. I agreed, letting him cut my rather long mane into a wobbly bob. The following day we left the city lights behind and off we went on our adventure. As excited as I was, it undoubtedly required some adjusting to fully embrace the whole 'backpacking on a shoestring' experience. From the get-go our travels turned out to be far more strenuous than I had expected and it wasn't long before I started doubting what had originally sounded like a dream-adventure. Always choosing the roads less travelled, I was generally the only girl around, trying to keep up with the boys until only a couple of weeks into our trip, while trekking somewhere in the middle of nowhere close to the border with Myanmar, I found myself wondering how I was going to hold up for yet another eleven and a half months. I loved the adventure, the jungle and the amazing scenery as much as experiencing new cultures and meeting the local people, but I wasn't used to the heat, the very different diet and the little sleep; and before long I got rather sick, with my body emptying at either end every half hour or so until I was throwing up bile. Yet the sorrier I felt for myself, the tougher Stephan turned, telling me to pull myself together. After another couple of weeks, however, I started to wholeheartedly adapt to the experience, changing my 'counting down' to 'Oh my gosh, the first month is over – there are only eleven more to go!'

In 1991 the whole backpacking scene in Asia was very different to what it is today. One would always meet a few fellow travellers along the way, but it was still a bit of a novelty for backpackers and locals alike, especially as soon as one found oneself even just slightly off the beaten track. We had agreed with our parents that we would try to contact them every second Friday. Mail took a long time and we wanted to make sure that our family and friends knew we were well and safe. Whenever we anticipated finding ourselves in a remote area on 'phone day' we would let our parents know in advance. There was no such thing as a public phone booth (let alone mobile phones), so making a call to Austria always turned into a half-day adventure, trying to find a 'call-centre' where an operator, using an antiquated phone, would attempt to place the call for us. At times it took hours for the operator to get through to either of our parents and then it was usually not much more than 'Everything's great, how about you? Good, thanks. Bye.' It was an exercise that would cost us about a day's budget.

The exciting thing was snail mail. Every few weeks we would give our family and friends an approximate schedule of when we would be at a major city so that they could write to us 'poste restante'. The anticipation of getting to a post office in a far-away place to see if there was mail waiting was immense. I still remember when we got to Singapore in late December and I even had a Christmas parcel waiting for me. There's nothing better than handwritten letters from family and friends when you are on a different continent and always on the move, not able to communicate much.

From the north of Thailand we slowly made our way south, travelling 'third class' on the cheapest train and bus fares, often seated among chickens and screaming roosters. By the beginning of December we had reached the far south and decided to take a ferry across to the Ko Tarutao National Park. The night we arrived we went for a walk along the beach. It was a beautiful beach set in a national park, but somehow had a weird feel to it. There were no food stalls, no locals trying to sell coconuts or pineapples or none of the hustle and bustle that we had become so used to. What we got in exchange were oodles of mosquitoes and sand flies. We had an early night that night. The following morning I awoke to an alarmingly high fever, chills and sweats. I could hardly move my head and my whole body ached. Stephan went and consulted a fellow traveller who we had met the night before and was a doctor by profession. Judging from my symptoms, the Swiss doctor believed I had contracted malaria. As a first-aid measure and to hopefully kill the virus, he suggested that I take six of each of the two types of malaria pills we had been taking on a weekly basis since leaving Austria. I did as I was told and, with no further resources on the island and feeling extremely weak, Stephan and I made our way back to the mainland, heading straight to the first hospital that we came across. As lovely as the resident doctors and nurses were, I was unable to properly communicate my symptoms and soon it became obvious that they didn't understand us the slightest bit. After several attempts of trying to explain to them – with hands and feet – that I was feeling very sick, one of the doctors handed me five different sachets of pills, as if hoping that one of these would sort me out.

With both Stephan and I starting to get worried, we decided to head to Malaysia (among travellers Malaysia was known as the place to go in a medical emergency). By the time we left the hospital it was already late afternoon and we found ourselves stuck for the night in Had Yai, a small town just north of the border. The following morning, we rose early and by 7am were piled into a so-called 'shared cab' and on our way to Malaysia. The trip soon came to an abrupt end when the cab broke down half way and we were left on the side of the highway, desperately trying to hitch a ride.

Our journey started to turn into a real ordeal. I was barely able to stand up, with a woollen sarong wrapped around my head and neck, shivering in the humid heat and feeling weaker by the minute. We eventually got picked up by a large flower delivery truck, which, once we had left the highway, seemed to stop at every corner. At long last we made it to Butterworth by early evening, from where we took a ferry across to Penang, an island off the coast of Malaysia that we had been told would be our best and closest option for medical treatment. Upon arrival at our final destination, we flagged down a rickshaw (a three-wheeled, human-powered passenger cart) and while I just sat there, all curled up and hoping for nothing more than a bed, Stephan directed our driver from guesthouse to guesthouse trying to find a free room.

After touring half of Georgetown, we eventually found a small Chinese hotel where we were given our own, clean room with *real* beds. This was pure bliss. But the best thing about that place was the lady doctor next door to the hotel who had studied in England for several years and spoke perfect English. She, too, suggested I had contracted malaria and that taking an overdose of Lariam and Fansidar, the malaria pills that we had been carrying on us, had been the right course of action. Apparently, nothing else could be done at that stage. Both Lariam and Fansidar were among the strongest malaria prophylaxis available at the time. And while 'feeding' my body with six pills each in one go – after having already taken them on a weekly basis for several weeks – might have killed the malaria, it also left me extremely weak. I felt like I had been put on a form of chemotherapy; everything I ate and drank tasted like chemicals. Each sip of water made me feel sick. I had such a strong chemical taste in my mouth that I could no longer handle drinking plain water, resorting to sugared soft drinks to try and overpower the taste. This was the first and only time I saw Stephan cry. We were both scared, and worried whether I'd recover enough to continue travelling.

If you told anyone today that the Tropical Institute in Vienna that we consulted in regards to vaccinations and malaria prophylaxis before we left Austria had recommended taking both Lariam and Fansidar for several months, they would shake their head in disbelief. To my knowledge, both medications have been prohibited in various countries, at least in the form available at the time. It took many months to regain my energy, but the effects of the malaria pills showed long after we had returned to Europe. By the end of our trip I had lost about half my hair and it continued to fall out in small strands for several months. I began to have nightmares about waking up bald but thankfully my hair started to grow back eventually.

Although I was still fragile, it wasn't too long before we were able to continue on our trip, moving on to the Cameron Highlands, in inland Malaysia, to get away from the heat. What followed was a nice, quiet Christmas in the mountains, New Year's Eve in Singapore – which, with all its restrictions, turned out to not have been a very good choice – and a couple of months in Hong Kong, where we made a temporary home of the infamous Traveller's Hostel on the 16th floor of the equally infamous Chunking Mansions block in Kowloon. It was time to supplement our budget. Among backpackers Hong Kong was rated as a pretty good place to find short-term work, a notion that proved itself right when within 20 minutes of scouting the area, I scored a job as a waitress at Mad Dog's, an English pub right next door to the hostel and Stephan was offered a position as a barman at the German Beer Café around the corner. While I commenced work literally a couple of days after we had arrived in Hong Kong, Stephan's job wasn't to start for another two weeks, which prompted him to travel to China in the meantime. Full of Stephan's interesting stories upon his return to Hong Kong – and his longstanding sentiment that I supposedly wasn't able to do anything by myself in the back of my mind – I decided to follow suit. I left work a couple of weeks before Stephan finished and embarked on a trip to China – on my own.

Travelling in China was a whole new experience. Upon arriving in Guangzhou, the town right across the border from Hong Kong, I faced my first challenge – getting to the hostel without being able to communicate on any level. I pushed myself into a bus crammed with locals and tried to follow the course of the road, comparing it with the map in my guidebook, in the hope of eventually identifying the right stop. This wasn't an easy task considering that the bus was so packed I could hardly see out of the window, let alone read any Chinese street signs. Stephan had already warned me that, once I crossed the border, nobody would speak or understand even a word of English. In the end I had no choice but to get off the bus without a clue where the hell I was. As it turned out, my instincts were still in good shape and, with the use of sign language, my map and the limited dictionary in the back of my guidebook (pointing out each word to a passerby), I eventually discovered that my destination was only a few minutes down the road.

Determined to prove myself and put together my own itinerary, the following day I embarked on a trip to remember. The first leg of my journey was a 17-hour boat ride to Wuzhou, which – as the only tourist on board – proved a good introduction to the

Chinese culture, especially when it came to staring and spitting. The male passengers were assigned one side of the boat. Women took over the opposite side. We had two storeys each with a small aisle in between. Each passenger was allocated a wooden plank as a sitting and sleeping area, with a 10-centimetre-high division separating one from his or her neighbour. The 'beds' hadn't quite been designed for Western frames though, forcing me to roll up my shoulders to avoid squashing the Chinese ladies on either side of me. For the whole trip it seemed like at least 20 pairs of eyes were on me, staring me down without even the slightest attempt at subtlety. Especially the men right across from me, who kept gazing at me as if they had been freeze-dried. Not knowing where to look – staring back at them wasn't a comfortable option – I decided to lie down and cover myself, including my head, with a sarong and try to sleep. Whenever I woke up and looked around, none of those eyes seemed to have moved. Not that I was sleeping much anyway with all that throat clearing and spitting going on around me. Not to talk about my excursions to the toilet, where trying to navigate my way through the mucus and the rubbish that was building up on the aisle en-route was a challenge in itself. Once I arrived in Wuzhou my journey continued with an eight-and-a-half-hour bus ride to Yangzhou. It was February and freezing cold and the glass was missing from several windows. I emptied all the clothes from my backpack and perfected the art of layering, putting on every single t-shirt, my only sweatshirt, and my rain jacket, finishing off with my sarong wrapped tightly around me. Although still freezing, the scenery was stunning and I very much enjoyed the trip.

My time in China was, without doubt, a great experience; it was challenging at times, but I loved it. I hardly spoke a word over the two weeks that I was there. There were no heaters other than the odd little black container filled with hot coals that was placed next to one's feet at selected cafés and restaurants, nor was there any hot water. But the times that take you out of your comfort zone are the ones you end up cherishing the most.

From Hong Kong, Stephan and I went back to Singapore, up the east coast of Malaysia, and across the country to Penang from where we crossed the Strait of Malacca to reach one of my favourite places that we visited in Asia, the Indonesian island of Sumatra. From Nias, a small island off the west coast of Sumatra, we managed to get onto a cargo ship that was heading south and was scheduled to anchor in Padang, the capital of West Sumatra, a few days later. The ship wasn't designed to host passengers and while we would have been more than happy to sleep on deck, this was not an option. Instead we were offered the beds of two crew members in exchange for extra money. Our cabin was a tiny one that we shared with other crew. It was extremely hot and humid with next to no air and an obvious breeding ground for cockroaches. I had never seen so many in the one spot; they were of the smallest kind, but you could feel them crawling all over you during the night. Due to the heat, we were each provided with an additional large cuddle-pillow to wipe off the constant flow of sweat during the night. The 'bathroom' was a small dark room in the hallway shared by the whole crew. The water in the *mandi* (a large tub filled with water that one pours over oneself using a plastic pan) must have been sitting in the tub for days and my first attempt at a refreshing 'shower' resulted in a rash all over my body, after which I decided to opt out of any wash routine for the remaining three days and chose to bathe in my sweat instead.

What was so special about this trip was the purpose of it. The ship had a big market in its hull carrying all kinds of consumables for the people who lived on the remote surrounding islands. Along the way to Padang it stopped at several different locations in the middle of the ocean, with natives from the islands approaching from every direction in their log-boats – some of them with plastic sails – filled with coconuts, bananas, wood or whatever else they had to offer in exchange for goods from the ship's market, like toothpaste, shampoo and cookies. It was such an awe-inspiring sight. The picture still remains clear in my head as much as the picture of our room when we arrived in Padang. Bed sheets had never looked that white, a bed had never seemed that big and a shower had never felt that good.

The following three months we spent exploring other Indonesian islands. From Sumatra we returned to Singapore, boarding a ship down to Java, from where we made our way to Bali and on to Sulawesi, Lombok, Sumbawa, Flores – with a side-trip to Komodo Island – and West-Timor.

I was very lucky to have had recovered from malaria as well as I had but, having grown up in the mountains and having always been very fit, it was a frustrating experience when at times the slightest bit of exercise, especially climbing the various volcanoes that we passed along the way, turned into a fighting game between my mind and my body. My mind was always more than willing but my body, more often than not weak and shaky, wasn't. For some reason it never seemed to occur to either Stephan or I to attribute the weakness to the after-effect of the malaria. Stephan kept pushing me and asking me to pull myself together when at times all I wanted was to lie down, cry and feel sorry for myself, not knowing what the hell was wrong with me.

After eight most amazing months in Southeast Asia, it was eventually time to move on to Australia and from Kupang, the main port on the island of Timor, we now boarded a short flight across to Darwin in the far north of the country. I was incredibly excited. I was about to set foot on the continent that, for years, I had been claiming to one day make my home.

As is often the case, however, expectations didn't quite match reality and my first impression of Down Under left me feeling rather irritated and, walking down the streets of Darwin, lost and lonely in a weird kind of way. I wished myself back to Indonesia, or Thailand, or Hong Kong – anywhere there was more life, more chaos, more people. I missed the hustle and bustle. We had become so used to crowded streets, to the noise, the hubbub and the colours – and not forgetting the many food stalls – that we weren't quite ready for the polar opposite. When we got off the plane at the airport, our first sight was a tall, rather white Australian lady with a cowboy hat who had come to greet the passengers on the tarmac, a large open space with no one else around. Downtown was marked by wide, empty, perfectly 'groomed' streets. Everything appeared way too organised to the point of feeling sterile.

My initial view of Australia clearly reflected my perception based on everything we had become used to over the previous eight months and it didn't take long for us to again fully immerse ourselves into the adventure, wishing we had more time to spend in that spellbinding country. Due to time constraints, we decided to first explore the outback and to then follow the typical backpackers' route along the east coast of the country. Sharing a car with an English couple, we drove from Darwin to Alice Springs and Ayers Rock (Uluru) in the so-called red centre of Australia, passing through the various national parks along the way. Next we took a flight to Cairns on the Great Barrier Reef. From Cairns we slowly made our way south to Sydney, hitchhiking all the way. This was in 1992, the year of the infamous 'backpacker murders' (a spate of serial killings with its seven victims being backpackers aged between 19 and 22), a horror story we only found out about on our final leg, when our ride, an ocker Aussie in a huge truck – one of the most warmhearted people we had come across – warned us to be careful because hitchhiking was no longer the way to go, at least not in New South Wales.

My original idea of 'a year in Australia' turned into a six-week stint. Once we reached Sydney – and with the final months of our trip rapidly approaching – we were left with no choice but to move on. Our next destination was New Zealand – best described, in its entirety, as a natural spectacle. With the country's extremely friendly and laid-back people and a hitchhiking culture that was still intact, it turned out to be yet another highlight on our itinerary. The least that people picking us up on the side of the road would do was drop us directly at our chosen backpackers (the new-age hostels, generally much smaller with more of a 'homely' feel than your usual hostel). The more likely scenario was that they would first invite us into their home for coffee and cake, or take us to their remote farm and offer accommodation for a night or two.

Continuing to make our way east, we were hit with yet another shock to our systems when we arrived on the island of Oahu, Hawaii, another six weeks later. I'd been very much looking forward to Hawaii, expecting everyone to run around in grass skirts (not literally, but kind of) and flowers in their hair. Instead, we were confronted by the sight of girls strutting along in high heels and red Ferraris zooming past. At least that was our first impression based on Waikiki, the touristy part of the island framed by five-star hotels, and following a very relaxed New Zealand that was dominated by checkered fleece shirts and utes (very small trucks). Life in Hawaii felt way too fast and trendy for us, so once we had given it the obligatory couple of days, we happily left for mainland USA.

Upon arrival in LA and eager to leave the city lights behind, we rented a cheap station wagon with a box of camping gear fitted to its rooftop and embarked on a tour of Arizona, Utah and Nevada, returning to LA via San Francisco and the famed Highway No 1. Last but not least and to ease us back into 'real life' we decided to spend a couple of days in Chicago, before flying to the Dutch city of Amsterdam, where Evelyn, my older sister, came to meet us – to hand me the baton while she set out on her year and a half away. It was the end to a most amazing year filled with experiences and impressions that were ours to keep; and that, without doubt, shaped me in various ways.

Chapter 3
Taking flight

Over the course of our year away and to stay true to his mission to rough it, Stephan had grown his hair and a beard and by the time we arrived back in Austria he looked rather rugged and 'suspicious', to the extent where at our final few border crossings – starting with our entry into the USA – my luggage was searched every single time simply, I suspect, because I was his girlfriend. As for my own appearance, after 12 months' travelling, apart from my jeans that were now ripped in more places than not and my boots that looked like they had seen a few jungle trails, I still looked as innocent and 'normal' as before we had left. Evelyn seemed a bit disappointed when she first saw me. I'm not sure what she had expected but there was really not much I could do about it then – it was too late for dreadlocks or whatever else she was hoping to see. My only option to spice up my looks for the rest of the family was a fake tattoo that I managed to get in Amsterdam and that I was hoping would do the trick to give my parents a bit of an initial shock when they came to meet me at the airport.

We arrived in Austria in late autumn, probably the most hostile time of year. I went straight to Bad Gastein, where two-thirds of the town was shut down as it was the off season. I was greeted with the vibe of a ghost town. Quite keen to get my brain cells into gear again, I spent the following few weeks in the hotel, mostly by myself, getting ready for the start of the winter season. It took a bit of adjusting but I found it surprisingly easy to get back into the swing of things. As agreed with Evelyn, I stayed working at the hotel for a year and a half. I was lucky in that I 'scored' two winter seasons, of which the second one turned out to be truly legendary. My parents had meanwhile moved to Salzburg with only the occasional visit and Bettina, my younger sister, had come to help me with the running of the hotel. We complemented each other perfectly and within no time perfected a system that allowed us to work our butts off *and* enjoy the advantages of living in a ski resort.

As much as I actually enjoyed working at the family hotel and living in a ski resort surrounded by a great group of friends – most of whom were only around during the winter season, the summer was a whole different story – I still very much felt that this was not where I belonged and that my calling was elsewhere. I had just turned 24 and I couldn't keep living my life ruled by a one-year-on, one-year-off arrangement. It was time to figure out what I *really* wanted to do and I could only do that if I was free, without the mental ties that came with having to return in yet another year's time. I anticipated difficult conversations with my family to follow but to my surprise my parents, as well as my siblings, accepted my decision without trying to hold me back.

I left Austria again at the beginning of June 1994. My immediate plan was to visit an old college friend of mine who was working in a hotel on Isla Margarita, an island in the Caribbean off the north-eastern coast of Venezuela, followed by a trip to Merida, one of the main cities of the Venezuelan Andes, to study Spanish. In mid-August another friend of mine, Arno, was getting married in the country's capital, Caracas, which would then leave me with a couple of months to travel around South America before eventually moving on to Whistler, Canada, for the winter season.

En route to Venezuela I stopped over in New York to meet up with both my sisters and to hand the baton back to Evelyn for one final time. The next stop was, as planned, Isla Margarita. It wasn't quite what I had envisioned the Caribbean to look like, but I had a great time with my friend Klaus, who showed me around the island and gave me a bit of an insight into the local life. The unfortunate side of the island was its crime rate. Whenever we went out at night I had to tie my hair and wear a cap while driving in Klaus' roofless

Jeep, it being too dangerous to be recognised as female. And the seashore didn't seem to be the safest place either. Due to several shootings over the previous weeks, guests had been advised to stay away from the beach after 4pm. Interestingly enough, however, this didn't appear to bother anyone other than me. It was the start of the soccer World Cup and almost no one out of the mostly German clientele seemed to have any intentions to leave the hotel at any time of the day. I still wonder if it wouldn't have been cheaper to watch the World Cup at home.

Back on the mainland, I went on a 14-hour bus ride up into the Andes where I had arranged to meet my friends Karina, Stephan (a different Stephan – my boyfriend Stephan and I had decided to go separate ways about a year earlier) and Schnovo in Merida. With a few weeks before Arno's wedding, we settled into a basic but nice apartment and got ourselves a Spanish teacher. About 10 days into studying Spanish we thought learning how to paraglide would be better. On a previous night out we had met a German guy, Frank, who ran a paragliding school with a couple of locals and it didn't take much convincing to sign us all up for a course. Growing up in the mountains, I had always wanted to take up paragliding but my mum, well aware of the accidents reported in the papers from time to time, had urged me not to. Taking the lessons in Merida therefore seemed a good choice; Mum wouldn't have to worry as she would never find out.

The outline of the course was a solid one, including theory, practical training on a small hill and a tandem flight from the top of the mountain. There was also going to be a written test before the eventual first solo flight. Unlike in Austria where, to launch your paraglider, you would usually run down a hill and pull it up behind you – with the option to back out at any time if you didn't feel comfortable or if the paraglider wouldn't pull up the way it should – the launching pad for our first solo flight was a small space adjacent to a gravel road close to the top of a mountain. In the middle of nowhere and with no car in sight, we were free to lay out the lines with the canopy in part sitting on the road behind us. The nature of the site meant that we couldn't rely on much more than a couple of steps to launch the paraglider and lift off.

There wasn't much room – literally – for error. Once set up, Frank gave us a rundown on what to do and what not to do and off he went, waiting for us at the bottom of the mountain, ready to deliver instructions from down below for our first 'real landing'. I'd be lying if I said that I wasn't sh… my pants when it came to my turn. We had one of Frank's colleagues up there with us and each student had a radio through which we received instructions, but that wasn't going to be much help if we made a mistake at take-off and ended up down the cliff. In the end, we all did well, and it was a huge adrenalin rush. This certainly gave us more of a kick than a Spanish lesson could ever have and we still learned a fair bit of Spanish while trying to converse with the locals.

The following day we went to Las Gonzalez, a popular location for paragliders and, due to its high Andean walls and strong thermal winds, well known among pros. Located about an hour from Merida, it was a rough, rocky ascent to the top. The ride itself had already warmed up my nerves when we packed a couple more guys into – or rather onto – the four-wheel drive, precariously hanging out the side of the Jeep just above the edge of the cliff while we maneuvered our way up. By the time we arrived on top – a small plateau also home to some wild horses – it was already late afternoon. The launch site, about 1500 metres above sea level with a descent of approximately 900 metres, was brimming with local paragliders, several of whom competed internationally. Watching the pros doing crazy acrobatics in the air was an inspiring sight. There were several tandem flights that were in line to take off and when my turn finally came around, Frank was hesitant to let me fly. Although officially that day was no longer part of the course, he still felt responsible. The sun was setting quickly and this was only my second flight. The problem wasn't just that darkness was approaching, but also that the location of the landing site was hidden by a cliff face to the right.

After some to-ing and fro-ing and having expressed my disappointment if I were to be forced to return via the road rather than the air, Frank suggested that he go first and turn on the lights of a car that was waiting at the bottom to make the landing site more visible for me as it was getting dark. Again, the take-off was more of a step off a cliff than a run down a mountain but conditions were perfect and off I went. The sun was setting in front of me and, with scenery like that of a Western film, I was gliding along in seventh heaven. I forgot everything around me for a while until it eventually occurred to me that it would probably be a good idea to look for the landing site. The night was moving in faster than I was comfortable with. There were no markers – street lights, buildings or other – to judge my distance to the ground, and together with an obvious lack of experience, I believed myself to be much higher up in the air than I actually was. Panic-fuelled, I looked for the supposed car lights when, out of nowhere, I heard voices right below me and spotted the shape of a light-coloured paraglider a few metres to my right. In a bit of shock, I was left with just enough time to do a sharp turn against the wind to break my speed and land – relatively – smoothly among some plants. It was a close call and my heart was racing.

When I confronted Frank about the car lights that obviously hadn't been switched on, it appeared that I hadn't kept myself in the air long enough to give him sufficient time – after his own landing – to free himself of his gear and turn on the lights of the car. There was no one to blame but myself; I was simply pushing my luck when I refused to take the car back down the mountain. Although still in shock, I thought I had managed well and I was proud of it. On our way back to Merida we stopped at a tiny village and, with the adrenalin still pumping, we got ourselves a few beers, sat on the wooden stairs of the village store, our feet in the dirt, big grins on our faces and chatted to the locals. This scene, to this day, still plays in my mind's eye from time to time. An unforgettable moment.

A couple of days later it was time to leave for Caracas to meet up with the 30 or so other Austrians who had flown in for the wedding. We attended the respective hen and bachelor nights and, with almost a week until the actual wedding, Stephan, Schnovo, Reto (a Swiss guy we had met paragliding) and I were keen on packing in some time on the beach. Tucacas, the gateway to the Morrocay National Park and only a three-hour bus ride from Caracas, seemed like the perfect choice. Once we had arrived at the destination, we booked ourselves into a cheap and rather dodgy guesthouse. Not quite trusting the place, we decided to take most of our belongings with us. While the boys ran off for their swim I stayed behind with our bags and lay down on one of the towels, keeping the bags at close proximity. Just as I was about to doze off I heard a weird noise. I opened my eyes and saw a local guy – who, minutes earlier, was sitting about 50 metres to my right – approach at full speed, leap over me and continue running. It took me a moment to realise what was happening. In his leap he had skilfully picked up three of the shoes we had used to secure the towels. Naturally, I jumped to my feet to chase him, but then noticed his friend in the bush and figured that they were waiting for me to run off so that one of them could freely take the rest of our belongings. I sat back down on my towel, frantically motioning to the boys to get out of the water, just to get a friendly wave back. As it turned out, the thief had managed to take one of each boy's shoes. Schnovo had 'hidden' his wallet under his one sneaker that was taken but due to the speed with which the thief had approached, he'd failed to spot that.

On a mission to find new shoes for the guys, we took off on a walk into town, three of us barefoot. While shopping we also equipped ourselves with a hammock and mosquito net each, in preparation for a sudden idea that had struck us. The following morning we had a local fisherman drop us at one of the many small, uninhabited islands in the national park to do a 'Robinson Crusoe' for a night.

Our designated island was tiny. We seemed to be the only living beings on it. There were plenty of trees for our hammocks, a couple of white sandy patches leading into crystal clear water and perfectly blue skies. The boys even caught a fish, which we ceremoniously grilled over an open fire at night. It was a small fish, just big enough to make for a good photo and give us all a taste, but we certainly were very happy campers. We spent the night singing, playing cards and drinking Cuba Libre until we all ended up sitting in a tree, pretty drunk, at 2am. The following morning we had a slow start to the day. There wasn't much to do other than prepare breakfast. As it turned out, we didn't have to worry about that either. Our food had been wrapped in plastic bags and tied up high on a branch, but still had been attacked overnight. We had managed to save our supplies from potential crawlies but had failed to consider possums. It was now up to the guys to organise fresh fish. They took turns, each of them hoping to triumph – the competition was on – but they failed hopelessly. As it was getting closer to 3pm, the time we had arranged to be picked up, jokes started popping about how we were going to survive if our fisherman failed to show. We all thought this rather funny, considering the boys' success rate in catching fish. But as it got later and later the jokes turned into worry and the worry into panic and by 5.30pm we were all jumping and waving frantically at another fisherman we spotted in the far distance. He seemed to be coming closer slowly, yet didn't appear to be seeing or hearing us.

With hangovers to nurse, no food and not much water left, the potential of a *real* Robinson Crusoe scenario slowly crept up on us. The sun was close to setting and we started to get seriously nervous. It wasn't just that we were facing a night without water or food but, other than the fisherman who had dropped us off, no one knew our whereabouts. As luck would have it, the lone fisherman whose attention we had been trying to attract eventually spotted us and came to our rescue. His was a tiny boat – actually more of a canoe than a boat – and, due to the tide as well as the night approaching, he quickly made it clear that it was too late to head back to the mainland, especially in a boat that was packed to its limit. Instead he offered to cut across the waves to a neighboring island, Cayo Sombrero.

The ride to Cayo Sombrero – a larger, well known tourist island – was a scary experience, to say the least. For some reason, the image of Pinocchio being eaten by a whale when he got lost in stormy seas kept popping into my head. Thankfully, though, the fisherman was a very skilled boatman and, after about an hour of maneuvering the huge waves at just the right angles, we arrived at Cayo Sombrero, soaking wet but intact and, above all, very relieved and happy. We ended up spending a couple of nights on Cayo Sombrero, still in our hammocks, but enjoying the luxury of a restaurant and a bar close by. Upon our return to Tucacas, we were determined to find *our* fisherman who had abandoned us. And we did. His story indicated that the motor of his boat had died half way to the island and that he would have picked us up the following day.

We returned to Caracas in time for our friend Arno's wedding and while the majority of the bridal party stayed in town for several more days, I was keen to return to Merida to fit in another week or two of paragliding, before travelling around South America. During my previous stay in Merida I had got to know a few local paragliders who were happy to take me under their wings, literally. And Frank had also allowed me – for the time being – to keep the same equipment I had learned with. I loved 'flying'. The adrenal rush aside, it was the cool surroundings and the very special atmosphere that came with it that made it so exciting.

For my final flight before packing my bags and leaving for my next adventure, we drove out to Las Gonzalez, my favourite spot. We had already been to another site close to Merida that morning and I had started to feel more and more confident. The wind was quite strong that day and I had to wait a while for it to die down before I was able to take off. Holding the lines in my hands, ready to step forward and pull the paraglider up behind me, all of a sudden I thought I was getting too cocky and careless – after all, I was still a beginner. I put the lines back down on the ground and made a knot in the straps of my helmet that had previously just been hanging there due to a broken clasp. I took a deep breath to remind myself to be more aware of what I was doing, adjusted all my gear, picked up the lines again and took off with a couple of steps.

The wind was still quite strong and the paraglider, slightly tilted, was steering me to the right alongside the cliff. I sat back into the seat and, just as I was about to steer out into the open, my shoelace got caught in a single, long, thin branch that was sticking out of the cliff. Breaking free from the branch within a couple of seconds, it shouldn't have been much of a deal, but with the relative speed I had already gained it was enough to twist the lines of the paraglider from top to bottom. I looked up and thought, *Oh shit!* The twisted lines meant I could no longer steer the paraglider. I was about 900 metres from the ground and was rapidly approaching another cliff right ahead of me. That wasn't a good prospect. I was gaining speed and there was nothing I could do.

Staying surprisingly calm, I had the following thoughts go through my mind in slow motion (I still remember word for word, as if it was yesterday): OK, *during the course they told us to pull the break lines if ever we were to crash into something ... it doesn't quite make sense to do this now as my lines are twisted and it won't have any effect ... well, I might as well do it anyway.* Then I looked at the cliff in front of me and wondered if it would be better to crash head-on or to turn sideways. *I better turn sideways.* That was my last recollection.

I passed out and only awoke when someone tried to take my harness off. I screamed. There was something seriously wrong with my shoulder and, although I didn't feel any pain in my lower back, I instinctively knew I shouldn't move. I was lying on my left side, curled up like a baby, presumably somewhere close to where I had first hit the cliff. I heard several voices from above me but I couldn't actually see anyone because I was stuck between rocks and a few plants.

Someone asked if I could feel my toes. The first thought that shot into my head was, *Thank god I have already done and seen so much in my life.* This thought would stay with me and shape the rest of my life. And yes, I could feel my toes, but I knew I was in trouble. I'd hate to think what would have been if I hadn't secured my helmet only moments before take-off. Falling in and out of consciousness, the only thing I remember is waking up at some stage, still in the same spot and looking at a pitch-dark sky, then lying in the back of an ambulance. To this day I'm not sure how I actually got off the cliff and into the ambulance. What still amazes me, though, is how the human brain works. I stayed totally calm and collected while in this extreme situation. My brain produced a clear string of logical thoughts – in slow motion – before switching off to spare me the experience and memory of the eventual impact when I hit the cliff.

Thankfully I passed out again soon after we left for the hospital; it would have been an agonising ride down the rocky road. When I woke up again, while driving full speed and sirens on along the main road back to Merida, one of the guys who accompanied me in the back of the ambulance tried to cheer me up and, referring to the sirens, joked about all the attention I was getting. All I could think was, *This would have been my one chance to get a ride in a helicopter but the Venezuelans show up in a four-wheel-drive ambulance!*

Upon arrival at the hospital I was put on a rollaway bed where I stayed for what felt like hours. I was told that one of the nurses had gone to get an injection, supposedly from the pharmacy around the corner. By the time they actually got the injection and put it on my bed next to me, my friends Karina, Stephan and Schnovo had arrived. They had travelled back to Merida a couple of days earlier and had been informed of my accident by the hotel staff. Carlos, a local paraglider who had become a good friend over time and who had taken me to Las Gonzalez that afternoon, had called the hotel earlier and urged the staff to please find my friends and send them to the hospital. When the doctor finally showed up to administer the injection that had been lying next to me for quite some time, it had mysteriously disappeared. The decision was made to forget about the injection and to proceed with the x-rays, the result of which were two fractured pubic bones and a complicated fracture of the humerus. The humerus had literally snapped in half – just below the humeral head – and the hospital staff now had to confer about whether surgery was necessary. The doctor in charge decided against it and I was wheeled into the plaster room. What followed wasn't far off a visit to a torture chamber. The nurse asked me to sit up, never mind the broken pubic bones and the yet-to-be-detected broken pelvis. When I told him that, in fact, I couldn't sit up, he grabbed my back and put me into a sitting position. That was my first scream. But it got worse. My right forearm had a huge open wound that ran all the way from my wrist to the elbow. Saturating a piece of cotton wool with pure alcohol, the nurse then rubbed it up and down that wound with not the slightest bit of sympathy. I was in a fragile state as it was and sitting up with a broken pelvis and broken pubic bones, having the alcohol rubbed into my wound, was simply too much. I let out more screams and eventually burst into tears. My friends tried to get into the room to see what was going on and offer their support, but the door was locked. The nurse then proceeded to apply a cast to my upper arm, without even attempting to put the broken bones in place. And the plaster itself was a brutal affair too – several centimetres thick on top and gradually getting thinner towards the elbow, it felt like it weighed a ton.

Once I was back in the hospital hall among my friends, Carlos suggested that I stay with his mum for a while so that they could look after me. What an extraordinarily kind gesture! I hadn't known Carlos for more than a few weeks, let alone met his mum, but this certainly sounded like a great offer and the best possible option. It was already late at night. Carlos had quietly disappeared to the pharmacy to buy a bedpan – a considerably embarrassing detail that hadn't even entered my mind at that stage – and upon his return I was shuffled back into the ambulance and taken to his mum's place.

The flat was a couple of floors up and without the luxury of a big enough elevator, I was tied onto a wooden plank and secured only by several loops of string. In a rather challenging mission, Carlos and the ambulance officers then slowly lifted me up the steep and narrow staircase. With my left hand struggling to keep the heavy cast from pulling my right arm down past my body, I was terrified of sliding off the plank. When we eventually reached the flat, Carlos' mum was already waiting. They put me into Carlos' bed and made sure I was as comfortable as I could possibly be. Carlos himself slept on the floor next to me in case I required any assistance during the night. In the morning I awoke to classical music and a bowl of fresh fruit salad. I will never forget their caring kindness, selflessness and generosity.

During the night I hardly slept. There was something not quite right with my shoulder; even the slightest move caused me excruciating pain. And although my lower back didn't hurt as long as I was lying still, it didn't feel quite right either. I mentioned my concern to Carlos and he suggested calling the ambulance and having me taken to a private hospital. While I was relieved at the mention of a private hospital and more specialised doctors, this also meant another move down the steep staircase, and I definitely wasn't looking forward to that.

Once we arrived at the hospital, the stress of the transport was quickly forgotten and replaced by a hugely grateful smile on my face when I was greeted by friendly, caring staff. I was given a nice, bright and spacious single room with a view of the Andes mountains and within a couple of hours of my arrival they had ripped off the cast, set my humerus in place and put my arm in a professional sling – rather than a heavy plaster that kept putting more stress on my shoulder. The doctor suggested I remain in hospital for at least a few more days for further checks. My left leg had been and still was splayed at the same angle as when I had crashed; I hadn't been able to straighten it, not even the slightest bit. This was accompanied by a strong feeling of pins and needles in my foot. Considering I'd been able to move my toes, I hadn't put further thought into it and simply counted on time healing all wounds.

A couple of days into my stay at the hospital I was taken to a special clinic for an MRI of my lower back and the images revealed a fractured pelvis. In the meantime I had asked my friends to please contact my family in Austria to let them know that I had a *small* accident, nothing major, and if they could please get in contact with my travel insurance company. I didn't want my family to worry. In the end, my brother got the close-to-full version of what had happened, with the request to dilute the story for my parents.

At the private hospital I had extremely caring nurses and I even had a phone next to my bed. When the insurance company, the 'Austrian Air Ambulance' OAFA, called and suggested they fly me back to Austria, I requested to stay in Venezuela. There was not much that could be done about a fractured pelvis, fractured pubic bones and a fractured humerus, other than lie on my back and not move for about six weeks. I figured that if I stayed where I was I could continue my travels a few weeks down the track. I still couldn't move my left leg but I was sure it was just a matter of time before I could stretch it out again. The hospital room was very comfortable and the staff was looking after me perfectly well, making it appear like it would have been a waste of time, money and energy to go through the troubles – and undoubtedly much higher costs – of organising transport back to Austria. Meanwhile my brother Heiner had been in contact with my younger sister Bettina who was living in San Francisco at the time and suggested she fly to Merida to check on me. My Austrian friends had left Merida to go travelling and Carlos had taken it upon himself to look after me, visiting me regularly and supplying me with fresh juices, special creams for my aches and all kinds of other gestures.

About one week into my stay at the hospital I got a call from Bettina, telling me that she would be coming to see me. Just as she was about to hang up I had this inkling to question her flight itinerary. When she had mentioned she was flying via Mexico City – which seemed odd – it dawned on me that there was another Merida in Mexico. I proposed that she double check and make sure that her ticket was, in fact, taking her to Venezuela. As it turns out, the travel agent had indeed made a mistake and booked her onto a flight to Mexico. It was late afternoon and only a few hours before her departure. Luckily she managed to have her ticket changed and make it to the airport just in time for her new flight which was now – due to the late notice – taking her half way around the planet.

A couple of days prior to my sister's arrival I was hit with a high fever and my general wellbeing started to go downhill. No matter how 'off' I felt, however, it was simply impossible to feel sorry for myself; I was so very happy and grateful for being alive and for getting off so lightly. Not to mention that back at the MRI clinic I had been told that had I cracked my lower back about half a centimetre up from the actual fracture, I would now be paralysed.

Reality slowly started to catch up. I still couldn't move my left leg and, with the onset of the fever and a general feeling of qualm, I began to wonder if it would be better to be taken back to Austria. By the time my sister arrived my insurance company was already organising my return flights. They were going to send one of their doctors to take care of the details at this end and to accompany me during the journey. Their organisation was extremely efficient and professional. With no arguing whether I was fully covered in regards to my insurance plan – or trying to find a reason to not pay for the expenses, as is often the case – it was a very smooth affair. There was not even a mention of the additional accumulated costs resulting from my original request to remain in Merida. The doctor arrived within a few days, sorted out all the paperwork – including the full payment for my two weeks' stay at the private hospital, for which I had assumed I would have to bear at least part of the cost – and within another couple of days I was on my way to Austria. My sister had decided to stay until I left, which I immensely appreciated. She organised a nice present for Carlos and was much needed moral support when I had to farewell my travel plans, as well as my beloved Merida and the beautiful people I had met over the previous weeks.

At the airport, I was – once again – lifted onto a wooden plank, which was then put across a row of seats in the back of the plane and secured with a couple of strings pulled tight around me and the bottom parts of the seats. Bettina was on a different flight to Caracas that had left about an hour earlier. She was determined to come and see me during her brief stopover, to make sure I was okay. I was absolutely stunned when, not long after we landed, she did indeed appear out of nowhere in front of my row of seats. All the passengers had left the plane and it was just the two of us. She had somehow managed to get through a couple of gates and onto the tarmac to find me in one of the planes. Bettina had tears in her eyes when she saw me lying there all by myself, wrapped up like a parcel. I assured her I was going to be alright and off she rushed to catch her onward flight.

I remained on the plane for what seemed like ages while my doctor left to organise the next steps. When he returned he had a couple of ambulance drivers with him. The plan was to take me to a hospital in Caracas where I would stay for about three hours before returning to the airport to catch the connecting flight to Europe. In my best Spanish I strongly argued that I didn't want to be taken to a hospital just to be unnecessarily lifted on and off the rollaway, ambulance and hospital beds to then return to the airport only a few hours later. This was supposedly my only option. I asked if I could possibly talk to a representative from the airport; I would be happy to be put on a rollaway bed and left somewhere in a corner of the airport.

The ambulance staff disappeared with my doctor in tow and upon their return I was told that they were going to take me to the executive lounge of our airline, the Dutch KLM. The lounge was a small but exclusive and beautifully decorated room. I was lifted onto a very comfortable white leather couch. There was no one else in the room. As I was about to doze off, my doctor, a very kind and caring man, left to explore the airport – but not before asking if he could get me anything duty free: 'Maybe a bottle of rum for your parents?' I was really touched by how well I was being looked after. I was going to miss Venezuela and its people, and it was comforting to have this friendly doctor by my side all the way until I would reunite with my family.

A couple of hours before takeoff, my doctor checked if I wanted to use the bedpan, suggesting that it might be more comfortable to do this prior to getting onto a packed plane. I agreed and proceeded to do what I had to do. Having been accustomed to a much more ergonomic bedpan than the travel version I had just been handed, while also dealing with the squashy nature of the couch, I failed to fully aim as intended, leaving a large 'water' mark on the expensive leather lounge. I freaked. The doctor tried to calm me, went to find some paper towels and did his best to lessen the effect under my lifted bottom – unfortunately with not much success. Literally five minutes into our effort, the door opened and two tall, handsome Dutch guys walked in with a rollaway bed, ready to take me to the plane. My face was already pink with sweat running down my forehead before they had appeared but when I saw them come through the door, I blushed to my limit. I felt the heat coming out of my ears. They were very friendly and, unaware of why I was in such frenzy, asked if I was ready for the flight. Being lifted off the couch, I figured that if I avoided catching their eyes, then they wouldn't see the wet mark that appeared right under my bum either. I just wanted to dissolve. For once I had wished that the airline had sent two shortsighted retirees. If someone asked me about the most embarrassing moment in my life, this would have to be *it*.

I was wheeled onto the plane and transferred to a bed that had been mounted on top of three three-seater rows, so taking up nine seats. The two handsome Dutch guys joked that everyone on the plane would envy me for my bed, and left. I slowly started to breathe again. It was an 11-hour flight and, other than a few small sips of water, I refused to eat or drink. The plane was filled to its last seat and, although my bed had a curtain that could be pulled, I was not going to be humiliated by half the plane listening to me doing my business and seeing the bedpan.

After yet another stopover in Amsterdam, I finally arrived in Vienna. There I was, back in Austria on 26 August 1994, not even three months after I had left *for good*. An ambulance was waiting on the tarmac and before my doctor said his goodbyes, he handed me a 100 schilling note just in case I needed money before my parents could meet me at the hospital. I never thought it was possible to have such a positive experience with a travel insurance company. The doctor had left his day job and his family at very short notice, flown halfway across the planet to attend to me and to sort out all the details in as little time as possible, just to return a couple of days later on yet another long-haul flight. Not once had he shown any anger or complained about the lack of sleep. On the contrary, he had gone way beyond the call of duty to make sure I was happy and to accommodate me in the best possible way. Later on I found out that the insurance-policy plan I had chosen would, in fact, not even have covered my accident.

Remembering a clause in my travel insurance that had said something along the lines of, 'If one has to interrupt a holiday due to an accident or illness, the insurer will compensate the insured person with a return ticket to the original holiday destination to allow resumption of the holiday', I contacted the insurance company several months down the track to enquire about my ticket back to Venezuela. I was even bold enough to ask if I could choose a different destination. They responded with a copy of the relevant terms and conditions, highlighting a paragraph outlining various policy exclusions. It contained a line that implied that dangerous sports like paragliding were not included in the policy. Their accompanying letter stated '... however, we still opted to cover all the expenses, a goodwill that, after all, cost us 216,000 schillings' (approximately AUD 24,000). I felt terribly ashamed.

In Vienna, I was taken to the Lorenz-Boehler Hospital, one of the best emergency hospitals in the country. Over the first few days I had regular early morning visits from the resident neurologist. Each time he had a different student with him, to whom he explained every move of his examination of my left leg, the one that I still couldn't stretch. He always followed the same routine, doing the same tests, and I always wondered *why* but I held back questioning his actions. On the fourth day he finally voiced what had been on his mind all along: he simply couldn't understand why I wasn't paralysed. I had all the signs that pointed to me losing the feeling in my left side at any moment; each morning when he came for his visit, he had expected to find me partly paralysed. But for some reason I had defied the odds. His eventual conclusion was that if the paralysis had not yet set in, he no longer believed it would.

Although I had always been very much aware of how extremely lucky I had been to have survived without more serious injuries, the neurologist's comments made me freak. Over the following weeks I had many sleepless nights or woke up in panic, terrified that I would not be able to move. I'm absolutely positive that the reason I didn't end up paralysed was that it had never occurred to me there was any such danger. Back in Venezuela no one had expressed any concern, a fact that kept me from tensing up. I had never had a reason to stress about my injuries, always believing that in a few weeks' time I would be fine and back on the road again. This allowed my body to relax. If I'd been in a panicked state from day one of the accident, I'm sure that the neurologist's prognosis would have been much more likely. I'm a big believer in the saying 'Things happen for a reason' and, to this day, I am still extremely grateful for the two weeks I spent in the hospital in Merida. Those two weeks provided me with the perfect environment to give my body the time and space to relax, and to recover enough to ultimately prevent me from spending the rest of my life in a wheelchair.

When my parents first arrived at the hospital in Vienna – they had since found out a few additional details regarding my accident – I was ready for a lecture from my mum, along the lines of: 'You should have listened to me' or 'I told you that paragliding was too dangerous'. But I received not even a hint of a silent reproach.

After a couple of weeks at the Lorenz-Boehler hospital I was transferred to Salzburg where I soon started physiotherapy for my shoulder, with a physiotherapist visiting me at my bedside daily. Not long into the therapy, I told the lady – working hard on the mobility of my shoulder – that I felt the humerus hadn't healed enough and that it was too soon for exercises. I could feel the part where my humerus had snapped in two – just below the shoulder – still moving to some extent and it wasn't hard to tell that the bones were not in line. Yet she kept pushing on, completely dismissing my concerns. Becoming more apprehensive by the day, I eventually convinced the resident specialist doctor to arrange another x-ray. The following night I dreamed that the doctor, followed by several nurses, walked into the room to inform me that the bones had grown together in the wrong position. I woke up to that exact scenario. The humerus had to be broken again and now complicated surgery was on the agenda.

I eventually went home after a total of two months in various hospitals. Weeks of intensive physiotherapy followed. Back in the throes of life my days became a bit more challenging. While in hospital, I had always been in a rather positive mood, having accepted that there was nothing I could do about my situation and that it would be just a matter of time before I could continue living my life. Out of hospital, however, it was a whole different story. I was only half functioning. While I was officially 'healthy' and out of bed, I still couldn't sit or stand up for any longer than a few minutes at a time and my days were guided by my scheduled physiotherapy sessions. Hanging around, not doing anything – other than physiotherapy – was not an option, neither for me, nor for my parents. Being forced to be either in constant motion or lying down, I was eventually appointed to clean up and reorganise the storage, laundry and maintenance areas of the family hotel in Salzburg. It wasn't the worst of jobs, but I would be lying if I didn't say I was sitting on hot coals, waiting to get fit enough to continue on my own path of adventure.

Chapter 4

Undeterred

My plans to spend a winter in Canada had to be put aside; I had been told I wouldn't be able to get back on my snowboard – ever – and, although I hadn't taken that statement too seriously, the upcoming winter would have definitely been too soon. I now sported a massive pin in my right upper arm that greatly restricted the movement in my shoulder and that sure wasn't meant to be put to any test. My best bet was to get as far away from the snow as possible, and South Africa seemed like a good choice.

I left for Cape Town in November 1994, six weeks after I had been discharged from hospital. It had only been a few months since the general election at which Nelson Mandela became South Africa's first black president. Several of my friends thought it too dangerous for a girl to travel to South Africa by herself but, as it turned out, it was one of the best times to visit the 'Land of Good Hope'. For my first couple of nights in Cape Town I booked myself into a backpacker hostel right in town. On my second day there I got talking to a group of fellow backpackers – three guys and three girls from Europe and Australia – who had met at the hostel and who were also planning to stay for the southern summer. They had teamed up to find a place to live long-term and had just managed to secure a large apartment in Sea Point, a seafront suburb. To make the place more affordable for everyone, they were now looking for one more person to share with. So here I was, having barely set foot into the country, already moving into a cool place in the best possible location – between town, The Waterfront (the Victoria and Albert Waterfront in the Table Bay Harbour) and the beaches – with the most awesome group of people. The following Monday, Katie, my room-mate at the new apartment, and I took off to The Waterfront to look for work and within an hour that mission, too, had been accomplished. We both managed to get a job at the Jolly Roger Coffee Shop, a restaurant right on the water, with the perfect view of Table Mountain and oodles of playful seals directly in front.

A couple of weeks into my time in Cape Town, I caught up with friends at La Med, a cool cocktail bar in between Camps Bay and the stunning Clifton Beaches, not far from where we lived. I fell in love with the place at first sight and although I had heard that it was difficult to get a job there, and that management had piles of applications to choose from at any given time, I felt it wouldn't hurt to apply (and add a couple of shifts to my working week). The following afternoon I returned to La Med and asked for the manager. We had a brief chat and I was handed an application form to complete. The form contained some rather weird questions but as I already had a job, I had nothing to lose and completed the questions without wasting too much thought. On my way out, I ran into a couple of friends and ended up staying at the bar for a few drinks. Later that night, while joking around with my friends just outside the bar, visibly tipsy, the manager who I had talked to earlier that day spotted me. Walking up to us, he told me he'd been trying to get hold of me and asked how soon I would be available for my first shift. Bingo.

My lower back was causing me trouble at times but, with the right exercises and the occasional afternoon in bed, it was manageable. I spent my working hours between the Jolly Rogers Coffee Shop and the La Med cocktail bar. The rest of the time, I made the most of every minute, out and about exploring Cape Town and its surroundings – not to forget the stunning beaches – and enjoying myself to the limit. The night before New Year's Eve, us seven flatmates went out for an early celebration as most of us had been rostered to work the following night. It was a great party and we didn't end up getting home until just before dawn. By the time I finally fell into bed, it was almost time to get ready for work again. Katie and I both had to start our shifts at 3pm, at The Waterfront and La Med respectively. It was going to be a long night and, considering our hangovers, neither of us had a clue how we were going to survive, let alone last the hours. Then I had a glorious idea. About a week earlier I had watched Matt, one of our flatmates and a tall, slim guy by nature, take a few drops from a small bottle labelled 'Dietetic Mixture'. I questioned why he, of all people, was taking a diet remedy. His response was that it gave him energy and helped him get by with less sleep than what he would usually require. Matt was mostly working late shifts at a restaurant and nightclub and it was this magic potion that got him through the nights. He suggested I give it a try; and, boy, could I tell what he was talking about. Not only did the couple of drops give me a real energy kick, they also made me feel even happier than I was already, resulting in me running around with a big grin on my face for the rest of the afternoon.

So Katie and I went to the pharmacy down the hill from our apartment, filled out the paperwork – the Dietetic Mixture was restricted to a single purchase per person – took a few droppers (as opposed to a couple of drops) of the magic potion each and off we went in our respective directions. It didn't take long before I started to feel rather weird and unwell. By the time I arrived at the bar, I was on a different planet. While everyone was rushing around, eager to get the place looking spick and span for the big night, I grabbed a handful of cutlery and napkins, positioned myself on a table outside in the sun, sunglasses on, and started to roll cutlery – in very slow motion. (Rolled cutlery wasn't needed that night.) And with everyone else busy to get ready before the doors opened, no one had time to question what I was doing. I completely lost the concept of time. At around 6.30pm we were called to a brief staff meeting and everyone had a table allocated to look after; mine seemed extra-large, with extra important VIPs (New Year's Eve tickets for La Med were hot property and certainly not cheap).

Once my guests arrived, I managed to pull myself together enough to take their drink order and proceeded to hand the order to one of the guys behind the bar. When I returned a mere couple of minutes later and my drinks weren't ready, on a tray, waiting for me to serve, I lost it. I went off at my colleagues behind the bar, then turned around and headed straight for the bathroom where I started to cry, then sob and eventually, when I noticed froth coming from my mouth, freak. My pupils covered almost the entirety of my iris and – as a total virgin when it came to drugs – it took a lot of assuring from a couple of my coworkers, who came looking for me, that I was going to be all right. There was no way I was going to leave that bathroom anytime soon. My colleagues took turns in checking on me and supplying me with pints of water, all during the busiest night of the year. I had no clue if 'my table' was being looked after or who had taken over, but that was the least of my worries at the time.

Fifteen minutes before midnight a friend came back into the bathroom and told me that management had called it a night for us – we were now allowed to join the party. I went to grab my bag and, still with tears in my eyes and a freakish look about me, I announced I was going to go home. But my colleagues wouldn't have it. They tried very hard to convince me to stay and have some fun but I was determined to leave. Then one of the guys dragged me to the bar, ordered four shots of tequila and made me drink three of them. Within a couple of minutes my anger, fear, embarrassment and whatever other emotion that had manifested itself over the course of the night dissolved into extreme over-the-top joy and enthusiasm for life and I ended up spending the remaining night on the dance floor. It was, indeed, utterly bizarre.

Back at the apartment in the morning hours of the new year I fell into bed and barely left the house for the rest of the week. I felt very ill for several days and both Katie – who hadn't reacted quite as strongly – and I swore never to touch this evil potion again. We had obviously left our common sense at home when we thoughtlessly overdosed on this 'diet remedy' but who would have thought it could have had such an effect? The Dietetic Mixture must have been in its composition a relative of the drug speed – not that I had ever tried it – but, I'm happy to say, it certainly was the best anti-drug campaign possible. I had assumed that New Year's Eve was my final shift at La Med but, to my surprise, one of my friends passed on a message from management that they expected me to return as soon as I felt better. My 'episode' was being treated as unnoticed and I never even had to face a lifted finger.

About a month and a half before I was due in Austria to have the pin removed from my humerus, I joined a five-week overland track through Namibia, Botswana and Zimbabwe. We climbed sand dunes, visited various game reserves and had locals guide us in *mekoro* (traditional canoes) down the Okavango Delta. We slept in tents or under the stars and heard lions roar during the night. We paddled past a dead body floating in the Orange River, visited the impressive Victoria Falls and went down the Zambezi in a raft (a great thrill but probably not the best idea in view of my restricted shoulder and the large pin in my arm at the time). My time in Africa was a very special and memorable one and, without doubt, the best possible side-effect of my accident. Had I been able to ski, I would have gone straight to Canada instead and who knows if I would have ever had another opportunity to experience South Africa the way I did, and at that time in history.

I returned to Austria at the end of the European winter. The pin from my arm was removed and another two months of intensive physiotherapy followed. Next on the agenda was London, a four-month interlude before moving to Canada for the winter. I decided it was time for some personal growth and found what sounded like the perfect opportunity – selling advertising space for *The World Travel Guide*. Back in high school my biggest fear had been public speaking – presentations and talks in front of the entire class. Every semester we had to choose a subject or a book that we were going to present to our fellow students and the teacher. The lead-up to each of my 'performances' forever entailed extreme anxiousness and sleepless nights; and no matter how well prepared I was, I always ended up with a mark way below average. Doing cold calls and 'presenting a book' to an unknown customer seemed like a perfect yet gentle enough start to improve my skills. I went for an interview with Columbus Press and got the job the same day. Equipped with a proposed script, a list of countries that were mine to call, the authority to discount advertising space by a significant percentage from day one and an alias that I was free to choose for myself, I was allocated a desk and my 'new career' was launched.

The World Travel Guide was a large, thick book that contained all the necessary information about any country, such as currency, visa requirements and health subjects, that one should be aware of before travelling. In 1995, the World Wide Web was yet to take over so it was a travel agent's bible, usually stowed somewhere underneath a desk, out of the sight of customers. My job was to cold call any kind of tourism business in Austria, Germany, Switzerland and South East Asia to convince their authorised signatory that an advertisement in *The World Travel Guide* would boost their business beyond measure. The problem was that I – personally – failed to see any value in advertising in that book. I knew about the guide through a subject in college dealing with the ins and outs of running a travel agency, yet, as a customer, purchasing my own airline tickets and finding out about travel requirements for any of the countries I had travelled to, I had never even seen the cover. In my opinion and, according to my understanding of the nature of the guidebook, an ad by any tourism business like a hotel, restaurant or tourist attraction would hardly catch the attention of a travel agent, let alone an actual client.

To test my theory, my first cold call was to the director of the Hotel and Tourism College in Austria that I had attended. Elated that I did, indeed, get him on the phone, I introduced myself by my alias and gave him my spiel about the importance of having his college represented in *The World Travel Guide*. To my surprise, he requested further information. Never having been a big fan of his, I happily proceeded with my effort to make this my first commission. After a couple more conversations with the former 'holder of my fate', he eventually decided that his budget was exhausted and that I should get back in contact the following year. It turned out that most of the businesses in Austria, Germany and Switzerland that I called were, in fact, aware of the guide – and that purchasing advertising space within would have no impact on their business. So I moved on to South East Asia.

My first potential client was the owner of a small hotel in the Philippines. She got so excited after listening to my spiel, she indeed thought that an ad in this 'King of a Book' would be the solution to her problems. I also made her feel very special by – sticking to my script – telling her that she was one of the selected few who were lucky enough to get presented with this rare opportunity. And that was all that was needed. She was ready to sign. I was shocked. Although proud of my newly gained sales skills, I started to feel like the biggest fraud. She was going to pay a lot of money – especially in her currency – for this ad and all this with no prospect, of that I was sure, of a return on investment. I concluded my call by suggesting that she have a think about it, discuss it with her husband and that I call her back the following day. However, I couldn't do it to her. When we talked the next morning, I told her I'd had a closer look at the nature of her business and it probably wasn't a good idea to go ahead with the advertisement. She sounded very disappointed but I simply couldn't proceed with the sale. I resigned the same day.

Still on a mission to work on my fear of public speaking, I wasn't going to let myself off that lightly. While I was well aware of courses I could attend instead, the thought made me feel sick. I would be way better off practising in a foreign country, with people who didn't know me and who would never see me again, ascribing the embarrassment of making a fool of myself a much shorter lifespan. To lift the stakes, and to take the exercise one step further, I applied for a job as a door-to-door insurance sales person. Again, I got the job without much ado, no experience needed. During an induction course that followed, the course instructor decided that, among the dozens of newcomers, he had a handful of stars in his class who he then pulled aside and branded the 'elite group'. I was one of them; I had no idea what had led him to believe that I was special – I hadn't opened my mouth once over the previous couple of days.

Five of us made up this so-called elite group. We were given a small car, a map of the London target suburb and the privilege to have our course leader as our mentor. Equipped with a name tag with the company ID, a serious-looking folder with all kinds of paperwork and a calculator, we drove ourselves to our allocated suburb, parked at the closest pub and off we went in different directions. Our instructions had been to knock on as many doors as possible, have a brief chat to the housewives and arrange appointments for the same night to give detailed presentations of the product once the husbands – the decision makers – had returned from work. The product was life insurance that was targeted to families.

On my first day I managed to chat to nine ladies and scheduled three appointments for that night. This was enough to get awarded the title 'my little star' by our course leader. The next best result by one of my colleagues was five doors that had been opened for a brief chat and two appointments. I had two big advantages – I was a female and I had an accent. Rather than feeling threatened, the individuals who answered the doors – indeed mostly mums – often felt intrigued and wanted to talk to me to find out where I was from. Once we had completed pounding our respective streets for the day, we all met at the local pub for a late lunch and shared our stories, to then take off again to face the serious part of the show. This was most definitely a huge step out of my comfort zone: sitting in the living room of primarily affluent families, at night, talking about a subject I knew hardly anything about. The scary part was conversing with the dads, mostly still in suits, who looked like they would know way more about insurance than I did.

My 'plan' seemed to be paying off, however, and over the following weeks I began to notice how I was gradually becoming more and more confident. The big knot in my throat that I'd woken up to every morning for several weeks started to slowly dissolve, until one day I stood in front of a door, hand in a fist, ready to knock, when all of a sudden I stalled, thinking to myself: *Enough! No more.* It was a case of 'mission accomplished'. It was only 11am, but I turned around and went straight to the pub and sat there, content, with a big smile on my face, waiting for my colleagues. When I told my supervisor of my decision, he was disappointed, looking at me with a frown and mumbling, 'But you were my little star!'. (Not that I had made him much money at that stage, but he had obviously believed in me.) All I felt was relief that I could now close this chapter and move on.

It was the end of August and time to make some real money before I left for Canada. I got myself a waitressing job in a busy café and everything seemed to be going to plan until I started to feel increasing pain in my lower back, as well as my left leg, to the point where I could hardly sit or walk, with the discomfort worsening by the day. I resolved to consult a physiotherapist and a chiropractor, as well as an acupuncturist. Eventually I was told I might have no choice but to return to Austria to spend a couple of months in a rehabilitation centre. I was absolutely devastated. With a nonrefundable ticket to Canada in my hands it was only two weeks before my proposed departure. I talked to my family, and my sister Evelyn suggested that I come to Bad Gastein for a few treatments with a special therapist she had recently employed at the hotel spa. She was positive he could fix me. Not setting my hopes very high, I still thought it was worth a try. So here I was, once again, on my way back to Austria. I kept getting sent back and I started to wonder if it was a sign that, maybe, I was meant to stay in Austria after all. This simply wasn't an option. Yes, I was a big believer in things happening for a reason, but the reason obviously had to be elsewhere.

The special therapist's name was Klaus, and the treatment method that he applied in my case was Akupunkt-Massage (APM). Klaus pointed out that my body was very much out of line, my sacrum was tilted and my lower back twisted; and as a result my legs weren't quite even. I could see what he meant and it all made sense. Once he got underway, however, the treatment soon started to resemble hocus-pocus rather than serious work and it wasn't long before anxiety set in. I had put quite a bit of hope in Klaus but that bit of hope quickly disappeared. I questioned him about what exactly it was that he was trying to do and, while his explanation sounded promising, I still doubted that this APM magic could produce results. Evelyn insisted I give Klaus the benefit of the doubt. Not having anything to lose – other than time – I agreed. Within a week and a half of regular treatments I was a new person. It was hard to believe; this was, indeed, pure magic. I left Austria literally two weeks after I had arrived and, at last, was on my way to Canada. My flight took me via Frankfurt where I met up with Asa, one of my best friends who lived in Sweden. She had flown in from Stockholm and was about to join me on my adventure.

We arrived in Vancouver, British Columbia, in late October. As we were sitting in the bus on our way to Whistler, driving up into the mountains along the extremely scenic Sea to Sky Highway, my heart was pounding; it had taken three attempts, but here I was – happy as a newly hatched chick. We booked ourselves into the Alta Lake Hostel, set right on the shores of the lake, with a view like one from a picture book. Just a few weeks before the start of the winter season, the hostel was packed with fellow travellers and it seemed that everyone was on the same mission – finding a way to stay for the season. There was a feel of desperation in the air because the general sentiment at the hostel was that it was next to impossible to find long-term accommodation. With a ridiculous amount of construction going on in town and a lot of the work dragging on for much longer than had been planned, all the flats, rooms and beds were still being taken up by construction workers. Most of the people at the hostel had already found work but thus far had failed to secure a permanent place to live. With the hostel only allowing a maximum one-month stay, and more and more people arriving by the day, the pressure was on.

Once we had taken in the various opinions and comments regarding the cold-hearted facts of 'the situation', Asa and I decided to rent a couple of bicycles from the hostel and get on our way early the following morning, a Monday. We checked when and where the local paper appeared first each day and took off at dawn, pedalling to Function Junction, a small conglomerate of shops and a small café at the south end of Whistler. Arriving just as the café opened, it seemed like we were the first ones in town to hold the fresh print in our hands. Ads in the accommodation section were limited but there was one that sounded just right: a guy called Daryl with a flat in Whistler Creek was looking for a flatmate. There were obviously two of us but as we were happy to share a room, we figured we had a chance. Giving it another half hour for the clock to hit an acceptable time to call, we phoned Daryl and he agreed to us coming by his place if we could make it within the next 45 minutes. Racing to drop the bikes back at the hostel, we hitched a ride for the rest of the way and, by 9am, it looked like we had a home for the winter – Daryl just had to get the okay from his girlfriend who lived in Vancouver. It was a small apartment (or rather, a small half of a house) and the room was just big enough to fit a second mattress, but the place itself – the location as well as the view – was more than what we could have wished for. Now all that was left to do was to find ourselves jobs. On the way to Daryl's we had driven past a couple of bed and breakfasts at which we now felt inspired to drop our résumés. The first one was a place called Haus Heidi. The owners, Jim and Trudy – a German couple who had been living in Canada for many years – were extremely friendly and welcoming and about 15 minutes into our conversation, we shook hands and I had a job. Trudy then suggested that Asa check out the bed and breakfast down the road. Another half an hour later, Asa, too, was all set. So here we were, at 11am on our first full day in Whistler, all done and dusted. It seemed surreal.

Daryl's girlfriend insisted on meeting Asa and me before allowing us to share a house with her man. The two of them were at the 'about-to-get-engaged' stage of their relationship and she didn't want to take any chances. I guess that the fact we came in a twin-pack had helped our case. The meeting went well and by the end of the week we had moved in. Daryl and his girl then took off to South America for three weeks, leaving Asa and me 'in charge' of the house and the dog. With our jobs not starting until the beginning of December, this was as good as it could get.

A couple of weeks into our time in Whistler, the pre-sales for season lift passes for the mountain opened. With the completion of a day's orientation course on the town and everything it offered – and an agreement that we would at all times display a helpful and respectful attitude towards the tourists – we qualified as locals and were now eligible to receive the locals' discount. Upon leaving the hospital after my accident 12 months earlier, I had been told I would no longer be able to do any high-intensity sports, let alone get back on my snowboard. Mine was a so-called carving-board, which meant that the snowboard bindings were at an angle to each other, posing a bit of a challenge for my pelvis and lower back; but snowboarding was my biggest passion and I wasn't going to give up my passion. Buying the early-bird ski pass for a full season and handing over a significant amount of money was like giving myself the assurance that I would be okay. Psychologically this was a major step; holding that pass in my hand was the equivalent to holding a ticket to a fresh start.

When Whistler and Blackcomb mountains finally opened their gates, Asa and I were among the first on top. I was confident I'd continue on my snowboard from where I had left off a couple of years earlier. But then reality hit. I couldn't even bend over to close my own bindings, neither standing up, nor while sitting down in the snow. I kept trying until Asa eventually had to come to my rescue and do it for me. The next challenge was just getting up, let alone standing on the board or doing a turn in that awkward position. I had tears running down my cheeks but I kept pushing myself. In the end I made it down the hill, just. It wasn't as much of an ease back into the sport as I had envisioned, but with the help of a renowned local physiotherapist, an extensive set of specific exercises and a lot of patience – a virtue that I hadn't been blessed with – I was back at my best within a few weeks.

My time in Whistler turned into the kind of winter I had always dreamed of. I worked five days a week – having two days off per week was a completely new concept to me – mornings at the B & B serving breakfast and cleaning rooms, and afternoons at a chocolate shop belonging to Trudy, the owner of Haus Heidi. I was up on the mountain every day. The chocolate shop was within the walls of the Chateau Whistler, a five-star hotel at the bottom of Blackcomb Mountain, meaning that I could literally ski right into the shop. I started my afternoon shifts at 4pm, just as the ski lifts closed, and with a change room and shower at my disposal downstairs from the chocolate shop, I was in a perfect position to capitalise on my season pass.

At winter's end, Asa returned to Europe while I decided to stay in Canada. Jim and Trudy weren't going to need any help at Haus Heidi over the summer months and instead asked if I would be interested in helping run a Wilderness Guest Ranch somewhere in the bush a few hours north of Whistler. The guest ranch belonged to a friend of Trudy's, a German gentleman who had inherited the ranch but apparently hadn't had the time and ambition to run it himself. Trudy arranged for a phone interview and that was that. I was about to go on a holiday with my boyfriend, Alain, who I had met several months earlier and – according to my new boss – by the time I came back, there would be a fax waiting for me with further instructions as to when, where and how I was to start work.

Alain was an avid rock climber. During the winter he had taken me to indoor climbing gyms to teach me the tricks of the trade and our holiday now was meant to be a climbing trip to 'Red Rocks' (Red Rock Canyon), Las Vegas. Following check-in at Vancouver airport, I was stopped at customs and told that I was not going anywhere. Apparently I didn't have a visa for the US. I politely pointed out that as an Austrian citizen I didn't need a visa, but as luck would have it, us Austrians were only allowed to enter the US once every six months without a visa; for any additional entry a visa was indeed required. Back in November I had crossed the border and visited Seattle for a couple of days and with that, my one free entry was gone. The customs officer suggested we contact the American Consulate, get a visa and come back the following day. If only it was that easy. We made our way straight to the embassy, just to be told that it wasn't a case of simply showing up but, rather, one had to make an appointment first. We then asked for an appointment and were advised that this couldn't be done in person; we had to call a certain number to do so. There was a catch to that too, however; one had to call from a private phone. The number we were given was a 1-900 number, a prefix that wasn't accessible from a public phone. This was in 1996, before the general use of mobile phones. We proceeded to a hotel and politely asked the concierge to place the call for us, offering whatever amount he believed that call would be worth and some extra. But, to no avail. After trying a couple of similar avenues without success, we returned to the embassy and told the receptionist of our plight. The bottom line was no personal phone – no appointment – no visa. A rather interesting concept. Adding to our dilemma was the fact that I had to leave the country by the following day. My six-month visa for Canada was up and with no time to squander, we decided to fly to Mexico instead. The new flight schedule didn't leave us any time to go back to Whistler to repack, so we arrived in Mexico with a whole bunch of climbing gear and not quite the right equipment for the beach. Nevertheless, we still had a great holiday

Returning to Whistler a couple of weeks later, there was a fax requesting I be at Green Lake just out of town on a certain day and time from where a seaplane would take me to the Yohetta Wilderness Ranch. I was stunned. Was I really that important, that they would *fly* me there? My chat with the owner of the ranch a few weeks earlier had been a brief one in which he had mainly inquired about my background and told me what he envisioned my role to be. It was a small guest ranch with only a handful of staff; my responsibilities would be to look after the guests and make sure that 'it was all running smoothly'. I hadn't seen a brochure and the World Wide Web hadn't spread to the bush, so I just went by the image I had created in my mind, which was a boutique four-to-five-star luxury 'pseudo-wilderness' ranch for guests to pretend that they had been to the real bush.

On the day, I showed up at Green Lake in a perfectly ironed white shirt, jeans and boots with a small heel. I felt that I looked the part. The ranch was located in the Chilcotin Mountains of Central BC, on the edge of Ts'yl-os Provincial Park. It was a one-and-a-half-hour flight over dense bush and I felt extremely privileged to have been given the opportunity of what I was sure would turn into the experience of a lifetime. During the flight I had a good chat with the pilot who even let me fly the plane for a while. It was fun and games until he pointed out the guest-ranch in the far distance – a small dot on a lake in the middle of absolutely nowhere. As soon as we landed, three of the four staff came to greet me or, rather, to check me out. They gave me a fairly skeptical look – to say the least – and it wasn't hard to tell that I wasn't a highly anticipated delivery. And my outfit didn't help either.

There was Claude (the camp chef), Linde (the horse whisperer – well, kind of), Norm (the resident cowboy – and he wasn't a tourist attraction, but the real deal) and Tom (a local guide of native Indian descent). Tom, Norm and Linde had been living and working at the ranch for many years and had always been more or less their own bosses. The three of them were basically part of the inventory and among them held all the necessary knowledge to run the show. Tom's ancestors used to own a significant amount of bush in the Chilcotin, the region that the Yohetta Ranch was in, and he knew the area like his own pocket. This was Canadian wilderness at its best and hosting guests and taking them into it came with a lot of responsibility. The current staff didn't quite agree with the vision of the new owner, Manfred, let alone with some young chick in a white shirt about to try to tell them what to do. After a brief introduction, Linde – about my age – showed me to my log cabin, one of a handful and usually reserved for guests. This naturally added to the separation that I could already sense between *them* and *me*. Claude and Norm had a bed in a wooden shack, Tom and Linde called tipi-style tents their homes, and the girl from the city, who didn't look like she'd ever got her hands dirty, was about to hang up her clothes in a guest cabin. Linde then gave me a bit of a lowdown on the property, its past and the recent changes. It appeared that the new owner's intention was to transform the camp into something more like a 'groomed retreat', similar to the image I had in my head prior to my arrival. This was a *wilderness* camp after all and Tom, Norm and Linde had no intention of playing along if it were to change significantly.

I fully agreed with what Linde was saying and I assured her that I wasn't there to change anything. My position was solely to meet and greet the guests and to make sure that they were happy. I didn't have any intention whatsoever of interfering with what they had been doing for years. And, although I felt that it wouldn't hurt to clean the place up a little bit and possibly exchange the old sleeping bags in the guest cabins with duvets (as Manfred, the owner, had suggested and was about to do), I thought it a good idea to keep that to myself.

The morning after my arrival Tom, Claude and Linde were preparing to go into town for a few days to get supplies of all kinds in anticipation of the first guests of the season. Norm was going to take them to a river where they would get into a canoe to paddle to the other side where another four-wheel drive wagon was permanently parked. From there they would continue on a rough dirt road to the closest town, several hours away. Linde had suggested I come along for the first part of the trip, to which I had happily agreed. Once we had dropped the three of them at the river, it was only Norm and me in the old truck. Before I had a chance to say anything, cowboy Norm made it clear that he didn't want to have anything to do with me. 'I don't know you, so I don't want to talk to you' were his exact words. There wasn't much I could say to that, other than 'OK'. It was a long, silent drive back to camp. And it was going to be an even longer, and above all awkward, couple of days until the others returned. There was no radio, phone or any such thing in the camp. To wash, we either went to the lake or, in my case, carried a bucket of water from the lake into the cabin, which had a small basin. For emergencies, the camp had a satellite phone that only worked in a very specific spot about 10 minutes – by truck – from camp. News was delivered every couple of weeks or so with the pilot, when dropping off guests and goods. It was mid-May and the nights could get pretty cold; a couple of times we even woke up to snow. Each of the guest cabins had a fire place and there was one communal shower with a big window and a view across the lake – without a doubt the most scenic shower I had ever come across – that offered hot water, as long as the log fire that was heating up the water was lit at least half an hour beforehand.

When Norm and I got back to camp, I tried to stay out of his sight as much as possible. I dismissed the idea of a hot shower before it even had a chance to enter my mind; it was all about looking tough now. If I had learned one thing over the previous 24 hours, it was that the camp was no place for wimps. When it came to breakfast, lunch and dinner, I took the safe road of grabbing a quick sandwich or whatever else I could find to have on the go. There was no way I was going to cook for myself and not offer any food to Norm, keeping in mind that he didn't want to have anything to do with me. I spent my days cleaning up the cabins and the main lodge. I hadn't been left with any instructions so I felt that this was the safest thing to do without stepping on anyone's toes. Yet, as it later turned out, the only thing that had in fact been expected of me – and one of the reasons why I had been left behind at the camp – was to look after Norm. Apparently I was supposed to cook for him and to heat the shower at night so that he could bask in hot water. Norm was as much a macho-cowboy as one could be and everyone had assumed that I had understood my role while they were away. It didn't take long, however, before the four of them started to warm to me and I soon joined them in front of

Linde's or Tom's tipi, playing cards or sharing stories while staring into the open fire at night.

The camp had around 30 horses, only about 10 of which were kept on site; the rest were left to graze freely in the many meadows surrounding Yohetta. Every so often the horses had to be swapped, providing each their fair share of freedom. During my first couple of weeks at camp, Linde showed me a few tricks of the trade, eventually allowing me to accompany her to 'exchanges' of horses. Leading a handful of horses each, we would ride off into the bush to find the free-roamers. Although Linde had a good knowledge of their 'favourite meadows', it was mostly guesswork, listening out for the sound of a bell that the lead horse was carrying around its neck. At times it took hours to find them. Once spotted, we would let loose the horses we had brought from camp, 'catch' a few grazers, one by one put halters around their heads and take them back to camp. For me, this was the stuff of little kids' dreams – riding through the most spectacular scenery, five horses in tow, no other soul around and not a sound other than horse shoes. On one occasion, during a week when there were no guests at camp, Tom asked me to help him cut a new trail. We were going to be gone for a couple of nights. Packing only the bare minimum – a bit of a challenge for someone who turns into a big wimp when cold – we rode along an existing path for a while until we reached a spot that Tom had declared the starting point for the new trail. We were in the middle of dense bush and every corner looked just like the one before, although obviously not to Tom. He knew exactly where he was going and where this new trail was going to take us. I found this incredibly intriguing. But first things first – the trail needed a name and it was going to be named after *me*. With a big chainsaw he marked the most dominant tree at the start of the new trail with my first initial. This certainly took me by surprise. I felt extremely honoured.

Tom went on to cut his way through the bush and my job was to walk behind him and to pick up all the branches and whatever else was in our way. After hours of hard work we reached a clearing not far from a small 'island' surrounded by a muddy stream that was going to be our camp for the night. We spread out our two canvasses, got a fire going, made some 'Indian bread' over the fire – as Linde had shown me – played cards and drank whisky. It was a beautiful, clear night and the full moon was shining bright above us. To complete the perfect 'Wild West movie scene', we were then treated to some intense howling from wolves at, judging by the sound, pretty safe distance. I had shivers down my neck. But, just like his whisky, Tom always had his rifle within close reach. He was a substantial guy, kind of like a big bear, with a warm heart and I felt safe as long as he was right there – and awake. When it came to bed time, Tom went to get our horses that had been wading in the water and tied them to trees closer to us. If any predator were to approach they had to cross the stream, the sound of which would alert us; that, together with the horses' nervous behaviour, would be all the warning we required. Tom then got himself comfortable and, within a couple of minutes, was off snoring away through the quiet night. He had had quite a bit to drink and the scenario that I now faced didn't give me much confidence. I stared at the full moon for hours, too scared to close my eyes. One of us had to stay alert. I moved my canvas closer to his and his rifle, just in case I had to quickly wake him. I had never been more petrified. This was bear country and the howling wolves didn't help. I survived the night without the slightest threat but with not much sleep either. We spent the next day clearing various existing trails, riding through the most breathtaking territory and – after another anxious though slightly more relaxed night – returned to the Yohetta camp the following day. It was good to be home, but what an unforgettable experience!

The first group of guests to spend time at the camp was a team of Italian fishing enthusiasts led by a gentleman called Giacomo, the owner of a fishing magazine. The purpose of their visit was to cast for fish in the various lakes in and around Yohetta and to then write articles about their wilderness experience. The day after their arrival we set off on what was meant to be a three-day horseback-fishing adventure in the bush. Claude, the camp chef, was the only one to stay behind. After hours of riding through dense bush, crossing crystal-clear rivers and meadows filled with masses of colourful flowers we reached the first lake. Along the way Tom had pointed out several fresh scratch marks on trees, commenting that they would be from grizzly bears that must have passed through not too much earlier.

At the lake Tom and Norm gave the Italians a run-down of the do's and don'ts, stressing that they should at least stay in pairs when fishing, while Linde and I went to prepare the overnight camp. We put up the tents for the guests, got a fire going, made camp-coffee and prepared lunch, which was meant to be served by 2pm. When by 2.15pm just three of the five Italians had shown up, Tom went to get the other two – Giacomo and his wife – only to return and inform us that they were nowhere to be found. Together with Norm he then took off to look for them. They were gone for hours. The remaining three Italians, Linde and I stayed back at the camp. No one was hungry and hardly a word was spoken. The air was extremely tense, to say the least. It seemed that we all had the same thoughts circling in our heads but none of us dared voice them: *Giacomo and his wife must have had an encounter with a bear.*

It was late afternoon by the time Tom and Norm returned. They had traced the couple's steps – or rather that of their horses – all the way to a river but that was all the news that they could provide us with. The plan was for Norm to ride to the top of the mountain behind us. Giacomo was a heavy smoker and we knew that he always carried a lighter on him. It was getting cold and the most logical move for them would be to light a fire to keep warm, to alert anyone looking for them and, above all, to keep safe from bears. The best way to check for smoke and a sign of a fire would be at dark and from up high. Again, Norm returned with no news; there was no fire to be seen anywhere. All that was left to do was for Norm to head back to the Yohetta Ranch at dawn and alert an emergency rescue team. And while Tom took off to search the bush again we stayed at the overnight camp, staring into the fire in silence.

By lunchtime the following day we heard the rescue helicopter approaching. Once we had watched it circle the area for a while, we decided to return to the ranch. We arrived 'home' late that afternoon and just before nightfall we had word that Giacomo and his wife had been found. The search troop had spotted them curled up in a ball, but safe and sound, close to Chilko Lake. As happy and relieved as we all were to see them alive and in one piece, it was hard to ignore the sheer stupidity that had created the anguish and drama. After having been left at the original lake next to our overnight camp, Giacomo and his wife had separated from the rest of the group to fish at a different part of the lake. A short while into their attempt to catch a trout or two, Giacomo thought it a better idea to try their luck at the famed Chilko Lake instead. According to the map he carried in his pocket Chilko Lake was only about 'a centimetre' away – *just around the corner*. Reality proved, however, that this one centimetre was a four-hour ride on horseback through dense bush, across rivers and with no sign posts. Giacomo had failed to recognise that this was Canadian wilderness, not a ride along a touristy trail in the Italian Alps. Apparently, Giacomo and his wife got lost soon after they had taken off. Rather than turn around, they kept going until, through plain luck, they indeed reached Chilko Lake (at 180 square kilometres, huge in size). Incapable of lighting a fire, they then huddled on the shores of the lake, waiting to be rescued. To top it all off, once they had returned to camp, rather than showing remorse and gratitude, Giacomo felt and behaved like a hero, re-telling his story with a big grin on his face; he now had, after all, combatted the 'real' wilderness and, in the first instance, made it to Chilko Lake on his *own*.

My summer at the ranch had indeed turned into a once-in-a-lifetime experience, the memories of which I will cherish forever. To be so far removed from the 'real' world, with no common luxuries, but the most stunning scenery, pitch dark nights filled with stars that glowed so much brighter than I had ever seen before, inspiring chats over camp fires with people who otherwise I would never have come in contact with, and the most amazing peace and quiet. Whenever a seaplane dropped off guests or supplies, every couple of weeks or so, we could hear it long before we could spot it in the sky. And the excitement when the plane eventually landed: there were always letters, chocolate and other surprises from family and friends. Any relevant news was delivered to us by the pilot, over a beer while looking out to the lake watching an eagle catch a fish.

I stayed at the Yohetta Camp until the start of the hunting season. Beside the fact that the camp would have been a lonely existence with everyone out in the bush for about 10 days at a time, the trophy-hunting thing wasn't quite my cup of tea. As much as I was excited about getting back to Whistler, seeing Alain and walking around the village, I was also a bit nervous; it had been around three months since I had left civilisation behind and it was now, without doubt, going to be quite a shock to the system to return. Manfred, the owner of the Yohetta Ranch, had been spending a bit more time at the camp towards the end of my stay and was about to drive back to Williams Lake, in the north-east of Ts'yl-os Provincial Park. He suggested that rather than calling in a plane, I drive out with him and take a bus from Williams Lake back to Whistler. Although this was going to be a very long trip, I didn't mind as it would allow me to see parts of the country that I otherwise wouldn't. After hours of driving on rough roads through the bush, we reached the highway and Manfred eventually dropped me at an intersection with a right-hand turnoff to the main road to Whistler, the best possible point to try to hitch a ride. It was too late for a bus and staying overnight was not an idea I entertained – I was too keen to get 'home'. Luckily, I managed to cover the whole 400-kilometre journey with only two different rides and arrived late that same night. As expected, it took several days to re-adjust to life 'outside'. It was an utterly bizarre feeling strolling around the – what now felt like – very hectic village streets. When I first walked into a rather large store, I almost freaked and had to leave again; the loud music, the noise, the people – it was all too much.

Within a few short months my vision of the perfect life had done 'a 180' and I was now dreaming of living in a beautiful log house in front of a lake at least a couple of hours from the closest town, with horses and dogs and a small seaplane parked at the lake shore. I could see myself running a B & B or a retreat, offering a healthy lifestyle and outdoor activities for city slickers. In the meantime, however, I would have to face reality and make some money. For the four weeks following my return to Whistler, I got a job at a circus trapeze that had been set up at the bottom of Blackcomb Mountain for the summer. It was a real-size trapeze, run by a very cool Quebecois couple – 'JC' and Dennis – where tourists, secured by a harness, could get a taste of what it was like to be an acrobat. My responsibilities were to have the waivers signed, help kids up the ladder, assist Alain – who had been working part-time at the trapeze all summer – on top of the platform and, last but not least, be the guinea pig for Alain's first attempts to become a 'catcher' (the person on the second trapeze, catching the clients who are swinging upside down and are game enough to let go on cue and be caught). It was a fun job and another opportunity to face my fear of heights following my paragliding accident.

Since I had returned to Whistler I had been looking for a more 'serious' job opportunity and in time I got offered what sounded like a pretty good start – a position as a tour and outdoor guide for a German tour operator. The job wasn't going to start for another couple of months and with Dennis and JC packing up the trapeze at the end of the summer season I would now have plenty of time at my disposal to join Alain on a road trip across Canada, followed by a couple of weeks in Quebec with his family and friends. At the end of September, just as we were getting ready for the trip, I had word that the tour operator with whom I was meant to commence work in a few weeks' time had gone into receivership. The following morning, out of the blue and with no knowledge about the status of my supposed Canadian job, I had a call from my brother Heiner, asking if I would be interested in running one of his restaurants. The restaurant in question – the Klug – was a gem of a place and close to my brother's heart. Set against the rock wall of the Festungsberg (a steep hill in the centre of Salzburg and home to the Hohensalzburg Castle), it hosted one of the most stunning restaurant-gardens in town. It had been a so-called 'problem child' – mostly related to the management at the time – within my brother's business and unless I was interested in getting involved, he was going to sell the Klug. As I do, I couldn't help but feel that things were, once again, happening for a reason. Bearing in mind that Heiner had called less than 24 hours after I had 'lost' the other job, his plea deserved consideration. I had been overseas for two and a half years – my stint at the hospital excluded – with ever-changing jobs, accommodation and circles of friends, and the idea of a more settled life started to sound more appealing than it ever had. I was 26 by then and I now tried to convince myself that it was time to get more serious – well, kind of, at least for a little while.

Chapter 5

Commitment or springboard?

The thought of a long-term commitment frightened me, especially with the prospect of settling back in Austria, so I eventually offered to help my brother out for six months. According to Heiner, however, six months wasn't an option; I had to stay for at least one year as anything less wouldn't make sense. I agreed, apprehensively. The agreement, however, came with another hitch. My brother was going on holidays in three weeks' time and was hoping for me to get back before he left. Rather than crossing Canada in Alain's van, we now had to fly to Quebec instead to be able to spend at least a week there and make the most of the stunning scenery during Indian summer (a period of leaves changing colour from green to vivid tones of yellow, red and orange).

I left for Austria in mid-October and Alain was to join me a few months later. There was no time to muck around upon my arrival. On my second day back in Salzburg, I was thrown into the deep end, to say the least. Heiner briefly showed me around the restaurant, introduced me to the staff as someone who was there to help out, and off he went on his holiday. The details of my exact position would be communicated to everyone upon his return.

A few years earlier my brother had renounced his interest in the family hotel in Salzburg with a view to doing his own thing. His entrepreneurial journey had started with the opening of a beer garden, continued with the addition of a pub as well as a trendy bar and by the time I had returned to Austria, he had built up a couple of other successful restaurants. At the same time, he was working on a new healthy-eating-feel-good franchise concept. And although Heiner was, to some degree, emotionally attached to the Klug he simply hadn't had the time and the head to deal with it on a day-to-day basis. On my first day 'in the office', Toni, the 'jack of all trades' who was in charge of maintenance as well as various other tasks at my brother's restaurants, greeted me with the words, 'Well, I wish you good luck!' Considering that he had chosen a sarcastic tone, I asked him to explain, to which he responded with: 'You will see.'

When Heiner returned from his holiday three weeks' later, most of the original floor-staff had left. Once they had realised that they couldn't rid themselves of me, one by one they decided to resign. Each night at around 11pm, the restaurant manager tried to send me home early with the reasoning that there were enough resources for the handful of customers left at the bar. In view of the fact that those customers were mostly friends of his, just like the staff he had employed, it wasn't hard to see what was going on. When his friends ordered expensive champagne, it was served in a wine glass and put into the system as 'house wine'. And when I wasn't looking, consumption wasn't registered at all. No wonder the restaurant wasn't making any money! In general the Klug was very quiet, which again wasn't a surprise going by the quality of service. It seemed like everyone who worked there was simply there to get drunk, cheaply, after work. It was hard to classify what was actually considered work as opposed to a break or being off work. Evidently neither the staff nor their friends hanging around the bar were thrilled to have the boss's sister around. They kept throwing me evil looks hoping that I would eventually stay away but, contrary to the manager's roster, I kept showing up at work early and only left once the bar had closed its doors. He certainly didn't want me there for the settlement of the accounts each night. But I wasn't going anywhere. With each day and each indiscretion exposed, the manager turned more and more belligerent until he eventually realised he had no choice but to leave his comfortable and very profitable job.

I hadn't spent much time in Salzburg since I had left high school. Staff within the hospitality industry were mostly being hired through word of mouth but, given I no longer had worthwhile connections, this posed a bit of a challenge. During my first few days at the Klug, an old friend of mine, Gabi, walked in one night. She was surprised to see me there and offered her help if ever needed. Although not quite expecting that she would, indeed, get a call only a week later, Gabi jumped on the wagon without delay. She was in between jobs and happy to help out; before she knew it, a couple of days per week turned into a full-time-and-a-half job, once all the former staff walked off. Gabi, too, had attended the hotel and tourism college. She was like an angel that had fallen from the sky just at the right moment. We worked our butts off, but at the same time had a lot of fun. It was a six-day week with – on average – 12- to 14-hour days. At the end of each night, generally around 2am, we would get a drink, turn up the music and sit on the bar-counter looking at each other, utterly exhausted but with big grins on our faces and proud of ourselves. Who would have thought, all those years ago …

I was on a mission to make the Klug into *the* place to go in Salzburg. The prerequisites, like an excellent chef and a cool interior and garden, were already in place; now all that was required was the right staff – people that customers would come back for. It was the ambiance that called for a serious makeover. Gabi eventually moved to Vienna for a new job but, over time and determined to the core, I gradually gathered a great team around me – mostly young, ambitious guys with not much experience but great personalities. And although it involved a fair amount of patience and 'flexibility' to train them, it proved worth the effort given the growing popularity and busyness of the Klug. This was confirmed one night, when – the restaurant packed to its limit and too much for the kitchen to handle – I walked up to several customers to apologise for the delay. While no one seemed to mind, it was the comment of one gentleman in particular – an internationally highly recognised businessman – that made me feel that we were heading in the right direction. I still remember his words: 'I don't mind waiting; I love sitting here, simply watching the staff. It's not very often that one gets to see cool, young people work with so much passion and commitment.' That, for me, was the biggest compliment.

One day, a television crew offered to film a short segment about the Klug for the local evening news. It was to be about the rare combination of excellent food and a relaxed atmosphere – the Klug was listed in the *Gault Millau Guide* and our chef, Gerhard Fuchs, was later rewarded Chef of the Year 2004 by Gault Millau Austria. The crew were going to come by one night and do a brief interview. Although I felt I had jumped a big hurdle by selling insurance in London a couple of years earlier, this was taking it a step too far. The thought of appearing on television was petrifying and not a plunge I was prepared to take; there was a limit and this was definitely beyond it. I told my brother that he had to make himself available for the interview. He refused, stating that the restaurant now was my 'baby' and that it wouldn't be right for him to take that spot. Only after I threatened to resign – this is how serious I was about crossing my boundaries – did he agree to attend the interview.

On the night, the restaurant was packed. The film crew arrived, we had a brief chat, they set up their gear and all we were waiting for was my brother. He had promised to come but I still started to get nervous. Then the phone rang; it was Heiner telling me that he was on his way to the hospital with his wife who had just gone into labour. *This can't be happening*, I thought. *It has to be a prank.* I was waiting for my brother to show himself, to jump out from behind the curtain and laugh. But he didn't. I told the television crew. They considered it to be very funny and made it clear that I now didn't have a choice but to step in – and up – after all. With the help of two glasses of prosecco that I downed faster than I could think, I told the gentlemen that they had two minutes and not a second longer and I proceeded towards the bright lights and the camera that was placed right in the middle of the restaurant. The interview went for at least 10 minutes. This was by far the furthest I had ever stepped out of my comfort zone; but once it was all over and I had expressed my anger at the crew about not sticking to the agreement, I was proud of myself (not that I was entirely happy with the end result, but at least it was another box ticked – one that previously hadn't even existed).

I ended up staying in Salzburg and managing the restaurant for a total of two years. Alain had come to Austria to live with me. We had a great apartment more or less in the middle of town and I earned a fair bit more than I could spend. I had great family as well as a fun group of friends around me. I cycled to and from work through a stunning, extremely safe city and the restaurant, although all-consuming, I had come to love. My brother had given me complete freedom in every respect, making me feel like I was running my own business. I basically had everything one could possibly wish for, while living in one of the most beautiful countries in the world. (I don't know how many times during my travels, whenever I mentioned that I was from Austria or Salzburg – I had given up calling Bad Gastein my home as more often than not people would look at me with a frown: '*What, Pakistan?!*' – I was met with big eyes and bright smiles.) Salzburg in particular appeared to be countless people's 'been there' or 'must go' favourite destination. My life seemed perfect. Well, on paper, at least, and when I rationalised it in my head. The fact was, I was not happy, no matter how hard I tried to convince myself otherwise. I couldn't pinpoint exactly what wasn't sitting right but I knew that if I didn't do anything about it then, I would get caught in a rut and eventually accept that plodding along was good enough. I was living a very privileged life and my sentiment was one that was hard for people around me to comprehend; but I knew that I had to leave. I had ignored that nagging feeling for long enough, mostly due to not being prepared to turn my back on the Klug before I felt that it was *where* and *what* I had it envisioned to be. But now was the time.

Chapter 6

Lucky country

My immediate choices were South Africa or Canada; I had fallen in love with both places and could see myself living happily ever after in either. It was now a matter of – first of all – going back to Cape Town on a brief holiday to look at the city from a non-backpacker's perspective; an exercise that, in the end, produced the sad realisation that unfortunately the atmosphere had changed and, compared to three years earlier, I didn't feel nearly as safe. With South Africa out of the equation, I now had to scrutinise my idea of moving to Canada. It was getting cold in Austria and, contrary to my initial enthusiasm, I could not fight the feeling that Canada might not be the best choice either. After two years in Austria I had to move to a warmer climate. I also had the creeping urge to take this step on my own – at least until I had a better idea about what I wanted in life. Considering that Alain was from Canada, going back with him would have been the easier choice rather than one I could confidently claim as my own. The problem eventually solved itself when, one morning, I woke up and suddenly knew that I had to go to Australia. It was a very strong sentiment that surprised even me. Although I had very much enjoyed my time in Australia six years earlier, at the time – and up until then – I had dismissed it with the mantra: 'Too far away; too many sharks; too big a hole in the ozone layer.'

So here I was, about to fulfil my childhood prophecy of emigrating to Australia one day. This wasn't going to be just another trip. I had moved around a lot over the previous years and, at the age of 28, I was ready to settle somewhere long-term. My family had always been very supportive of me but when I told friends that I was going to move to Australia, the general consent was that I was running away from something, that it would be impossible to attain a permanent visa, and that they bet I would be back within a couple of years, at the most. My final two weeks in Salzburg were very intense, to say the least. I worked until the very last minute to ensure a smooth transition to my successor at the Klug, while at the same time packing up my life and selling whatever there was to sell. There was also the separation from Alain after three years together. By the time I stepped onto the plane, I was a walking zombie.

I touched down in Australia on 1 October 1998. Not having been overly impressed with Sydney first time round, I had decided to give Melbourne a try. It was the southern hemisphere spring and still rather cold when I arrived. The Esso Longford gas explosion – a catastrophic industrial accident – had occurred six days prior to my arrival and there was no gas, hot water or heating for the time being. I tried very hard to develop a love for Melbourne but after freezing my Austrian butt off for two weeks, I decided this wasn't what I had come for and took an overnight bus to Sydney. With backpacker accommodation out of the equation – I had to prevent myself from getting into the travelling spirit – I booked myself into a cheap hotel in Sydney's Chinatown. My room was just big enough to fit a bed and my suitcase and, together with its small barred window – the iron bars of which were decorated with old tea bags that obviously once belonged to residents from the upper floors – made me feel like an inmate and did nothing to lift my spirits. I dropped my bags in the cell and walked down to the harbour. Sitting on a hill in the botanic gardens adjacent to the Opera House I started to cry, questioning what the hell I was doing moving to Australia. With no working visa, next-to-no energy and a hotel room that felt like a prison, it struck me that I was no longer a 21-year-old carefree soul sparkling with fire. I was utterly exhausted and all I wanted to do at that stage was to sleep for two weeks and not worry about a new home or a job. I didn't know anyone in Australia, let alone Sydney. It was my gut instinct, this strong inner knowing, that had pulled me to the opposite side of the world. I hadn't given the how and what much thought. Things had always worked out; something would come up, of that I had been sure. But here I was now and the thought of a fresh start and the effort and energy this required made me feel sick. Just before I had left Austria I had been given two contacts for potential jobs but at that miserable point I couldn't have cared less about either of them.

My first plan of action was to find a place to live; I had to get out of that room. Each morning I would sit in the same café, the local paper spread out in front of me, running through the 'shared accommodation' section. I was so stuck on the European model where one would always strive to live in or close to the city centre that I was looking for this in Sydney too – a shared apartment somewhere in town. On my first visit to Sydney six years earlier we had skipped exploring the beachside suburbs; with more than enough beaches over the previous months in Asia and along the Australian coast, it was the city itself we wanted to discover. No wonder Sydney had failed to impress at the time. I arranged viewings for several places, mostly apartments in tall dark buildings and, with nothing to compare it to, I thought this was as good as it got. Interviews with potential flatmates generally didn't go particularly well. I wasn't in a good frame of mind nor was I in the mood for making an effort to 'sell myself'. It was almost like I was hoping to get a 'no' so that I could feel sorry for myself.

I had left Austria with two possible job opportunities, both handed to me without asking. The first one was from Dieter Mateschitz, co-founder of Red Bull – the energy drink – and a regular at the Klug, asking if I would be interested in taking Red Bull to Australia; and the second was from a cousin of Niki Lauda, who was also a regular at the restaurant and had organised for a recommendation letter from Niki Lauda for Lauda Air Australia. Mr Mateschitz had given me the contact details of the Managing Director of Red Bull New Zealand and suggested I get in contact with him to discuss opportunities. Red Bull had been facing legal difficulties in entering the Australian market but had recently advanced to the approval stage. I managed to talk to the gentleman in New Zealand a couple of times whereupon he chose to ignore my emails and calls. From our first conversation I had the impression that he had no plans to hand any responsibility to anyone else, let alone to someone who had connections with the owner. I had offered to fly to New Zealand to meet with him, but even that suggestion was met with an instant 'no'. Not wanting to push any further – there was no sense in trying to work for or with someone who didn't want me there – I eventually gave up. My attempts with Lauda Air in Sydney turned out much the same. No one could have cared less about my letter of recommendation from the big boss; well, at least the gate keepers couldn't. And with my current headspace and level of confidence, I let that one go, too.

While initially I hadn't put much weight on either of these options, once I had received a double rejection, I used it wisely to wallow in self-pity. One night I called my brother from my hotel cell and, staring at the bars on my window, I told him about my misery: how I couldn't find a place to live and how neither Red Bull nor Lauda Air were prepared to give me even the chance for an interview. I expected nothing less than a good portion of sympathy but instead what I got was a lecture; a lecture about how I should get my act together and appreciate my freedom. *I was free to do whatever I wanted. I was in Australia, for goodness sake! I was single, I had no kids and no other responsibilities whatsoever; the world was my oyster. If my brother were in my shoes, he would embrace that freedom of mine and the adventures that it would bring with it, to its fullest.*

I don't know where the negativity in my head had come from as this was not me, but that stern talk from my brother sure had an impact. While right after the call I was upset and angry beyond measure (how dare he not buy into my misery!) Heiner certainly got me thinking. By the following morning I had managed to find the switch in my brain. I was sitting in the same café, with the same paper, looking at the same sections of the paper, but now, as if by a miracle, excitement was pouring out of my every pore. I had a big smile across my face, feeling like the luckiest girl – free to choose and do with my life whatever I wanted. And, as my brother had said, for goodness sake, I was in Australia. It's unbelievable what a change in perception can do to one's mental state. This was a big lesson in life and one that I would think back on. My brother's words were the best thing that could have happened to me at the time. Any commiseration would have confirmed and given permission to my gloom and thereby dug a deeper hole.

As it happened, that morning in the café I decided to broaden my view of Sydney and I arranged a viewing of a shared flat in Cremorne, a suburb on the lower north shore. I took a ferry from the Opera House across to 'Old Cremorne' and while I was wandering around Cremorne Point trying to find my way, I passed several streets lined with stunning homes just metres from the most beautiful bay. In awe, the insuppressible thought *One day, I would love to live around here!* induced even further inspiration. This was certainly a very different Sydney to the one I had experienced so far. I had presumed that Cremorne Point or Old Cremorne couldn't be far from Cremorne but, as it turned out, it was a different suburb up the road and the address that I was looking for was a good half-hour walk. The apartment wasn't quite what I had in mind, but it got me venturing out of the city and the inner suburbs. The following day, while again looking through the 'shared accommodation' section of the paper, I noticed two separate ads for rooms in shared houses in Cremorne Point. I was ecstatic. Never in a million years would I have thought that in a posh suburb like that there would be such a thing as *shared* accommodation – and a house, rather than a flat?! The monthly rent for each of the advertised rooms was well within my budget and I arranged two viewings for that afternoon. I loved both places as much as the people I would be sharing with and by day's end it was in my hands to choose. There I was, two days after my breakdown on the phone with my brother, going from being miserable about not finding a place to live to moving into a house literally around the corner from where I had dreamed of living in 'one day'.

Next on the agenda was the hunt for a job. The day after I moved into my new home, I once again turned to the classifieds section of the daily paper that I had come to know so well. My commute into the city would be a three-minute walk to the ferry, followed by an 18-minute ferry ride across the most beautiful harbour. I thought how cool it would be to find a job in walking distance from where the ferries docked at Circular Quay, in town, right between the Opera House and the Harbour Bridge. I called the first number I came across within the hospitality section of the paper: a short ad with no mention of location. It was Tuesday, 3 November around 3pm. The phone seemed to ring out and just as I was about to hang up someone answered with a rather annoyed voice. I gave my 'I'm looking for a job' spiel but was interrupted half way through and asked to hold for a couple of minutes. I heard lots of voices screaming in the background and eventually another voice came to the phone, asking me what I was thinking calling during the Melbourne Cup.

The Melbourne Cup is Australia's premier thoroughbred horse race and, for a few minutes a year, during the main race, the nation stands still. It was quite an achievement of mine to manage to call bang-on those three minutes. But luck was on my side and I was asked to come in for an interview later that afternoon. I started work the same night. The restaurant was in The Rocks, literally five minutes' walk from Circular Quay and right across from the Opera House.

The Rocks is the historical precinct of central Sydney and my new workplace was a small restaurant and café, The Sydney Cove Providore, housed in an old building with a very special atmosphere. My spirits lifted the moment I walked in; the place was full of character and the staff seemed lovely. As for Robert, the owner, within a couple of days he started to treat me like his second in charge. He also almost immediately offered to act as a so-called business sponsor so that I could remain in Australia long-term. Although I very much appreciated his offer, being a waitress for longer than necessary wasn't quite what I had in mind. I still didn't know what it was that I actually wanted to do, but in order to retain the freedom of choice for when I finally *did* figure it out, I somehow had to get my hands on a so-called 'Independent Skilled Visa' – a visa that would grant me permanent residency without being tied to a specific job. This feat wasn't going to be easy; thinking about it rationally, in my case it would be virtually impossible. Independent visas in Australia were tied to a points system and I simply didn't have enough points, no matter how much I tried to twist and turn my circumstances. At the time, the points system comprised three sets of criteria that could award an applicant various points – skills (education, profession and work experience), knowledge of the English language and age (the highest number of points were given to 'under 30s', meaning that I just scraped through). Without a university degree and my profession not on the 'most-wanted' list, the skills part represented the obvious deal-breaker. Robert suggested I talk to an immigration lawyer who he'd had dealings with previously. I was still hesitant as a sponsorship for the position of waitress was simply not an option; but when he kept pushing, I thought it wouldn't hurt to meet with the lawyer, if only to have a chat. As it happened, the lawyer specialising in business sponsorship who Robert had made the actual appointment with was tied up on the day and his colleague, David, agreed to meet with me instead. The lucky coincidence was that David only dealt with Independent Visas and consequently suggested we check my options in that regard. It didn't take much for him to acknowledge that I did not, indeed, have enough points. The number of points required at the time were already on the lower end but David nevertheless recommended that I get all the paperwork in place, just in case. Immigration authorities change the number of points from time to time and he believed that there was a slight chance that they would be lowered even further at some stage.

It took weeks to gather all the information, stats, certificates, letters and official documents required. Remarkably, one of the conditions in my case was that I had to have held a management position for two years – a small detail that I had in no way been aware of when I had decided to extend my 'sojourn' at the Klug in Austria to exactly two years. Another point on the agenda was to undergo the IELTS test – an international standardised test of English language proficiency for non-native English language speakers – which I thankfully passed with flying colours, awarded the highest possible points within that category. Once the extensive to-do list was completed, it was then just a matter of hope and, above all, lots of patience. I decided to utilise David's services rather than attempting to deal with it all by myself, as the stakes were simply too high. I was determined to stay in Australia and I was happy to pay the additional fee if it meant increasing my chances even a tad.

I stayed at Sydney Cove Providore until February 1999. After five months of running up and down the same stairs between the kitchen and restaurant, it was simply time for a change. I had enjoyed working there, but considering that waitressing wasn't quite my dream job, I felt that adding more variety might help my case. I decided to have a look around my own neighbourhood, on the other side of the bridge, and to canvass the streets of Cremorne and Mosman. Within a few short hours I had three different jobs in hospitality that I later complemented with a casual office job at a one-man-show marketing office. With each of the jobs I was lucky to be able to choose which and how many days a week I wanted to work – ticking the variety box. To add fun, spice and purpose, I then also got my competitive streak involved. One of my jobs was as a barista in a cute little, but very busy, coffee shop in Mosman, where I loved to challenge myself to make as many coffees simultaneously as possible. This wasn't Austria though, where one had the choice of an espresso, large espresso, long black or a cappuccino. Rather, what I was dealing with were soy flat whites with not too much milk, skim double shot cappuccinos, decaf macchiatos with hot – but not too hot! – milk on the side plus a shot of vanilla, and so forth.

Another of my new jobs was at a fine dining restaurant where I set myself the task of memorising all orders, drinks and food without the use of a notepad, slowly increasing the size of tables that this rule applied to (more than once customers would bet that I wouldn't be able to remember the full order and I would end up with a bigger tip as a result of it). And then there was the job at an extremely busy pub in North Sydney, where my position was that of a 'runner', taking food from the kitchen to the tables. I chose to work lunchtime Fridays, the busiest time of the week, declaring the job as paid exercise; the heavy plates were my weights and I exerted myself with power walking, trying hard not to run so that I wouldn't look too ridiculous. To balance it all off, there was my one day 'at the office', which was a good and subtle enough way to introduce myself to business English and learn a thing or two about marketing. All these jobs – although fun – were a big step back from the responsibilities I had held back in Austria. This didn't bother me, especially in view of the bigger picture – permanent residency in Australia. I was, without doubt, making the most of my 'transition time' though; not only did I quite enjoy going to a different workplace each day with all the variety of experiences this involved, I also met a lot of new people and made many new friends.

Although David, my immigration lawyer, was on the case, I kept calling the immigration office every couple of weeks to check if the number of points required to obtain permanent residency had, by any chance, changed. Eight months into the exercise, I was told that the points had been lowered from 115 to 110, matching exactly what I had on offer. I kept asking the lady on the other end of the phone if she was sure this was right and she kept responding that it was indeed the case. My calls had become so routine that receiving a different answer to what I had heard a zillion times before was no longer something I counted on. I still didn't dare accept her response as true and went on to call another immigration branch that, too, confirmed what I had been told in the first place. There were no words to describe my excitement. For a while I just stood there in disbelief, my heart racing and – tears in my eyes – murmuring a continuous stream of 'oh my gosh, oh my gosh'. Eventually I collected my thoughts and emotions enough to call my lawyer's office, just to be told that David was on holidays. I passed on the great news to the receptionist who simply countered that there was no way that what I had just told her could be true as they would know about it. Having received confirmation twice, however, her response failed to deter me from my excitement and I suggested she call the immigration office herself to receive validation. A couple of hours later my phone rang with David calling from his holidays, instructing me to immediately take all the paperwork I had collated and completed over the previous months and drop it all off at his office. I did as told and by the Monday after, when David returned from holidays, my application was couriered to the Australian Embassy in Austria. It was received by the embassy on 28 June. The points were raised again to 115 on 1 July.

When I had first found out that the points had been lowered, I contacted my South African friend Liezl, who had been going through the same process but with a different lawyer. She, too, hadn't had enough points and her lawyer, too, wasn't aware of the changes. Contrary to David, however, he didn't see the urgency and took his time submitting Liezl's visa application. By the time it had reached the Australian embassy in South Africa, the points had been put up again and Liezl eventually had no choice but to leave the country. The fact that neither of our immigration lawyers had been informed or been aware of the change in rules seemed odd. The points had only been lowered for a couple of weeks and it appeared to have been a somewhat secretive mission; possibly to reach a certain number of immigrants by the half-yearly mark, or to open the doors for someone with the right connections who otherwise wouldn't have got into the country. Who knows? I was extremely lucky to find out about it in time and to have had the entire paperwork ready, allowing the submission process to fit into the narrow window.

Alain had been understanding of my need to take off to Australia by myself, and had gone back to Canada soon after I left Austria. We had been keeping in contact and, six months into my time in Sydney, I decided to go and visit him in Whistler to see how we felt about our relationship now I'd had time by myself. We spent a couple of weeks together and by the end of it both of us knew I had made the right decision. My visit to Canada was an important one on several levels. Canada had always held a special spot in my heart and, other than checking in on the relationship with Alain, I also had to confirm that Australia was where I was truly meant to be. My trip turned out a 'mission accomplished' and by the time I returned to Sydney and my cherished abode, any doubts had been put to rest. I was still living in Cremorne Point – not far from the shared house I had originally moved into, which had been sold by its owners five months into my stay. Now I had the added bonus of a view of the Sydney city skyline, looking straight out to the Opera House and the Harbour Bridge. Each morning when I got up and glanced around I found it hard to believe how lucky I was. My apartment was right at the gorgeous Cremorne Point path that led around a couple of beautiful bays dotted with sailboats of all sizes. The vegetation – giant plants that in Austria were only found at florists and in miniature sizes – was stunningly beautiful, especially for someone who had grown up in the snow. I had lorikeets (small, bright coloured parrots) and cockatoos regularly visiting my balcony and whenever I phoned home, family and friends would think I was somewhere in the bush whereas, in fact, I was only a 10-minute ferry ride from the centre of a major international city.

Months passed and the only news that we had had from the Immigration Department was that they had received my application and that it would be evaluated; a process that could take up to 18 months. There was no guarantee that I would get the stamp of approval but both my lawyer and I were pretty confident. About seven months into the waiting game I eventually heard from David that the Immigration Department had requested further information. According to David, this was a good sign; once it got to the stage of the office actually looking at my application, it was supposedly only a matter of weeks before a decision was made. I had a friend from Austria visiting in 10 days' time and we were booked to fly to Tasmania – an island state off the southern tip of Australia – for a two-week holiday. The information I had been asked to provide was substantial and it had to be in original format – that is, original certified copies of the English translation. With a serious time constraint on my hands, I was now facing the challenging task of collating the requested documents and having them translated and sent to Australia to arrive before we left on holidays. Many late-night overseas phone calls later, I had arranged for all the paperwork – in the required format – to be couriered to Sydney, with a guaranteed delivery time the morning of our departure. On the day, we arranged to meet the gentleman from the courier service down the road from where I lived and where our taxi would be waiting, everything timed to the minute. On the way to the airport we rushed past my lawyer's office where I dropped off the envelope, leaving David with the request to call me should there be any problems. By the time we arrived at the airport it was almost a straight walk onto the plane.

There was a reason for the rush. My Australian visa was running out in 10 weeks' time and there was no chance whatsoever to get it extended, let alone leave the country and be allowed back in even on a tourist visa after what would have already been one and a half years in Australia. As relieved as I had been to get the requested paperwork to my lawyer in time, upon my return from my holiday I found out that David's perception of my situation hadn't quite matched mine. Still in the belief that everything had gone according to plan, a couple of days after I arrived back in Sydney I had a message from David's secretary asking to arrange an appointment. Another few days passed before I walked into David's office and eventually saw the envelope that I had fought so hard to get delivered prior to my departure to Tasmania (and that I believed had been forwarded to the immigration office that same day) sitting right there on his desk. David opened the envelope, pulled out the paperwork and placed it in front of him, ready to commence our meeting. Simply speechless, I shifted the documents towards me, tears rolling down my face and onto the originals. Then just sat there staring at the pile in front of me. I felt like David was playing with my life; it was my future sitting on his desk and, although he should have been very much aware of this, he obviously didn't care. I was just another client and he was getting paid regardless of the outcome.

It wasn't only that time was running out in regards to my Australian visa: I had also been offered a dream job at the 2000 Sydney Olympic Games with the condition that I could prove the legal status of my work permit. My flatmate Catherine was an HR manager at SOCOG (the Sydney Organising Committee of the Olympic Games) and had arranged an interview with the department heads of the Olympic Village. The position on offer was 'Resident Centre Supervisor', essentially ensuring that the athletes were well looked after during their stay. The job was to commence on 1 May, four and a half months before the start of the actual games, and the deadline to confirm receipt of my 'permanent residency' was Monday 27 March, seven weeks away. Displaying very much a laissez-faire attitude, David tried to calm me down by saying that he hadn't dared to send off the papers as they were. He felt that the documentation I had provided wasn't quite sufficient and that I should organise changes/additions to a couple of the documents. (The amended papers would have to be, once again, translated and couriered, eating up precious time.) I questioned why he hadn't told me sooner – as I had clearly asked him to before I left on holidays – and emphasised that it was now too late for any changes. David replied by saying he could send it all off that day but that he wouldn't take responsibility.

I felt the changes he appealed for were a simple cover up of his negligence so, without hesitation, requested that he send the papers as they were straight away, and I only left David's office once I had witnessed the courier pick up the envelope. After exiting the building I went to hide in a little side street and started to cry hysterically. I knew my behaviour was over the top but I simply couldn't stop sobbing. With so many emotions attached to that visa and my life in Australia, it was hard to be rational.

There was nothing left for me to do, other than to wait and hope. The Monday of the week of 20 March – a week before my deadline with SOCOG and two weeks before the expiry of my Australian visa – my boss at the marketing office where I was now working three half days per week followed up his 'good morning' with an enquiry on the progress of my visa. With full confidence, I told him I was going to get it that week. He laughed and asked how I was so certain and I simply responded that I just knew. (It had to be that week – I wanted the job at the Olympics too badly for it not to be.) When I returned to his office two days later, I was welcomed with the same question. The exact scenario repeated itself on Friday morning and all I could say was that the day wasn't over yet. That night I worked at the fine dining restaurant in Cremorne. I started my shift at 4pm and by the time I got to work I still had no news from David. I was upset and strangely confused. The presentiment that I would receive my visa that week was such a strong one that at no point had I doubted it would be the case.

According to my current visa I would have to leave the country in 10 days' time. Friends had been asking me what I was going to do and where I was planning to go, and I kept telling them that I wasn't going anywhere. There was no space for a 'no'. And I had no plan B. No matter how often I had been told that one always had to have a plan B, it rarely worked for me. Having a plan B meant that I doubted myself from the get-go and would have taken away from the conviction and determination that I otherwise had. Should plan A ever turn out to be a no-go, I could always come up with a plan B then, but it simply couldn't be part of the initial plan.

I couldn't comprehend what had gone wrong. I kept checking my mobile phone during work that Friday night, but there were no missed calls and I had no message from David. It was bizarre, but I felt as if someone had betrayed me, as if someone had promised me with all his heart that I would get my visa in time and then failed to deliver. I got home just after midnight and more out of habit than anything else I pressed the button of the home phone answering machine and there it was: 'Hi Sabine, it's David. I have good news for you … '

The following Monday, literally two and a half days after I had heard from David and four days before my 30th birthday, was D-day for my job at the Olympics. I called my future boss and gave him the news. The next call was the owner of the marketing office. We had always got along very well and, for all his sarcasm the previous week, he was ecstatic for me. Third in line was the restaurant where I had worked two nights earlier. Management had recently changed and I had no respect whatsoever for my new boss. She was very rude to all the staff, but especially with me, and I couldn't wait to hand in my resignation.

Chapter 7

Fun and Games

I had to pick up my Permanent Resident Visa outside of Australia. It was going to take a couple of weeks for the paperwork to be processed and forwarded to the embassy in Auckland, my closest pick-up option. And with my existing visa about to expire on 7 April, that was the latest possible date to depart Australia. I wasn't sure how long I would have to stick around Auckland before my visa would be available but on my second visit to the embassy, two days after I arrived, I held my passport with the 'stamp to freedom' in my hands. I still get chills when I think about it – it meant so very much to me. And the timing couldn't have been more perfect.

I started work at SOCOG on 1 May 2000. After a year and a half of living a kind of backpacker life, it was such a great feeling to walk into an office on Monday morning to be part of something – at that point in time for me – more real, but above all hugely exciting. For the first couple of months we were located at the SOCOG head office in Ultimo, close to the Sydney city centre. My team consisted of Martin and Lisa, the Resident Centre Managers – the coolest bosses one could wish for – and 15 Resident Centre Supervisors, of whom I was one. I had never worked in a Monday-to-Friday, nine-to-five environment, let alone in a humungous open-plan office; the people on my floor seemed like a great bunch and the buzzing atmosphere could be felt from every angle.

The Sydney Olympic Village had been constructed specifically for the Games and was said to be one of the biggest athlete villages ever built. With housing for over 15,000 competitors and team officials, there were 21 Resident Centres scattered around the village that would become the contact point for the athletes and their teams. Participating at the Games were 199 nations, plus four individual athletes from East Timor. (Athletes compete as independent Olympians at the Olympic Games for various reasons, including political transition and international sanctions.)

Back at head office, our team of 15 was divided into five groups, each of which had to take ownership of a special project. The task that I was working on with my two colleagues and my boss, Martin, was to create a roster for the period of the actual Olympic and Paralympic Games, for a total of 90 supervisors – us 15 plus another 75 who were to start work in a couple of months' time – as well as approximately 800 volunteers. The Resident Centres were varied in size and each nation had a specific Resident Centre allocated, in general the one closest to their housing. Producing a roster of such gigantic proportions brought with it considerable challenges, for example, the subject of languages. We had to ensure that, where available, the language skills of paid and volunteer staff correlated with the nationalities attached to each Resident Centre, while at the same time taking into consideration volunteers' specific availabilities and special requests. There were three shifts that had to be covered daily: morning, afternoon and overnight. Rather than getting stuck with the comparatively limited computer scheduling system that we had at our disposal, we decided to revert to the good old manual system. Having typed each of the volunteers' names, availability, language skills and special requests into a word document, one below the other, we printed all those sheets of paper and cut out each of the names with its details. Armed with a big pile of snippets – 890 in total – we then retired to a big meeting room where we had all the Resident Centres laid out, numbers one to 21, each represented on an individual piece of paper with the number of the Resident Centre as well as the allocated nationalities showing on top, and three divisions, one for each shift, underneath. The paper snippets were then sorted by language skills and availabilities. Now it was 'only' a matter of going through the two piles of snippets and allocating them to the individual Resident Centres, which, in our case meant gluing them onto the corresponding sheets. This may sound pretty straightforward, but when one takes into account the very specific special requests from some of the volunteers it became a bit more challenging. As daunting as the project had appeared to be to start off with, the four of us had a lot of fun in the process, at times spending nights with wine and pizza, bent over snippets and arguing over whose was the best solution. Once we had finished the first draft of our 21 pieces of what resembled modern art, we entered all the information into the computerised scheduling system, printed the 800 volunteer rosters and sent them out in the mail, well prepared for the inevitable influx of phone calls to request changes.

Two months into our time at SOCOG, our team moved to the Olympic Village, about 19 kilometres west of the Sydney central business district. We settled into an unfinished Chef de Mission office and prepared the training program for the 25 supervisors who were about to join us, as well as the 800 volunteers who were to be trained and inducted soon after. Whenever I talked to my family, it was first and foremost my mum who took in every word of my accounts about our preparations for the Olympics. She considered it extremely exciting that I was going to be a part of it. One day, about three weeks before the opening ceremony of the Games, I asked Mum if she would be interested in coming to Sydney to work as a volunteer. Although thrilled at the sound my proposition, she was convinced that she was way too old. (Mum was 60 at the time.) I kept assuring her that she most definitely wasn't too old and she eventually agreed to me checking with my boss, Martin, if it would still be possible for her to join. Martin rushed her through the accreditation process and, in her typical cool and uncomplicated manner, less than a week later Mum was in Sydney, ready to join the large team of Resident Centre Volunteers.

The morning shifts at the Resident Centres during the Olympic Games started at 6am. In view of the amount of time we were going to spend at the Olympic Village, Cheryl – who had been part of the rostering team and with whom I had become close friends – and I decided to look for a small place in close proximity to the Olympic Village to 'hole up' in for the duration of the actual Games. Lucky as we were, we found a small and rather cheap two-bedroom apartment in Lidcombe, a suburb in western Sydney adjacent to the Olympic Village. Martin had offered to lend us a mattress, allowing Cheryl and I to share a room while subleasing the second room. My usual flatmate, Catherine's brother, and a friend of his, who both also worked at the Athletes' Village, moved in and now it was simply a matter of 'Let the Games begin'. By the time the Chefs de Mission and their teams arrived, the Olympic Village was in full glory and every possible scenario – security, athletes' laundry or team procedure for the opening ceremony – had been rehearsed and documented. Cheryl and I had rostered ourselves for the same shifts, regularly rotating mornings and nights. Neither of us were morning people and, with regular 5am wake-up calls, every minute in the morning had to be accounted for. Sharing a room that, with the additional mattress, was only big enough for one person at a time to stand up and move around, we quickly managed to work out a routine that would allow us to get ready while preserving our minds in an alpha state. Our turns in the bathroom, the use of the mirror in the room, the signal for when it was time to leave the house – all happened in silent agreement. We managed to get to our respective Resident Centres without speaking a word other than 'Talk to you later' once we got off the bus. After the first three mornings of ordering the same cheese sandwich at the Chinese bakery along the way, we no longer had to use speech for that either – it was a simple 'same' from the guy behind the counter, followed by a nod from us. Yet once we had entered the Olympic Village, it didn't take long for us to wake up; by 7.30am at the latest, I would have a call from Cheryl telling me that she just saw Pat Rafter (my celebrity crush at the time) walk past with his shirt off or I'd call her, giddy with excitement that Muhammad Ali had just come up to me for a brief chat. Whenever possible we also always made sure we took our lunch breaks together. We had so much to talk about, none of which could possibly wait until later that night. We always stayed at work at least a couple of hours longer than we had to, followed by a loop around the village just to see who else we would run into.

I was at Resident Centre number one, right at the main entrance to the Olympic Village, Cheryl was about half way down and Mum had been placed right at the other end. Mum was staying in my room at the apartment in Cremorne Point and had become good friends with the parents of my flatmate Catherine, who were also volunteering at the Village. Mum's shifts were quite different to mine, having adjusted the times in line with her long commute, but we still caught up whenever we could.

On the night of the Opening Ceremony, Martin called me at my Resident Centre and requested that I meet him at the main entrance of the Village in five minutes' time, and to tell my staff that I wouldn't be back until much later that night. His tone was urgent but I had no idea what was going on. On my way to the meeting point I ran into Cheryl; she, too, had received a call from Martin. By the time we reached the Village entrance, Martin was already waiting in a car and urged us to get in. Both Cheryl and I thought something bad had happened. As it turned out, Martin had just received three free tickets – A grade – to the Opening Ceremony, and Cheryl and I were his pick of the draw to join him. Our seats were among the most expensive, right in the bottom corner where all the athletes entered the stadium. Words can't describe how I felt being part of this huge spectacle, with an atmosphere as electric as it could ever be.

Operations during The Games ran as smoothly as one could have possibly wished for. There was a huge buzz all around, in the Athletes' Village as much as in the city. I had heard of a lot of locals having left town to avoid the chaos expected due to the traffic, packed hotels and restaurants, and drunken spectators, but rather than chaos the city was wrapped in an immensely joyful atmosphere that we all wished would last forever.

My time working for SOCOG and at the Athletes' Village was certainly one to remember. But unfortunately it all had to come to an end and, a week after the Closing Ceremony of the Paralympic Games, it was time to say goodbye to the excitement of the previous six months and to face the 'real world' again. Like many of the now thousands of unemployed ex-SOCOG people, I decided that the events industry had my name written all over it and set out to find the perfect job. A friend of mine had handed me the contact details of the owner of a reputable event management company, together with a referral, and I was now facing the unappealing task of constructing a résumé' for the first time in years. Although, other than the Olympics, I didn't have much to show for within that industry, I was still convinced I would make the perfect candidate. I hit my first hurdle when it came to writing the cover letter. Being Austrian and rather conservative when it came to rules and regulations, I was used to starting each letter with the formal address of 'Dear Mr/Mrs/Dr/Eng', assuring that every title – be it a doctor, engineer, etc. – that confirmed your educational status was included in the salutation. (For example for an aristocrat with two doctorates, it would be something along the lines of 'Dear Dr Dr Baron van Miller'.) Now my friend told me I had to change my address to 'Hi John'. Really? I couldn't quite fathom addressing a possible future boss in his 50s, and whom I had never met, by his first name. This seemed just wrong. Eventually I settled for 'Dear John', but it still didn't sit right.

The 'Dear John thing' seemed to work and I got invited for an interview with the big boss. The interview went surprisingly well and I was asked back for a second meeting to discuss details. It was only a small company but it ticked all my boxes: a cool office in a groovy suburb, a very likeable and relaxed boss and, above all, a role organising large corporate events – mostly conferences and incentive tours – in rather exotic overseas locations. I showed up at the second meeting feeling pretty confident, only to be told to first gain experience in the travel industry, as well as the Events Pro computer system. With a lot of talent out there after the Olympics, John had obviously decided to employ someone more qualified. He was very kind and apologetic and promised to give me a chance once I had done as suggested. Though I was disappointed, it was hard to deny his point. I called the company behind the Events Pro system to enquire about a training course but the next one wasn't for another couple of months and I didn't want to wait that long. I followed up by suggesting that I meet with a trainer at the head office in Brisbane – 950 kilometres from Sydney – for a one-on-one course. This wasn't what they usually offered but, as I appeared so desperate, they decided to make an exception. Next on the agenda was a Certificate II in Travel and Tourism, including Fares and Ticketing I and II, the part John required in particular. It was a two-week course and I was surprised by how much I enjoyed it. Once completed and with both certificates in hand, it was time for the experience part so I proceeded to send my résumé to every travel agent and events company I came across through the paper, online or word of mouth.

Up to that juncture I had never had any difficulties finding a job, although they had been mostly jobs that weren't very demanding in terms of skills. This time, after sending out a gazillion applications, I received only a few responses – and these were mostly negative. I managed to arrange an interview with a small travel agency but as soon as I discovered the low-down of the duties, I had no choice but to decline: I would have died the certain death of boredom.

Involuntary unemployment was a completely new concept to me and one I found extremely hard to deal with. During the week I spent all my waking hours researching companies, taking apart the classified sections of the various papers and searching online job websites, but come the weekend I couldn't sit back and relax, feeling that I didn't deserve to do so. I was determined not to get back into hospitality. With a Permanent Residency Visa finally in my possession, it was now about career progression. I had sworn to myself that once I had the freedom to do what I wanted, waitressing would be out of the equation. Some mornings I stood on my balcony watching people walk to the wharf to catch the ferry to work, wondering if they appreciated the fact that they had a job. As hard a phase as this was, it certainly was a good lesson; further down the road, whenever I had a bad day at work, this period would always be at the forefront of my mind. In the end it got to the point where I had to step down from my high horse and be open to compromise. Friends had been telling me all along that Flight Centre – a large and very successful chain of travel agencies – was always looking for people; to me, however, this had been an absolute no-go zone. In my mind, working for Flight Centre equalled working at a supermarket checkout. Without wanting to degrade anyone working at a checkout, my biggest test in life had always been monotony: I was after a stimulating challenge. But, despite weeks of doing everything in my power to avoid it, the day came when I grabbed the phone and called the Flight Centre head office. A phone interview, a meeting with the team at my potential new office, and a week's training later, I started my new job at Flight Centre Central.

So much for perception. Contrary to what I had expected, my new job was demanding, especially during the first couple of months when everything was still very new. Ours was a busy office; there were only four of us in the team and we were each more or less running our own show. At the time the system was quite a manual one where the agents had to figure out potential airline carriers and routes themselves. The final sales prices for airline tickets, tours and packages were mostly left up to us to determine at the time of the sale – we were typically given net prices and, apart from the occasional set fare, we could decide ourselves how much to charge. The more creativity one possessed in regard to uncommon routes or finding alternatives for busy and expensive flights, the greater the chances of making the sale, and the higher the commission. There were also plenty of additional incentives to work towards, mainly involving travel, which made the job even more appealing. Everyone was held responsible for their actions and with a huge number of fare rules, special conditions and deadlines that one had to be aware of, mistakes were to be prevented by hook or by crook to avoid any financial loss being deducted from one's commission. Then there were the unforeseen and extraordinary challenges like September 11 with clients stranded all over the place, and a couple of days later the collapse of Ansett Australia – Australia's second largest airline at the time – leaving several thousand passengers and many clients high and dry.

My time at Flight Centre certainly taught me plenty about multi-tasking, efficient problem solving and thinking outside of the square. With the in-house computer system slowly becoming more automated and the work more routine, however, I started to get bored. And once I felt that I had achieved what I had come to achieve in the first place – namely experience in the travel industry – and with my one-year anniversary not too far off, it was time to think about the next move. After spending a year in an office, I couldn't help but dream of alternatives to sitting in front of a desk, every day, all week. As much as it was a welcome change for a period of time, I felt that the strict Monday-to-Friday, nine-to-five life wasn't quite for me; it simply wasn't in my DNA. Both my parents' parents were self-employed, as were my parents and all three of my siblings. Having my own business wasn't an idea I'd entertained thus far, mainly out of fear of losing my freedom and being tied to one location. But I was now in my early 30s and, although the thought of working in the events industry was still an appealing one, I started to get slightly attached to the idea of being my own boss. Until one day I woke up and had the solution – I would work my way towards owning an outdoor adventure company.

Chapter 8
Exploring new horizons

A couple of days following this eureka moment, I met up with Cheryl, my friend from the Olympics. It was a Friday night and as we walked into a packed pub, she ran into a friend of hers, who was with a couple of visiting English friends. The English friends were in town to help with the promotion of the CCUSA program (Camp Counsellors USA). They had both been camp counsellors the previous year and now, over a beer and full of enthusiasm, recounted their time as activity counsellors in outdoor adventure. It didn't take much to convince me; there was a reason why we had bumped into these people literally two days after I had decided on my possible new future. The camp would be a great way to see if taking people on outdoor adventures was indeed something I would want to make my career.

The following Monday I resigned from my job at Flight Centre. The one-year anniversary I had committed to was still about six weeks out but now that I had a plan and an approximate start date for the new job (that I was yet to apply for) I thought I might as well give as much notice as possible. Although the original purpose of my time at Flight Centre had been to gain travel experience for my future career in organising corporate events overseas, I never thought of it as a waste of time. It gave me valuable insight into the travel industry, which would prove useful no matter where my career eventually took me. As advised by my friend's friend's friends, the application and interview process for the CCUSA program was straightforward. A couple of months later, following a brief interlude in Egypt and Europe (taking advantage of the very special conditions we enjoyed at Flight Centre, I had booked myself a round-the-world ticket, ensuring that I'd make the most of my time before life became more structured), I found myself on my way to Honesdale, Pennsylvania, a small town with a population of approximately 5000 people about two and a half hours north-east of New York City. The camp, Camp T, was an independent, co-educational sleep-away camp for six- to 17-year-olds. It was about 15 minutes out of town, on a small lake and surrounded by bush. With its stunning setting, it seemed like the perfect playground for kids. There were more activities on offer than one could have possibly dreamed of, from arts and crafts to drama classes and every kind of sport. The team I had been allocated to comprised a great group of people from various parts of the world. Our department – outdoor adventure – offered an array of fun activities like rock climbing, mountain biking, kayaking, a high ropes course, zip-line and the so-called 'leap of faith', a jump off a platform high up on a tree while secured by a rope and harness. If I'd been there as a child, I would have felt like a kid in a candy store.

However, Camp T was a rich kids' camp, and at least half of the girls aged 12 and over appeared to have rather different motivations for their summer 'in the bush'. The main reason a fair few of the girls picked outdoor adventure as their chosen activity for the morning or afternoon was to parade themselves along the track around the soccer field while the boys were playing a game. We tried our best to convince them that rock climbing was cool and that the ropes course was fun, but to no avail. Rock climbing posed a great risk to the freshly painted fingernails, the ropes course was out of question with the helmet likely to destroy the hairdo, kayaking put carefully crafted make-up in danger and mountain biking would get the shining designer outfits dirty. I was absolutely stunned, especially considering the amount of fun that was on offer. What a waste of a childhood. It was really sad to watch. Late afternoon, during 'off time', the battle to 'stand out' in the bush continued with a fight over the showers and mirrors. The camp was powered by generators and almost every night from about an hour before dinner the electricity around camp was cut off by the simultaneous use of every available hairdryer in the girls' quarters.

The seven-week summer camp came with a hefty price tag, equivalent to a five-star hotel, only the accommodation featured large dorms and the food was the lowest quality – there was nothing nutritious about it whatsoever. Every meal was dominated by fried and heavy foods; not quite what one would expect from an outdoor camp where kids were meant to spend a fun and healthy summer. As one of the older counsellors, I made various attempts to talk to the owner about nutrition, but it seemed like profit was the only incentive.

All in all, my time at camp was a great experience and certainly an eye-opener. We staff had plenty of fun among ourselves and there were more than a few great kids, who I was sad to see leave at the end of summer. A couple of weeks prior to waving goodbye I had bought a cheap car and my plan now was to cross the continent in a bit of a zigzag between the northern states and Canada, with a friend from my outdoor adventure team, Caroline, joining me for most of the way. A road trip across America had been on my to-do list for a while and there were specific cities, towns, national parks and scenic roads that had to be ticked off.

Our journey took us from Honesdale to Toronto (Ontario, Canada), Chicago and through Wisconsin and Minnesota up to Winnipeg (Manitoba, Canada). We then drove back south via North Dakota and South Dakota to Wyoming where we spent a day in Laramie with a good friend from camp. From there we continued across Wyoming to Jackson Hole, and up through the Yellowstone National Park and Montana back to Canada, crossing the Canadian Rockies and eventually reaching Whistler a couple of weeks after we had left Pennsylvania. After spending two days in Whistler, my old stomping ground, and passing on a few insider tips to Caroline who was to stay for the season, I continued on my own, driving down the west coast from Vancouver to Los Angeles.

Along the way I caught up with a friend of mine, Mark, who invited me to stay for a night at the hotel where he was working as the Front Office Manager. The Ritz Carlton Half Moon Bay was a five-star luxury property 35 kilometres south of San Francisco and, after three weeks of living a backpacker's life, sleeping in the car, hostels or cheap hotels, I was now going to be treated to some lavishness. The only hitch was that having just spent a couple of months in the bush, followed by a road trip, neither the car nor my wardrobe seemed quite appropriate. Searching through my luggage I eventually dug out a dress and 'ironed' it with a wet towel. Rather than putting it on straight away I decided to get changed just before I arrived at the hotel to avoid the dress getting crinkled during the drive (plus I didn't want to look all dolled-up leaving the backpackers). The plan was to stop somewhere close to the hotel, freshen up, hide the car out of sight of the hotel foyer and walk into the Ritz Carlton pretending I was a sophisticated hotel guest. As it happened though, my entrance didn't quite go to plan. Turning off the highway and following the main road towards the hotel, I found myself on a long, open boulevard lined with luxury properties on one side and a stunning golf course on the other with nowhere to pull over. As a last resort there was still the Ritz car park but, as luck would have it, I missed a turn and I ended up on a one-way loop that took me straight to the main reception area, leaving me stranded right in front of the hotel concierge. Without delay, a prim and proper gentleman approached me and my old car and asked if he could help. He motioned for the car key and offered to valet-park it. I was so embarrassed; I wished to dissolve in air. I was still in my shorts and t-shirt, my backpack was lying on the back seat with my clothes all over it and there was a For Sale sign with the price and my contact number glued to the window. I quickly ripped off the sign, stuffed my dress and shoes in my bag and handed him the dirty red and white Canada sling with the key on it. I then proceeded through the main entrance in the hope of finding the closest bathroom without getting noticed; the last thing I wanted was to embarrass my friend.

It was funny to see Mark in an exalted position, all serious. I told him about the concierge and my not-very-appropriate arrival but he only laughed. He showed me to my room and suggested I make the most of my time at The Ritz. I didn't know what to do first. I could have a bath in the huge tub – the first bath in months – lie in the king-sized bed covered in crisp linen and enjoy the stunning view over the bay and the golf course, or go downstairs and have a bite and a drink at the outdoor restaurant. It was such a fantastic treat. I couldn't help but think of Julia Roberts in *Pretty Woman*.

The following morning, refreshed, energised and driving through the most beautiful scenery with the windows down and the music blasting, I was in a dreamer's heaven. I felt as free as one could possibly feel and my mind went wild, piecing together the puzzle and creating my future in my thoughts. The 2000 kilometres down the west coast from Vancouver to Los Angeles were very inspiring and productive and, by the time I reached the City of Angels, I knew exactly what I wanted to do with my life. My time at camp had been enough to dismiss the idea of making my passion of the outdoors my livelihood. Not only did working in that field not necessarily mean one got to engage in the activities in the way I had envisioned, I also couldn't see myself doing it on a day-to-day basis; I would be missing something. I had to be involved in a project that was challenging and fast-paced, something that would give me a real kick. So, 13,000 kilometres and various ideas and options later, I decided to take my brother's franchise business to Australia.

Over the previous few years Heiner had created a new business called My Indigo. The concept was to offer healthy, light, nutritious food, organic and fairtrade where possible, in a feel-good atmosphere. I had always felt that Sydney was lacking in healthy, affordable food options, especially when it came to limited-time lunch breaks. The choice was mostly between expensive restaurants or rush-in, rush-out salad bars with no atmosphere. My Indigo would fill that void. I could already picture its success and rapid expansion Down Under. I was passionate about good-quality food and I identified with the ethical and environmentally aware side of the business, together with the style and fit-out of the stores. As soon as my vision had ripened enough to 'make it public', I called Heiner and asked for his thoughts. He suggested I come to Austria and spend a couple of weeks within the various departments to familiarise myself with the operations and to discuss my plans further.

I arrived in Los Angeles three days before my scheduled flight to New Zealand, a brief stopover to ski the Southern Alps on my way home to Australia. In view of the limited amount of time available to sell my car, I had put a 'For Sale' sign in the window. If I managed to sell it before I reached LA I could always take the bus for the remainder of the trip. With no interest along the way, however, the pressure was now on. I thought my best bet for a quick sale would be to target fellow travellers at the hostel that I had pre-booked, and the easiest way to do that would be to park right in front of it. Parking at the hostel, however, was limited and all the prime spots were taken upon my arrival. I waited in a restricted zone close by and about half an hour into the game, a truck that had been parked right outside the entrance left, so I dived into the empty spot like a hyena.

The following morning I had a call from a woman asking to go for a test drive. She was the owner of the hairdresser right opposite the hostel and had spotted the sign from her window. By late that afternoon it was all done and dusted. The car was sold, the papers exchanged and the change of ownership documented by a woman in a shop down the road – I never knew that the sale of a car could be that easy. Back in Austria bureaucracy would have had me running around town, waiting in several queues and most probably being told to return the following day. This was the perfect start to my new life as a businesswoman. I had bought the car for $1250 and managed to sell it – 13,000 kilometres later – for almost twice as much. Back at camp friends had been in disbelief that I had been prepared to waste that much money on a car. As I later found out, two of the cynics had also bought a car. Unlike me, they had only paid a few hundred dollars, but had to bury their rattle box in a junk yard after breaking down somewhere along their road-trip, losing their initial investment and ending up stuck in the middle of nowhere. I had purchased my car from a local working at camp who was happy to get rid of it and, while I never cared much about cars, other than their shape and colour, I was very much aware that I had cut a great deal at the time. The car had been very well maintained and not having had any incidents or issues with it along the way, I felt justified in asking for what I felt it was worth. In the end, I managed to make more money with a road-trip across the country than I did over 10 weeks at camp. This sure put a big grin on my face.

I arrived back in Sydney at the beginning of October and, with my departure for Austria timed so I could spend Christmas with my family, I now had two months to kill. Before leaving for the States I had subleased my room in the two-bedroom apartment I had been sharing with a friend, allowing me now to move straight back into my old place. I registered with a temp agency and kept myself busy with a couple of jobs in travel while in my spare time I investigated the perfect location for what was going to be my first My Indigo store. At the beginning of December my flatmate announced that she would be moving out just before Christmas. While she felt bad for leaving me with such little notice, to me, the timing couldn't have been better; the second bedroom could now be turned into my office.

Upon my arrival in Austria, fuelled by eagerness, I was set to throw myself right into the business side of things. On my second day back in town I found myself exploring the various My Indigo stores, organising a tour of the production kitchen and presenting my vision to my brother. A couple of days into our discussions, as we were driving along in his car, Heiner told me that, having had a good think about it, he felt it was too soon to take My Indigo overseas as a franchise business. Rather than going ahead with it all now, he would feel more comfortable if I could give him another year or so to fine-tune the concept. There were still several areas that required improvement and the business simply needed more time to mature. Heiner then suggested taking an Austrian food and beverage cost control software system to Australia instead. He had recently had a system called Smart (not the real name) installed in several of his restaurants and, although it was still quite new, he felt enthusiastic about it. It seemed to be the solution to several of his problems and he was wondering if there would be a market for it in Australia.

Having grown up in a hotel and having managed one of my brother's restaurants for a couple of years, I knew quite a bit about cost control. Back in Sydney, working in the various restaurants, coffee shops and pubs, I was always stunned by how little control there was. None of the places I had worked at had any systems in place – manual or computerised – and I couldn't help but wonder how much money was going out the back door or down the drain.

This situation appeared to be the same just about everywhere. Without giving it much more thought, I agreed to my brother's suggestion, already picturing myself educating the Australian market. A few minutes into our conversation and still in the car, we had Thomas, the owner of the Smart software company, on the line and Heiner asked if they would be interested in his sister taking Smart overseas. Two days later Thomas met with me in Salzburg for a presentation of the product. Another couple of days later I was at their office in Graz, three hours south-east of Salzburg, receiving training on the system. Armed with an installation file, an electronic manual and a handful of brochures, I returned to Sydney with a completely different vision than the one I had left the country with three weeks earlier. It was January 2003.

PART II

'You can blow out a candle but you can't blow out a fire'
– Peter Gabriel ('Biko')

Chapter 9

Persistence and grit

Back in Salzburg, when Heiner and I first talked about Smart, a friend of mine, Trevor, popped into my head as a potential business partner. As soon as I arrived back in Sydney, I arranged to catch up with Trevor to present him with my business idea. He conducted his share of market research and got back to me with the conclusion that yes, he agreed, it certainly looked like there was a market for it and he would be interested in doing this with me. I then locked myself into my new home office for a couple of months and went through the user manual of Smart, page by page. I checked every bit of functionality, no matter how small or potentially irrelevant, set up a 'test restaurant' and simulated all the processes I could possibly think of. In mid-March I returned to Austria with all the questions I had collated, the translation errors I had detected and several suggestions for market adaptation. And then came the most challenging part of it all – the technical side of things, such as installation, set-up and interfaces to various other systems. Over the previous years, since personal computers and laptops had become mainstream, I had only ever worked with very basic systems and the term Information Technology certainly wasn't part of my vocabulary – at least not in that sequence.

Meanwhile, after a couple more meetings to discuss details, Trevor called one day asking to catch up that afternoon. I could sense there was something wrong and arrived prepared. Trevor then told me that as much as he had tried, he just wasn't passionate enough about selling an IT product and that unfortunately he would have to withdraw from a potential partnership. Disappointed but at the same time grateful that he was being honest and that we'd had this conversation at an early stage, I asked him to at least help me with a business name. Straight away Trevor threw several suggestions at me and when he called out 'essence', I stopped him. Yes, that would be it! But it would be es**sense**, with an 's' instead of a 'c'. And that was that. There was a lot one could do with that word; it felt right. I had a name for the business.

On my third day back at the Smart office in Graz, when Thomas started the technical training I managed to follow him for about the first 10 minutes, after which I switched off and reverted to my fake-it-until-you-make-it facial expressions. I didn't have a clue what he was talking about. Without any kind of IT base knowledge there was no use in trying to get him to explain the various terms that were all foreign words to me. I took notes in as much detail as possible while still pretending it all made sense. It was now time to come up with a plan B. While Thomas went on one of his cigarette breaks I called a friend of mine, Josef, who I had met in Australia a couple of years earlier. Josef, now back in Austria, had contacted me at the beginning of the year to see if I knew of a company to sponsor him, opening the doors for him to move to Australia long-term. Josef was a computer programmer. Putting one and one together, he now seemed like the perfect solution. With no time to get into details, I asked Josef if he would be available to catch up. He lived in Vienna, about three hours north-east of Graz and we arranged to meet in a couple of days' time, once I had finished my training at Smart. In the end, it didn't take much to convince Josef to come on board. While I wouldn't be able to pay him a huge salary, through *essense* I could at least provide him with his ticket to permanent residency in Australia.

A couple of years earlier I had inherited some money. As I'd had no use for it at the time other than to invest it, I had handed it all to my brother whose business required an injection. We had agreed that he would pay it back whenever I needed it and now was the time; he would transfer a certain amount each month, enough to cover my costs. The only challenge now was the business sponsorship for Josef. I was very much aware of a rule that required a certain ratio of Australian versus foreign employees, meaning that a business was only allowed to sponsor an overseas worker if there were Australians working in that same business. The first immigration lawyer I met with confirmed just that; considering that *essense* at that stage was a one-person show, there was no way I could sponsor an Austrian. I would have to employ several Australians first. However, this was not an option. I *needed* Josef, no matter what. He spoke German, which was paramount, apart from the fact that it would have been next to impossible to find a local IT specialist who would be prepared to work out of my kitchen for a salary below market. I decided to blow my budget and see an immigration specialist from Deloitte. Bringing forward my rather tricky situation, I conveyed to the woman who had been allocated to my case that unfortunately I wouldn't be able to take no for an answer. I was very much aware of the law, but considering that I was in the process of introducing an Austrian product to the local market and would only be able to do so with the help of a German-speaking IT specialist, there surely would have to be an allowance for that. Her response was that it wasn't going to be easy but she was positive that she would find a way. Less than four weeks later Josef was sitting in my kitchen, ready to help me conquer the market.

I was very passionate about the product, Smart, and the thought of helping hospitality businesses tap into their full potential. It was a big learning curve, however, especially considering that the Australian mentality varied greatly from the Germanic way of thinking. Whereas profit, efficiency, high-pace, etc. was part of the middle-European make-up, Australians were a lot more relaxed, not only with how they addressed each other. Rush hour started at 4pm and on Fridays the bars and pubs began filling up at lunch time. For hospitality businesses it appeared that a packed establishment was good enough for management – no cost control needed, not even if this meant a significant increase in profits. It wasn't a lack of appointments and meetings with potential clients that was the problem, but rather that CFOs and business owners didn't want to spend any money unless absolutely necessary. The business was doing well, so why invest money in a new system (or any system) and, above all, the time operating it? There would be work involved in maintaining the system as well as ensuring the integrity of the information fed into it and this didn't sound very appealing. It seemed impossible to get anyone to look at the bigger picture. It was all about keeping it simple, even if that meant less profit. In part it was hard to argue with that attitude, considering one of the reasons I loved Australia so much was the relaxed approach to life.

Looking back, I still have to smirk at the picture in my head when Josef and I first set out on our mission to convert our first client. During those initial meetings – as inexperienced as we both were – we must have looked like an immigrant husband-and-wife team trying to make a living. Both of us with the same strong accents, laptop in hand, we went from meeting to meeting, passionately praising what we had to offer. With each appointment though, our approach slightly changed until – I dare say – we looked the part and managed to present the business in a much more sophisticated way. By September that year, we had moved the office out of my kitchen and into a one-bedroom apartment in the city that we converted into a cool working space. We were getting more professional as time went by but success was still a long time coming. Carrots kept dangling in front of our faces, but whenever we came close to sealing a major deal, the CFO or business owner would put us off, suggesting we talk to them again in six months' time or similar. Our biggest hurdle was that all-important first local reference. No one wanted to be the guinea pig and take a risk.

About four months into the official launch of *essense*, I received a call from a German company called GUBSE, a software development company with a Property Management System (PMS) for the hotel and accommodation industry. Their product was called SIHOT and one of its modules, SIHOT Control, was the Smart system that had been white labelled and integrated into their own product. GUBSE had heard that I had taken Smart to Australia and were keen to have SIHOT represented in the South Pacific. SIHOT was quite well known within the German market and had made some inroads into Spain but other than that was not a widely popular product. Their sales manager, Gerd, forwarded me a variety of information and I agreed to give it some thought. I talked to several contacts within the industry in Austria to see whether they had heard of SIHOT and to receive feedback but it appeared that it hadn't made it across the border – at least not in a way that would have encouraged my deliberation. Eventually I came to the conclusion that although the system, judging by its user interface and functionality, looked quite intriguing, it was too soon to take on another product.

Soon after, we exhibited Smart at our first trade show, the highly respected Royal Sydney Fine Food Show. Our budget was quite limited but we made the best of what we had and managed to attract a few interested parties. To my surprise, we had more visitors enquire about whether we provided a Property Management System than showing interest in the Smart system that I was so passionate about. In view of the fact that this was a fine food show, not a hotel show, it appeared that the market must have been rather desperate for a new player in the hotel-system arena. After the fourth enquiry about a PMS, I responded that we were in the process of introducing a new, state-of-the-art system to the market and that the highly anticipated Australian launch of a system called SIHOT had been scheduled for the end of October. As the Smart company was already working closely with GUBSE, this move now made sense. Maybe the way to go would be to make SIHOT our main priority and sell Smart as an add-on module, shifting the focus to hotels, rather than restaurants. That same night I called GUBSE and happily announced that I was now ready to take their product on board. Two weeks later I was sitting in their office in Germany attending a week-long, in-depth training on SIHOT PMS and its modules. I hadn't worked in a hotel since I had distanced myself from the family hotel 10 years prior, at which time most IT systems were still pretty basic. With no experience in hotel computer systems as such, I also felt an obvious lack of insight into competitor products. As with Smart, during the training at the GUBSE head office I had to – for the sake of avoiding embarrassment – resort to various instances of nodding in agreement where in fact I had no clue what my counterpart was talking about. Back at the office in Sydney, I – as ever – worked my way through the user manual, page by page, setting myself daily targets of pages to be studied. The SIHOT system was far more comprehensive than Smart but it didn't take long before I knew it inside out. I was now convinced I had a winner on my hands. With only basic research into the competition, I decided not to get too hung up about it but instead focus on how we could stand out. I was too far into the game and obliterating my enthusiasm with any discouragement wasn't something I felt the need for.

As much as I loved and adored the relaxed, laid-back nature of Australia and its citizens, when it came to doing business, this often proved quite a challenge. Like, for example, the simple act of signing up for business insurance. While serving possible commission on a silver tray – rather than a sales representative knocking on my door – getting someone to actually talk to me turned into a wild-goose chase that involved endless calls and emails with seemingly no one interested in my business. There was hardly a returned call let alone a quote. Yes, I was a small fish in a big pond but I was still stunned by how little ambition many of those people seemed to possess, and this was only one of many examples. At times it would drive me to despair. Being put on hold on the phone forever, followed by the promise of a callback when, by the time I'd hung up, I already knew that *I* would be making the follow-up patience-testing calls. I repeatedly had to remind myself that this laissez-faire attitude was part of the culture. As hard as it was to accept at times, I obviously couldn't glorify the unperturbed Australian attitude in day-to-day life while condemning it when it came to doing business. On the upside, however, it seemed like a great opportunity to turn my negative experiences to my advantage. I was a perfectionist at the best of times and when it came to customer service and how we were going to present ourselves, we were going to excel and deliver – I was on a mission, one that seemed achievable considering the present standards.

With their main operations in Germany together with two small offices in Spain, GUBSE only had one English-speaking client, a hotel in London that formed part of a Spanish hotel group that GUBSE had struck a deal with years earlier. There was next-to-no software or technical documentation in English and the language files within the system were somewhat faulty. We had to invest a lot of time and effort in getting the system market-ready, and were still going to be faced with the challenges of the lack of a local reference client. Whereas Smart was a computer system that 'supported' a business, a Property Management System – with its reservation, check-in/check-out and so forth features – basically 'carried' a hotel and any faults or defects could be far-reaching. This was a much bigger project now than Smart had been and we were determined to get it right from the start.

We also needed to consider the marketing side of things. The folders GUBSE had provided us with might have worked for the German market, but I hadn't seen their concept (a couple of dolphins peeking out of the ocean) as quite suitable for the South Pacific region. As long as we kept the logo, we were free to make changes and do whatever we felt necessary to succeed. Keeping in mind the Aussies' almost unrestricted love for anything European, especially when it came to cars, as well as the age and gender of the average GM, CIO, CFO or CEO in the industry, we felt that developing a marketing concept more in line with fast cars and new technology would be more appropriate and appealing.

Our competition was mostly local and international companies that had been in the market for years. It was a very male-dominated industry and everyone seemed to have known each other for decades. If I was to make an impact that would match my grand vision, I had to enter the market with a bang. The ideas were there; the only hurdle was the budget. The plan was to get SIHOT and *essense* engrained in people's minds and create the vision of a large, successful company before we directly approached clients. And while we had already made an inroad with *essense*, it was nothing truly worth mentioning. In view of my rather badly negotiated contract with GUBSE, which encompassed the same conditions that had been set for their local distributors (I was still a rookie and there were lots of lessons to be learned), I now approached their board for support. But all I was granted was $8000 and a loan for $20,000.

When we eventually felt ready to make our mark, Josef received his Australian Permanent Resident Visa and left the company. He had been a big support but it was time for him to return to being a software developer and receive an adequate salary. Following his resignation, I put the word out that I was looking for 'another Josef' and, as luck would have it, as seemed to be so often the case in my life, I heard that a friend of a friend by the name of James was about to return from overseas and would be in the market for a job in hospitality IT within a week. James had lived abroad for several years and had counted on it taking months to find the right job, so he was happy to start off on a relatively low salary. James didn't just join the company with the right attitude and ambition; he also came with the added bonus of having worked at the front office of the Melia White House in London, the *one* hotel – the only one in the world – that was using an English language version of SIHOT. How lucky can one possibly get? This simply bordered on miraculous. With his existing understanding of SIHOT and further knowledge passed on by Josef, James was up to speed in no time and we were finally ready to go.

Building on our experience with Smart, I was aware of the challenges that we would ineluctably encounter and, as a first step, thought it a good idea to approach hotel schools to get students – future front-office staff – to use our system. It was about the all-important 'first reference' and a reputable hotel school would be a good start. Years earlier, the general manager of the International College of Management in Manly, Sydney's most prominent seaside hotel school, had been one of the managers at the Olympic Village. We hadn't worked together directly but with a bit of help from Martin, my past boss at the Olympics, I managed to arrange a meeting with him. Several presentations and discussions later and, understanding the importance of training students on various systems rather than just the one that had been dominating the industry for years, he agreed to have SIHOT implemented at the college. With this our first client was birthed. Our second client signed soon after – an exclusive five-star resort in Fiji, with its head office in the United States. Jetting between California and Fiji for the install and client training, together with a rather challenging set up, this wasn't the easiest first 'real' installation but James managed well.

Yet things didn't get easier. While we had several hotels showing interest in and being intrigued by our system, we kept being told to come back once we had more references from the Australian industry. It was a frustrating and stressful time, to say the least. Nonetheless, the more people urged me to admit defeat and stop investing money into a futile project, and the more competitors and authorities in the industry belittled me, the more determined I became. I knew I was on the right path and was convinced that the big break would be just a matter of time. I had never gone to university nor worked in the corporate world, leaving me without knowledge and experience to draw on outside of the hospitality industry. This wasn't just an investment in my business but was also my time to learn and grow. The money that other people had spent on their education, I was prepared to invest now. I had read many business books, especially biographies of people who I had looked up to, and one of the biggest messages I took from each of those stories was to never give up if you believed in something.

By the end of 2005 I was desperate. Something had to happen soon and it had better be big. By then we counted a couple of smaller hotels and three of the country's most prestigious hotel schools as our clients, but it wasn't enough to sustain the business. Whenever a potential client decided to engage an industry consultant in their search for a new system, we were always left out of the tender process, no matter how much I tried to challenge the usually weak and random reasoning behind it. The initial stumbling block had been the usual argument that we had come so accustomed to hearing – the lack of a reference client in Australia. But even after we had signed several local hotels, we still remained a no-go zone for consultants. There was always a reason why we couldn't receive a copy of a tender – reasons that never seemed to apply to any other company, no matter what size. I wasn't part of the 'old-boys' club' and, whatever agreements, deals and bonding went on in that club, they certainly didn't include me.

At the beginning of 2006 word got about that a major hotel group was looking for a new software system. MFS Ltd was a publicly held investment firm that had recently purchased several hotel and resort brands and established a hotel operation by the name of Stella Resorts Group, at the time boasting a portfolio of approximately 90 managed properties. What they now required was a standardised system to allow for efficient management of the newly formed hotel group. Its head office was located in Surfers Paradise on the Gold Coast, a one-and-a-half-hour flight from Sydney. I contacted Geoff, the CIO of Stella, to request a brief introduction and, to my surprise, he agreed. Taking into consideration the size of my company, compared to the size of the project I was going to discuss, this was a major achievement.

Chapter 10
Wheels and deals

My meeting with Geoff was informal. I managed to give him a quick spiel on SIHOT and, although he had never heard of it or of *essense*, it appeared to awaken his interest. By the time I left his office I had Geoff's word that he would include us in the upcoming tender process. I was ecstatic; I was going to be given a fair chance – that's all I had ever asked for. Ten days later I had Stella's Request for Proposal (RFP) on my desk. It was a comprehensive document – to say the least – and the due date was even more frightening. We had a mere seven days to complete what seemed like a task worth three times that amount of time. And the challenge didn't stop there. Point four of the RFP included several questions and requirements that should have had me throwing the document straight into the bin. It was all about how long the company – *essense* – had been established in Australia and New Zealand, the number of existing installs in Australia and New Zealand, the total staff within the company, etc. While the request for this kind of information was to be expected, it certainly wasn't an encouraging introduction to my make-or-break deal, but I chose to ignore that part for the time being and focus on the areas giving me more confidence. We divided the document into technical and non-technical chapters and James and I got stuck into our respective parts without delay, putting our heads down, not to be lifted for the next seven days.

James had a huge task ahead of him and my challenges included trying to squeeze information out of GUBSE. Back in Germany,

GUBSE was looking after a couple of hotel groups that were similar to, but smaller than, Stella and I considered it important to include the relevant details. Denying us noteworthy support, GUBSE dismissed our efforts as a waste of time and suggested we focus on individual hotels instead. What I did receive, however, was a pitiful 'smile' through the phone for believing that we even had the slightest of a chance. The mere fact that a company such as Stella couldn't possibly be serious about the project if they expected such an extensive RFP to be responded to within seven days meant that GUBSE weren't going to flog a dead horse at their end.

Other than the client references I had requested, there were also a couple of questions in regards to specific functionality that I had put to GUBSE. Again, it might have been easier to move a mountain than extract any information from them. I wondered why they had contacted me in the first place and suggested I take their product to Australia, if they hadn't thought I could make an impact.

James and I spent every working minute on the response, until all hours into the night, including the weekend. And just because we were on such a roll, James even decided to take the task beyond the call of duty and create an appendix with all the bells and whistles that SIHOT had to offer outside of the officially required functionality. To address our shortcomings regarding the company details and client history I included a so-called Company Summary Page, acknowledging that SIHOT was new to the Australian market and that *essense* was still a young company but at the same time highlighting the benefits that this would bring. With only a handful of clients in Australia, we would be available to dedicate our time and focus almost exclusively to *their* project. SIHOT was a proven system overseas and as a crucial future reference client in Australia, Stella would be guaranteed a lot of love and care.

There was one more hurdle – trust accounting. A significant part of the Stella Group properties required an integrated trust-accounting module to accommodate the scenario of a strata title. A strata title allows for individual ownership of a resort's rooms and apartments. The resort would still be managed and operated as a 'normal hotel' but the accounting – the trust accounting – called for a specific system that could handle a complex set up. A pre-condition to be included in Stella's tender process was the existence of a 'trust module'. Several months earlier I had contacted GUBSE and advised them that for me to be successful in the Australian market, we would require this additional module. More resorts seemed to be strata titled and the lack of a trust-accounting module would limit my target market to the extent where it wouldn't be feasible to continue with my efforts. GUBSE was naturally reluctant to oblige but once I suggested that I would have the development of the module financed by a local partner – not that I had the slightest idea who – and that I in return collect 100 percent of the profits, GUBSE quickly reversed their decision and offered to add the module to their portfolio at their expense. (A similar hotel and property model started to emerge in Europe and GUBSE understood there might be a broader use for a trust-accounting module in the future.)

Within the Stella Group RFP, we now had to respond to an extensive chapter relating to trust accounting, its functionality and the way it would handle certain transactions. As a basis for the development of the module I had provided GUBSE with a specifications document I'd acquired from an industry consultant but it only covered the most basic requirements. GUBSE had started writing the module but at the time of the RFP had only completed about 30 percent of the fundamentals. Again, to make up for our shortcomings, I suggested that the module being in its infancy was highly advantageous as it would allow Stella to get involved in the development process. Stella would have the opportunity to receive a system fully tailored to their needs and requirements. We had a potential case of a win-win situation on our hands, where Stella could have all the issues addressed that they were facing with their obsolete system and *essense*/GUBSE would have the advantage of building on the experience of the largest trust-accounting client in the country. With this we could create a system that would quite likely leave our competitors stranded.

Our response to the RFP had to be on the CIO's desk on 16 February 2006 by 5pm; any documents received thereafter wouldn't be considered. I called Australian Air Express to find out the latest possible flight that would get our bundle to the Stella Group's office in time. Under sweat and over endless cups of coffee and take-away food, James and I worked on our response, fully zoned into our respective areas and oblivious to anything else happening around us, until the very last second, followed by a mad dash to the closest office service centre – a sophisticated laser printer hadn't yet made it into the office budget – where I had the requested four copies colour-printed and bound. This was followed by an even bigger dash to the airport, ignoring various road signs and providing the occasional fellow driver with ammunition for road-rage. Parking the car right in front of Australian Air Express, I sprinted to their office, hurriedly requesting the paperwork – just to be told that I was too late for the current flight and that my documents would have to go on the next one, reaching the Stella office first thing the following morning. I was shattered. No matter how hard I tried, the gentleman behind the counter kept repeating himself, saying that their truck had already delivered the mail to the plane, which was about to take off. I kept telling him that my package had to get onto that plane. Soon, another gentleman approached the counter to see what was going on. Looking at me and the desperate state I seemed to be in, he sympathised and offered to take one of their buggies to deliver the item to the plane himself. There was still a chance that he would make it before takeoff. Anxious as one could be, I paced up and down the shop praying that he would return with good news – and he did. Fifteen minutes after he had left me with a glimmer of hope, he appeared with a big smile and without my documents. That angel of a man had handed my package directly to the pilot with the request to pass it on for urgent delivery as soon as he arrived on the Gold Coast. I just wanted to give him the biggest hug, almost crying with relief. What an effort and extraordinary service. This man was my hero. To top it off, he had also arranged for the local delivery guy to give me a personal call as soon as he had handed over the package to Stella. I received that call at two minutes to 5pm that day. As it later turned out, most, if not all, of my competitors had requested an extension on the deadline for the RFP, stating that it was impossible to respond to the tender within such a short period; never mind that they each had a much bigger team at their disposal, along with a much larger pool of experience.

Approximately two weeks after we had submitted our response to the RFP, I received a call from Adrian, Stella's project manager at the time, to say that we had made the next round and were invited to present our system to a team of decision-makers the following week. According to Adrian our response had been the best presented and had awakened the most curiosity; they were awaiting our presentation with great anticipation. Now it was time for another case of 'fake it til you make it'. There was no way I could show up at a presentation of that calibre with just James and me. Australia is a small country when it comes to target market in hospitality. There were the usual international hotel chains with their head offices overseas and only a limited number of local hotel groups – on average much smaller in size than the Stella Resorts Group – that would allow the selection and decision-making process to stay in the country. Replacing a hotel group's existing system would be an enormous undertaking while at the same time a huge opportunity that most likely would only come along once in my career. Word had it that a total of 12 suppliers had submitted a proposal to Stella and only six of these had made it to the presentation stage. Soon bets were being made as to who would eventually get the deal. As always the usual suspects sat at the top and the ranking seemed to stop at five. Across the field *essense* was being dismissed as non-existent. It didn't bother me. It made me more determined. I had heard that several of our competitors had organised for high-level support to be flown in from their overseas head offices for the presentation. I contacted GUBSE suggesting they follow suit and send one of their board members or at least their sales manager or IT manager to join us at the presentation. I received a straight-out 'no'. There were a couple of trade shows coming up in Germany and Mr Gruber (not the real name), the CEO of GUBSE, believed it to be more important to focus their attention on those solely. While his response didn't come as a surprise, I was disappointed.

In their RFP Stella had also requested information about either an existing 'revenue management module' or an external such system that could be interfaced with the PMS (the Property Management System). I was well aware that SIHOT had an existing interface with 'IDeaS', an internationally highly recognised revenue management system, and while SIHOT also had its own somewhat limited module, it seemed better to get the local IDeaS team involved. I arranged a meeting with the CEO, Graham, and offered to include his company in our upcoming presentation. Graham politely declined and instead suggested he hand me some flyers that we could distribute on the day. This was not what I had in mind; I needed another person there with us at the presentation to take our head count to at least three. I went on to question his professionalism and how a CEO of his reputation could possibly let go of an opportunity like the one I had just put in front of him. Yes, *essense* was a small and, as yet, still insignificant company but he better not underestimate what was to come. I had a big vision and it was up to him to choose to be part of it. Even if *essense* went no further than the presentation, partnering with us on that occasion would put him in front of one of Australia's largest hotel groups, and all this without even having to go through the usual process of courting a client to acquire a first meeting. When we parted after lunch he had promised to think about it. After a couple more phone calls and to finally shut me up, he eventually agreed to send his sales manager, Nick, to join us at the presentation.

With no experience whatsoever in meetings of that size and importance, we entered the Stella Resorts Group Head Office in Surfers Paradise the best prepared we could have possibly been. Equipped with expensive-looking and sophisticated marketing material, I wore heels that gave me the extra bit of confidence that I so desperately needed. Being almost the only woman in sight, I had to stand tall to avoid being looked down on – literally. Height was important; at least at a stage where my poise was still very much *put on* rather than real and natural. This was new territory for me and a big step out of my comfort zone. At the same time, without doubt it was a huge buzz. The conference room started to fill at the same rate as my anxiety grew. Someone once told me that in order to command respect, he would always go to the bathroom shortly before the start of a meeting and be one of the last to re-enter the room. This seemed like a good idea. Rather than standing there, nervously watching the members of the 'judging panel' appear one by one, I left and, just before I re-entered the room several minutes later, I took a deep breath, pulled back my shoulders to make myself even taller and gave myself a pep talk. *Now* I was ready for the challenge. There were approximately 15 people in the room, including the Group CEO, CIO, IT Manager, Project Manager and several area and hotel general managers. I started the meeting with an introduction and then handed over to James for the software presentation. James did a fantastic job – even I was impressed with the in-depth knowledge of the ins-and-outs of the system he had gained over a relatively short period of time. During and following James' presentation I had several rather intense non-IT related questions directed at me but, all in all, we must have done well as when our time was up, we were met with enthusiastic applause by the whole room. In all the excitement I almost forgot to give our friend from IDeaS a chance to shine. It was great to have Nick there – head count aside, considering the size and reputation of his employer, being associated with that company sure didn't hurt our credibility – and I believe that in the end it turned out to have been a mutually successful exercise.

And indeed it was. Ten days after our presentation I received an email from Stella stating that due to the success of our first presentation, *essense*, together with just one other contender, had made it into the final round. The product we were up against during that next stage of the evaluation process was a system called Epitome. The system of choice of a couple of the hotel groups that Stella had recently purchased, Epitome was already installed in a significant number of Stella Hotels and Resorts. To everyone in the industry it was obvious that *essense* had only been chosen as the obligatory second finalist and that this was a clear indication that Epitome would emerge as the winner. Our last competitor standing openly admitted that for them it was the best possible outcome to have us there with them in the final round – we were really just a placeholder. For me, however, this was serious business now and, no matter what, I had to get GUBSE to start playing for keeps too. If successful, a contract with Stella would most likely represent the biggest deal in GUBSE's 20-year history. According to Adrian, Stella's project manager, the emphasis of our next meeting would be to discuss trust accounting and the significant development work associated with it, as well as the system's multi-property capabilities and existing overseas clients. Without doubt most of these subjects required the presence of an authority from within GUBSE. Any kind of development work would occur at head office and, when it came to existing overseas clients with a multi-property set-up, it certainly wouldn't give us much credibility if James or I were to comment on GUBSE's behalf. After much ado, Walter Schmidt (not the real name), the IT Manager and one of GUBSE's board members, agreed to join us at that meeting. He was going to bring his wife and make a three-week holiday of it.

The meeting was an informal affair with only the CIO, CFO and the project manager present. It was done and dusted within a couple of hours but none of us left the Stella office feeling confident. Although Walter's English skills weren't too bad, there appeared to be the odd miscommunication and I felt that his abrupt German way hadn't given the meeting the smooth course we had been hoping for. After the meeting, James and I headed straight to the airport to return to Sydney and Walter and his wife were about to start their tour of Australia, flying to Sydney the following day. On their second day in town, Walter came by our office for a brief catch-up and chat about Stella and the possible next steps. Walter still didn't see much of a chance of us eventually sealing the deal and in the end concluded our conversation with the statement: 'All that women in our industry are good for is trade shows.' His candid chauvinism aside, I found that declaration a rather interesting one, especially considering both James and I felt that if we failed to be awarded the contract with Stella, it would certainly in part be due to his not very impressive contribution earlier that week.

As it turned out, it wasn't all bad and a couple of weeks later we had another request from Stella to attend their head office, this time to give a presentation of the SIHOT Central Reservation System (CRS). This was the beginning of April 2006. The subject of central reservations was a completely new world to both James and me and, up to that stage, hadn't been part of either the Stella Group RFP or the conversations that had followed. Stella had their own IT team who had been busy working on and improving their proprietary CRS but they had now decided to consider other options. The date that Stella had suggested for the presentation was in three days' time but we managed to defer it to the week after. The following Monday I had a new staff member, Grant, start with us. He came with extensive experience in central reservations, having worked for the IDeaS Revenue Management Company years earlier where he had spent a significant time dealing with large hotel groups. With only a few days until the presentation, on his first day at his new job Grant was greeted with relative urgency and, without further ado, got stuck right into the subject. Grant was extremely committed from the get-go, voluntarily staying back each night to speed-train himself on SIHOT and, together with the occasional Skype conversation with GUBSE at all hours of the night (they finally started to cooperate, although they would never make themselves available after-hours), by mid-week he had managed to create for himself a complete picture of the CRS capabilities within SIHOT extending to the smallest detail. We found ourselves back at the Stella head office on the Gold Coast on Thursday that week. It felt like Groundhog Day – same meeting room, same number of people, even if from other areas of the business – only this time the ice had been broken and I felt significantly more confident. Grant had a very mature and professional demeanor. He owned the room the minute he started to speak and at the end of his presentation the attendees erupted into a standing ovation. It was surreal. Just as we said our goodbyes, Rolf, the Stella Group CEO, approached me and congratulated me on the presentation. System aside, he was very impressed with Grant's honesty and the fact that rather than making up favourable responses on the odd occasion when he didn't have the answer, Grant offered to get back to whoever had asked the question once he found out the correct response. According to Rolf this was the first time he had heard anyone say such a thing during a crucial presentation. No other supplier took the risk to display 'a weakness' of any kind and it gave him a lot of confidence in our company. His words stuck with me and whenever I employed a new staff member in the future, I'd recount this little episode, stressing the importance of honest and sincere communication.

Not long after that final presentation I had a call from Adrian, advising me that we had won the contract and suggesting I return to their offices to discuss further details. Although up to that juncture I had always believed we stood a chance to seal the deal, Adrian's words made the world stop around me. I felt like I had just scored the winning goal in front of a packed stadium. I was in Melbourne at the time and, on my way to a meeting, froze in the middle of a walkway. It was too hard to comprehend. *We did it, oh my goodness, we did it!* I must have looked like a weirdo, talking to myself with a huge grin on my face, shaking my head but otherwise motionless. Straight away I called James and Grant to tell them.

A couple of days later I found myself in a meeting at the Stella head office with Adrian and Sunny, the Stella Group CFO, where we laid down the basics. Several emails and phone calls followed until all of a sudden communications started to halt – 'the *essense* deal' was being put on hold under the pretense that other areas of the business required urgent attention. I soon found out that the CEO of the competitor company that had made the final round of the Stella Group product evaluation had commissioned a European hospitality IT consultant to conduct investigations into GUBSE and SIHOT. The resulting report was forwarded to Stella, together with an accompanying letter by the competitor's CEO, warning Rolf, the Stella Group CEO, of the big mistake he was about to make. GUBSE, as the developers of SIHOT, was a comparatively small company with not much to show for themselves outside of Germany and, in his eyes, the risk that Rolf would be taking in signing with *essense* would be way too high.

As a consequence of the lightly damaging but mostly irrelevant report, Stella naturally felt compelled to check a few details. In the end the report managed to intimidate the Stella Group project team enough to request yet another presentation. I was appalled. I told Adrian that after an in-depth response to their RFP, two very detailed presentations, several further meetings (at their head-office 900 kilometres up the coast) and a handshake to seal the deal, I was not prepared to start from scratch. We would be happy to clarify any open questions but I did not see any value in going through the whole evaluation process yet again. Adrian agreed and the request for another presentation was dropped, but many more phone calls, emails and meetings followed. I kept asking for a draft of the contract and kept being told that their in-house lawyer was working on it.

Another two months passed and I still hadn't seen a first draft. It seemed like Stella wasn't prepared to commit and I was no longer prepared to waste my time. It got to the point where Sunny – the CFO – refused to take my calls so that he could escape any kind of pressure from me. This game could go on forever and I had to put an end to it. I sent an email to Sunny and Adrian informing them that if I hadn't received a letter of intent by close of business that Friday, I would withdraw the offer we had agreed upon months earlier. When by Friday night I had received no answer to my email, let alone a letter of intent, I followed up with another email, telling Sunny and Adrian that the deal was off and if ever Stella decided in the future that it still wanted to go ahead with the implementation of SIHOT, we would have to renegotiate. I received a response from Adrian by return email apologising profoundly and assuring me that he had put a lot of pressure on Sunny to react, but unfortunately to no avail. I told Adrian that I had been patient enough and that my decision was final. This was a strategic move on my part and I was hoping it would pay off.

The following Monday, first thing in the morning, the CEO, Rolf, called my mobile. I recognised the number and decided to ignore it. Rolf left a message asking for an urgent call back. I let two hours pass before I dialled his number. When I eventually talked to him after what was a very anxious wait on my part, he apologised for whatever had happened and promised to have the letter of intent to me within the next few hours. The deposit should be in the bank account by the following day. I advised Rolf that in recent times we had been treated with considerable contempt and that I wasn't prepared to sell my soul for a business deal. I very much loved what I was doing but when it came to the point where my time was reduced to playing power games with Sunny, I would rather take a step back and let one of my competitors take over. Everyone else in the industry very obviously was crawling on their knees for Stella but I wasn't one of them. In my eyes, this was a humungous project that required both parties to work together in a sincere and respectful way and, unless that was the case, I would no longer be interested. Rolf assured me that things would be different from that point onwards and asked me to get in contact with him straight away should there be any further issues. As promised, I received the letter of intent together with a payment confirmation for the deposit that day.

The Stella Group's plan now was to shift the focus to the Central Reservations System (CRS) and only once the CRS was implemented, the rollout of the PMS into the individual hotels would follow. Over the following few months Stella purchased another four (mostly smaller) local hotel groups and while for *essense* this was the best possible news, for my competitors it was yet another blow. Before long we made new friends from within companies who were keen to form 'partnerships' with us while at the same time we attracted animosity from the one or other competitor who had missed out. There was also word that I had bought my way into Stella or that I had won the deal due to a 'favour'.

While my growing team was busy working with Stella and GUBSE on the specifications of the central reservation and trust-accounting systems, I sat through endless meetings with Sunny to puzzle out the intrinsic details of the contracts. Sunny was of Chinese background and did full justice to the widespread reputation of Chinese CFOs for being the toughest people to negotiate with. It didn't take much to realise that Sunny wouldn't be happy unless he had a win-lose situation on his hands. Over the course of my dealings with him I learned my fair share and after pulling my hair out for so long, I eventually became more skilled at playing my cards. All I was after was a fair deal; once I felt we had reached that point, I simply had to make Sunny feel he had won and I had lost. During each of my meetings with Sunny, he had at least one competitor's proposal on his desk, strategically placed to intimidate me. His antics, however, were so obvious that they failed to have the desired effect. I was well aware that other competitors were still knocking on his door and that the letter of intent wasn't a guarantee of anything. But the project was well on its way and I was confident that even if Sunny – at this late stage – changed his mind, he wouldn't get past anyone else involved. My dealings with Sunny did, nonetheless, cost me a lot of sleep and energy. Every time we agreed on the exact content of a clause, he would forward the amended draft with the wording crafted in a way that would again favour Stella and disadvantage *essense* and undermine agreements already in place. He had to call the shots and was only ever content when he had the final say. Knowing Sunny – and after all those months of negotiations I did know him pretty well – there were two clauses I had to insist on. The first was an obligation to install our system into at least 50 percent of the Stella properties. (The purpose of the project had been to implement SIHOT across all properties, but in view of the fact that no one ever signs anything that says 100 percent I would have been happy with 50 percent. Once the system had been rolled out into a significant number of hotels, the rest would follow.) Secondly, the Support and Maintenance Agreement had to be a five-year agreement. These two clauses were crucial to protect all of the efforts that had already gone into the project, not to mention the costs of employing a team of specialists and having them undergo in-depth training of the SIHOT system in order to deliver on D-day – and thereafter. As much as I was prepared to give in with other areas of the agreement, for me this part of the contract was non-negotiable. Naturally Sunny wasn't happy about this and called a meeting with Bob (the CEO of the hospitality part of Stella), Daniel (the in-house lawyer) and me in their head office. It was obvious to me that – being cornered by three powerful men – the purpose of this meeting was to put pressure on me to drop these clauses; yet I arrived at their offices with a mission to stand my ground. The two clauses reflected the Stella project team's promises. Unless Stella had never intended to do as they had said, these clauses should not pose a problem. Following my meeting on the Gold Coast, several more emails went back and forth and in the end I got what I had asked for.

By mid-September 2007 GUBSE was ready to deliver a fully customised Central Reservation System to Stella and to pilot the system for 30 of their hotels. The transition to a new, sophisticated system was an enormous task and required intensive preparation from all parties involved. If anything were to go wrong, the hotel group's operations could have stopped, with major implications for the business. The process of the cutover was being carefully planned and involved many people, including GUBSE, who were flying a couple of staff members from Germany to assist with final preparations.

Outside of Stella, things had started to pick up. We had added several more hotels from the various corners of the country to our books and had even managed to install the Smart food and beverage cost control software as well as a European spa management system (that I had brought on board earlier that year) in a couple of sites. With the business gaining momentum I was able to gather a great team around me and we eventually moved the *essense* office to bigger premises. The staff – all guys; I was yet to have a female apply for a position – got along very well and I was very proud of the atmosphere in the office. Everyone seemed to enjoy what they were doing and our customers and industry colleagues repeatedly complimented me or my employees on the standard of the services received. While the big rollout of the SIHOT Property Management System into the Stella Hotels wasn't going to commence until the CRS project had been finalised, we continued to implement SIHOT into individually selected Stella properties that urgently required a new system. Operations out of the *essense* office were running very smoothly and everything seemed to be going according to plan. The finished trust module was 'handed' to Stella on 11 March 2008, two and a half weeks prior to the agreed upon deadline, and the trust pilot – a newly built resort hotel acting as the pilot site for the trust module – followed soon after. The installation and go-live of the system went perfectly well and the official auditors who visited the property to review the trust-module '...were happy that SIHOT Trust met all the requirements'. (A trust-accounting system is subject to very strict legislative requirements in Australia and an auditor's approval was crucial.) Over time and as to be expected of any project, but especially one the magnitude of Stella – where new, fully customised software was involved – issues of various types, both software- and operations-related emerged. Stella's obsolete trust system was rather limited, simple and very user-friendly, whereas the SIHOT trust module was a highly sophisticated system fully adapted to Stella's growing needs. What hadn't been considered, however, was the level of training required for staff working with the new software. Whereas it seemed that the use of their old system was very intuitive and did not involve extensive thought processes, SIHOT required users to be much more attentive, especially when executing the less repetitive functions. It soon became obvious that more in-depth staff training was needed and operational procedures had to be reviewed. Software-related issues were being referred back to GUBSE and attended to according to a list of priorities in line with the purpose of a pilot phase, which was to identify faults and iron them out for follow-on projects.

Not long after *essense* had received the letter of intent from the Stella Group, signs started to emerge that – with the initial risk and substantial investment required to build up a new market taken care of by *essense* – GUBSE had bigger plans for 'their' presence in Australia. The Stella project was being hailed as the largest IT project in the history of the industry in Australia and had put SIHOT on the global map. The related enhancements to the system had placed GUBSE on a level playing field with major competitors. According to GUBSE the Stella Group should be associated with GUBSE, rather than *essense*, and it wasn't long before Mr Gruber contacted me and suggested the use of the name SIHOT for my company. To be exact, he advocated I drop the name *essense* and rename my company SIHOT.

Chapter 11

Trouble brewing

I kindly declined Mr Gruber's offer, stating that I had bigger plans for *essense* and was happy with the name I had chosen for my company. At the latest ITB (Internationale Tourismus Boerse) in Berlin, the world's largest tourism trade fair where GUBSE had showcased their SIHOT system, they had supposedly been approached by a couple of international hotel chains so it was important that their marketing material now reflected the existence of a subsidiary in Australia. I suggested naming *essense* as their distributor instead (as had already been the case on their website), but – as I was well aware – this was not in line with Mr Gruber's vision. I asked if he intended to invest in *essense* or what sort of incentive he had thought to offer, but there was no such thing. The fact was, I had poured a humungous amount of hard work, energy, time and money into the business – and the Stella deal – not forgetting the risk that I had taken upon myself by introducing an unknown product into the Australian market. I was certainly not prepared to be reduced to GUBSE's marionette. I was stunned that Mr Gruber could have come up with such an idea, especially in the blunt format that he had presented it. Although it was difficult, I managed to stay calm and sincere during our conversation, now well aware of the vulnerable situation I was in, having put all my effort and money into someone else's product.

It didn't take long before marketing material emerged claiming that GUBSE did, indeed, have a subsidiary in Oceania. Even

GUBSE's website now reflected that claim. Where a couple of months earlier *essense* had been listed as their Australasian distributor, it was now GUBSE who supposedly had an office in the region. Any mention of *essense* had been removed from the site. Walter Schmidt, Mr Gruber's fellow board member, was even bold enough to contact one of my employees, Mark, and ask for his help in regards to double-checking the English version of a press release that spoke about the Stella deal and GUBSE's 'local office' – again with no mention of *essense*.

The next step towards creeping their way into taking over *essense*'s market was the adaptation of their website to the SIHOT marketing material we had created in Australia. Where originally GUBSE had represented their company in shades of light- to sky-blue with a rather conservative design of dolphins and ocean, it was now changed to a black background cut up by strings of bright colour and a fast-paced, trendy design, mirroring our Australian representation of the SIHOT product. While this was more proof of the obvious significance of the Stella deal and the general impact that *essense* had made for their company, GUBSE had to make sure that whatever was happening in Australia would be directly associated with them, clearly disregarding the image they had created for their company in Germany over the previous 20 years.

Back in the office, James and the rest of the team noticed that GUBSE was starting to interfere with our relationship with Stella and suspected that they were on a mission to push us out. GUBSE continually failed to inform us of significant development changes to the Stella central reservation and/or trust-accounting systems, making it difficult at times for our 24-hour support team to do their job without having to involve the GUBSE second-level support. Several email and Skype discussions about the correct flow of information notwithstanding, GUBSE kept choosing to ignore their part and do as they pleased. They made our lives harder by the day. Instead of working with us, they started to work against us, at times rather aggressively. I discovered that GUSBE had already interfered with my contract negotiations with the Stella Group months back, such as when Bob and I had already agreed on the payment conditions for the CRS license fees and GUBSE decided to talk to Stella behind my back to offer them very different, completely irrational and – for *essense* – highly disadvantageous conditions. It became clear that, even back then, GUBSE's actions were paving the way to create an impression within Stella that they would be better off bypassing *essense*.

At the end of September 2008 I received an email from GUBSE requesting I fly to Germany for a meeting to discuss and amend some terms within our contract – the distributor agreement. At the meeting a couple of months later, I was sat down with the three board members, the Director of Sales and the son of Mr Gruber, Andreas (not his real name), who was in charge of the development work at Stella and who would step into his dad's shoes at some point in the future. Once the obligatory chitchat was out of the way, we moved straight on to my contract and the 'unsustainable commission structure'. The commission schedule within the contract awarded *essense* – among others – 50 percent of the support and maintenance fees collected from its clients for the provision of first-level support on a 24/7 basis; the remainder would be passed on to GUBSE for any second-level support and access to regular software updates and upgrades. *essense* was also to receive 10 percent commission for any development work and other services that GUBSE was to collect from a client referred to by *essense*. GUBSE now urged me to 'voluntarily' drop those clauses in the case of Stella, saying this was only fair in view of the 'phase' the Stella project was in. The Central Reservation System implemented at Stella still produced several bugs and additional functionality kept being requested by the client. GUBSE was faced with a workload that could not be covered by their mere 50 percent share of the support fee – they now required the full amount. Never mind that they were already being paid for the development work itself and the 'bugs' and additional functionality had nothing to do with support. They were happy for me to keep my share of the support fees for the PMS (the software installed in the individual hotels) part of the deal but not for the CRS, regardless of the fact that I had four people sitting in my office providing 24-hour support. The monthly support fee for the CRS was a significant amount of money that I had worked hard for – and my staff continued to work hard for on a 24/7 basis. Naturally, I was not prepared to give that up. Yet it didn't take much to understand that for GUBSE this was a non-negotiable 'offer' – take it or lose all. They weren't very coy in their dealings with me, as evidenced by one of the questions they posed during our meeting, which echoed my conversation with Mr Gruber many months earlier: was their system now known under the name of *essense* or SIHOT? GUBSE 'understandably' had to figure out if their product was too closely associated with *essense* and if getting rid of *essense* altogether could unearth any issues. Still pretending I hadn't caught on to their intentions, I responded that although we had marketed it as SIHOT, people in general called it 'the *essense* system'. Again, I was well aware of the fragile situation I was in and I figured that although I had the right to insist on the existing paragraphs in our contract, it might be wise to let go of *something*. The amount of development work and number of services that Stella still required from GUBSE seemed measurable and giving up my 10 percent share in this regard would be something I could live with – although not happily, especially when viewed as a matter of principle.

In GUBSE's eyes a compromise wasn't acceptable and they decided to send their Director of Sales to take me out for dinner that night and sweet-talk me. The following morning, when we reconvened at their office, Mr Gruber's first question was, 'So how was dinner?' He looked at me with an expectant smile. I replied, 'If you mean have I changed my mind in regards to giving up my share of the support fee then no, I haven't.' GUBSE continued to pressure me from every angle of the table but if I had any self-worth, then I had to hold my ground. I found it more and more difficult to stay respectful and polite. The scenes confronting me were rather surreal and hard to comprehend; I had delivered GUBSE what turned out to be the biggest deal in their 20-year history – without any noteworthy support from them – and here they were, consumed by greed and ego, pushing me into a corner with such brazen intensity that it was hard to fathom. Not once since we had received the go-ahead from Stella had there been a pat on the shoulder or an actual 'Thank you, well done!' from GUBSE. I don't know how many people in the industry congratulated us, including comments like, 'So, how did GUBSE react? They must be celebrating you like a hero!' but all we ever got was arrogant paternalism. As soon as the letter of intent had been signed by Stella, GUBSE's belittling and laughing at us for being naïve enough to take part in the Stella Group tender process had overnight turned into avarice.

It was now the end of November 2008. Back in Australia, we continued to install SIHOT PMS into selected Stella Hotels with two new properties about to be opened in South and Western Australia. Just before Christmas we were asked to install the SIHOT system at one of their properties in Melbourne followed by the installation of the SIHOT trust-module at a resort in Queensland early in the New Year. And finally, with the CRS project as well as the pilot phase for the trust-module completed, the much anticipated SIHOT PMS rollout into *all* the hotels across the Stella portfolio was now set to commence in February. We were on a roll and everything seemed to be running smoothly.

In mid-January I received an email from Mr Gruber saying that he was going to come to Australia in a couple of weeks' time to meet with Stella 'to discuss the CRS project as well as contracts regarding consulting work through GUBSE' and that he most likely wouldn't have time to catch up with me. In his email he had cc'd the Stella Group General Manager for IT, Garry. I responded saying that I would certainly make the effort to fly to the Gold Coast to meet up and asked Garry if there was an agenda for GUBSE's visit as yet. I also stated that I thought it was important that I or one of my key managers be in attendance. Garry's response was a brief 'thanks, but no thanks'. The meetings that had been requested were between GUBSE and Stella and representation from *essense* for those meetings was not needed.

Garry's email confirmed what I had feared all along and what was now about to happen. The fact that Mr Gruber's email to me was in English – his knowledge of the English language was limited and we had never before communicated in English – and that he had cc'd Garry in a personal email to me was bizarre enough in itself. The email had obviously been drafted by Stella. GUBSE's intentions had now turned into a team effort. Mr Gruber had not been involved in the Stella project, other than a couple of contract clauses that required his input, and the only rational conclusion to that email conversation was that Mr Gruber was coming to Australia to rid themselves of *essense* – the middleman – and to amend the existing contracts with Stella accordingly.

At that stage there was nothing I could do other than sit and wait. And the wait wasn't a long one; the events that followed came thick and fast. It all started with an email from Stella indicating that the imminent SIHOT PMS install at their Melbourne property had been cancelled. No reason was given. A few days later we were told at the very last minute and for no reason that we would no longer be required to install the trust module at their Queensland resort, notwithstanding the fact that one of my employees was already on a four-hour flight to the location in the far north of the country. The following day we found out that the trust module at the pilot site was going to be de-installed on 1 February. (Again we were denied a reason.) Finally, another two days later we were informed that all SIHOT installations at Stella had been put on ice. When we kept requesting the rationale behind these decisions, we were eventually told that 'the decisions were driven by reasons that the greater business deemed necessary'.

The significance of the de-installation of SIHOT and its trust module from the pilot site was enormous and far-reaching. The *essense* contracts with Stella were tied to 'a working trust module' (and as such a successful trust-pilot) and, without such a thing, the software-license agreements for both the Property Management and Central Reservation Systems were practically worthless. Stella and GUBSE were obviously on a mission to give the impression that the trust-system wasn't working – regardless of the facts – and with this make it easier to dispose of *essense*.

On 15 February Mr Gruber and his son Andreas arrived on the Gold Coast. It was a Sunday night and I opted for a final attempt to reason with them. I called and talked to Andreas – his dad had never been one of many words, let alone courage. Andreas and I exchanged a few polite words, which I followed up by telling him that I had a strong inkling that the purpose of their time in Australia was to push out *essense* and to re-assign the contracts, and that I was hoping their business ethics would be strong enough to not go ahead. He sounded uncomfortable with what I had to say and, without responding, changed the subject and ended the conversation a minute later.

At 3pm the following day I had an email from Garry (Stella's IT Manager):

> As a matter of courtesy, I wish to advise that SHG (Stella Hospitality Group) do not currently intend on renewing the Software Support and Maintenance agreement with *essense* beyond its 12-month anniversary. We anticipate serving notice 60 days prior to the anniversary date.

> SHG believes that it will be better served by a direct relationship with GUBSE, given the documented shortcomings related to service and support to date.

My response was just as brief and to the point, stating that the support and maintenance agreement was a five-year agreement and that I was not aware of any shortcomings related to service and support. Garry's email had been an obvious attempt to intimidate me and to test my reaction. The two contract clauses I had insisted on earlier so fervidly – that the Support and Maintenance Agreement was to be a five-year agreement and that Stella had to install our system into at least 50 percent of their properties – were the exact two clauses that now stood in both GUBSE's and Stella's way for an easy transition and, at the same time, my only foundation for justice. In their eyes Stella's obligation to install SIHOT into a minimum of 50 percent of their properties – with the software and services to be delivered by *essense* – had already been dealt with through uninstalling the trust-pilot. It was now only a matter of discrediting the support and maintenance agreement, and what better way to do that than to relate it to supposedly bad service and support.

I could picture Garry, Kylie – Stella Group's new project manager who had taken an obvious liking to Andreas – and father and son Gruber in the meeting room together waiting for a call from me to go off at GUBSE. Instead, I decided to await their next move. At about 8pm that night I received a call from Mr Gruber communicating to me how shocked he was about what had happened and how he had had 'no clue whatsoever' that this was what the meeting with Stella was going to be about. I couldn't help but wonder what planet Mr Gruber thought I was from. GUBSE had been anything but subtle about their intentions from day one and I was stunned that he thought I would buy his story. I stayed calm and told him that, for me, there were three solutions to the 'unexpected problem' at hand:

1. GUBSE buys the Stella contracts from me
2. GUBSE takes over the Stella contracts and we formulate another contract between our companies reflecting the exact same conditions as *essense*'s contract with Stella. (This was to counter his ridiculous argument that GUBSE had nothing to do with this decision and had, indeed, no idea.)
3. I take legal action.

Mr Gruber sounded rather shocked as this was certainly not the response and reaction he had expected. He suggested that I fly to the Gold Coast and meet with him over dinner to discuss the situation. Supposedly, Stella was very unhappy with *essense* and unless GUBSE took over, they would drop the project, which was an outcome that GUBSE could not – under any circumstances – afford. What Mr Gruber could offer me, however, was for GUBSE to subcontract *essense* to continue to do the software installations, training and 24/7 support. This was an interesting proposition considering that – according to him – Stella was unhappy with *essense*'s services. I made it clear that this was not an option that I would consider even for a second. I had given him my three options and it was now his choice. If he would like to talk in person, he would be more than welcome to come to Sydney but I had no intention of going to the Gold Coast, unless our meeting would involve representation from Stella. Mr Gruber concluded our conversation with a threat, stating that if I dared to take legal action then my distributor agreement with their company would be cancelled and, as per Stella, '*essense* would be guaranteed to never again set foot into any of the Stella properties'. The second part of the threat didn't resonate though, considering I was *already* being kicked out.

I'm not sure what Mr Gruber expected. Did he really believe I would accept his overture to pick up the crumbs and probably even thank him for his grand offer? He obviously needed us to take over the services part of the deal – the software installations, training and support – for the time being and until they had employed and trained their own team. In his eyes I was fully dependent on GUBSE – it was no secret that at that stage SIHOT represented approximately 95 percent of the *essense* business – and he obviously anticipated me holding on to whatever I could or, better, gratefully accepting whatever I was given.

We had always had a good relationship with Stella and at no point had there been any complaints about our level of support. To the contrary, over the previous couple of years we had gained a reputation for *the finest support in the industry*, reflected in the many written testimonials from our clients – including an IT manager as well as several hotels from within the Stella Group – raving about the efficiency and can-do attitude of the *essense* team.

It was certainly extremely disappointing to find out that Stella had decided to get on board with GUBSE and to cut out *essense* but still I couldn't blame Stella quite to the same extent as GUBSE. Only two months earlier in December 2008, Rolf, the Stella Group CEO, had parted ways with Stella. The Global Financial Crisis was in full swing and I can only assume that Bob, as the CEO of the hospitality arm of the Stella Group, would have been under a lot of pressure. The rollout of SIHOT PMS was about to commence and, with Stella well aware of GUBSE's willingness to deal with them directly, they had clearly decided to take the bull by its horns and save the business a significant amount of money.

Another aspect that I can only assume would have played a part in supporting GUBSE's move and that would have stemmed from Stella's middle management was the fact that I was female, younger than most of my peers and the sole owner of a company that had just signed a contract threatening 'to make me rich' (as it had been put many times over). More than a few people didn't quite feel comfortable with this. On several occasions I had suffered passing remarks from within Stella such as, 'So what's the plan now – are you going to retire to a tropical island soon and sip cocktails all day?' Although said jokingly, these kinds of comments always had a grudging and resentful tone.

Chapter 12

Refusing to run

To prepare myself for the legal dispute that was undoubtedly to follow, I summarised my conversation with Mr Gruber in an email to him. I concluded with a statement of utter disappointment in their actions, especially in view of all the time, money and effort I had put into their product and the resulting success I had served them on a silver platter.

The following day, Mr Gruber called and informed me that he was at the airport and on his way to Sydney. A couple of hours later we were sitting in my office holding a polite conversation that led nowhere. The situation was one that I had seen coming for a long time and I surprised myself by how calm I managed to stay. It was evident that Mr Gruber had been fed the content of what to say and what not to say by the Stella in-house lawyer. He kept repeating himself, saying that the events of the previous couple of days had nothing to do with GUBSE, but instead were due to Stella no longer being willing to work with *essense*. No matter how much I challenged his excuse, I kept receiving the same response, making him sound like a stuck record. Stella had obviously drilled Mr Gruber in the art of not saying much to avoid saying the wrong thing. I told him that I had already given him my three options, which were as fair as they could possibly be under the circumstances, and that it was now solely his choice.

The truth was that I had nothing to lose. Picking up the breadcrumbs and taking on the role of GUBSE's puppet was not something I was prepared to do. Yes, undertaking the software installations, client training and support would have given me a sustainable income – until GUBSE had their own staff trained and ready to roll – but would bear no relation to what my business and the Stella deal were actually worth. Either way, it was not about money; *essense*, for me, had never been about the money. It was a passion. Building something from scratch, disregarding people's predictions and advice, believing in my vision and my staff, and eventually beating the odds – all this had given me a big kick. I felt alive. I loved what I was doing; I loved my office, the people I was working with – in and outside of the office – and our clients. Every morning I was excited about going to work. The general atmosphere in the office was one of drive and excitement and I felt that my staff were growing with me. There were also stressful and challenging days, of course, but all in all I couldn't have been happier with what we had created. Having someone take all that away from me and treat me so unethically and disrespectfully was not something I could accept or live with; I had to stay true to myself. I would have resented GUBSE and Stella for years to come had I accepted Mr Gruber's ridiculous offer. Besides, there was no way I could have kept working with two companies that were screwing me and that I no longer had any respect for whatsoever.

Mr Gruber ended up spending a total of an hour and a half in our office. He eventually understood that if I wasn't going to change my mind – and he was obviously not allowed to venture outside the couple of sentences he had been given – there was no sense in continuing our very monotonous conversation. He asked me to go online to change his flight to the earliest available and to cancel his hotel booking in Sydney. I happily obliged. Another 15 minutes later he was back in a taxi and on his way to the airport.

The day after I had received the 'thanks and goodbye' email from Stella, followed up by Mr Gruber's phone call that night, I contacted my lawyer, who had been involved in reviewing my contracts with Stella. The conclusion of our meeting that followed was plain and simple advice 'to run as fast as I could' as Stella – a multibillion dollar company – 'would with certainty kill *essense*; they'd drag out the case until *essense*'s finances were dried out'. To cement the bleak picture he was painting, my lawyer told me of a similar case he had recently dealt with where the owner of a franchise business eventually had to close shop after having run a successful business for 10 years.

I was shocked. My understanding was that it was a case of obvious betrayal and deception, with valid existing contracts. There was no way I could take his advice. How could things ever change, if this was a legal representative's reaction to a typical case of David versus Goliath? It surely couldn't be that easy for large companies to screw small businesses. I left my lawyer's firm with utter disappointment. Back in the office, I sent an email to various contacts whom I felt might be able to provide me with details of a *good* litigation lawyer. Within a few minutes I had several suggestions and later that same afternoon I found myself sitting in a meeting room of yet another law firm, talking to a gentleman called Damian. Recounting my case once more, this time around I received a very different response. Although it wasn't going to be easy, Damian believed I had a good case and offered to take it on. Moreover, he would charge a success-fee only. A week later Garry (Stella's IT Manager) had a letter from Damian on his desk. It concluded with a summary of *essense*'s position:

> Our client does not accept that Stella has any present right to terminate any of the Agreements including the Support Agreement …

After listing the various points of breach of contract – starting with Stella's 'secret meeting' with GUBSE that *essense* hadn't been welcome to join – and the potential steps that *essense* was going to take, Damian summarised:

Our client demands that you:

1. Immediately arrange for payment in full of outstanding invoices. [From the beginning of the year and with the onset of the series of 'surprise' events, Stella had also stopped paying their monthly recurring CRS support invoices, while *essense* continued to deliver its services.]

2. Withdraw your email of 16 February 2009. [With this, Garry had advised me of their intention to contract directly to GUBSE '... given the documented shortcomings in service and support'.]
3. Confirm that you will continue to observe your contractual obligations with our client including but not limited to your obligation ... to install the PMS Software into at least 50 percent of your properties.
4. Undertake that you will not conclude any agreement with GUBSE during the term of the Agreements with our client that would have the direct or indirect effect of taking the benefit of those contracts from our client.

In accordance with the procedures provided for in the Support Agreement our client puts you on notice that this letter should be treated as notice of a dispute and an attempt to resolve a dispute in accordance with Clause ... Our client would also be prepared to arrange a meeting to be attended by the senior management of both parties. If the matter does not resolve and you fail to provide the assurances sought in points 1–4 above, then we are instructed to have the matter referred to mediation under Clause ...

Our client reserves its rights to take whatever action that might be required to preserve its position including seeking any necessary orders from the courts.

Over the next weeks, several letters between our respective lawyers followed, during which time Stella also withdrew their email of 16 February 2009. With Stella's senior management not willing to meet, mediation was eventually scheduled for the end of April. It had been our intention to involve GUBSE in the mediation process, but our suggestion was rejected vehemently by both Stella and GUBSE.

Mediation took place on 29 April 2009 at a local mediation lawyers' office on the Gold Coast. Stella was represented by their new CFO, Steven, and two lawyers of a large, renowned law firm. I was surprised to see not one familiar face, not one person I had been dealing with over the previous months or years. None of the people present had been involved in the project to date, let alone the contract negotiations. But, then again, I doubted anyone from within Stella who had had any dealings with *essense* would have had the guts to look me in the eye and lie, or to repeat what they had said on paper (through emails or via their lawyers). From *essense*'s side it was my lawyer, Damian, Mark (our Director of Sales) and me.

Mediation was an 'interesting exercise'. At no point did the representatives from Stella mention the presence or existence of any issues with *essense*, its staff or the quality of its services. Instead – for a special surprise effect – they produced a letter from GUBSE that read:

Dear Sir or Madam,

GUBSE takes the position in agreement with SHG (Stella Hospitality Group) that the pilot of the SIHOT PMS with trust-accounting was deemed unsuccessful and therefore was removed by mutual agreement.

Signed
Otto Gruber

The letter – undated and signed by the CEO of the company that had written the bespoke module – clearly served the purpose of underlining and strengthening Stella's claim that the SIHOT trust-system wasn't working and, with this, dissolved Stella's commitment to, as Damian put it, '… observe their contractual obligations with *essense* including but not limited to its obligation to install the PMS Software into at least 50 percent of its properties …'. Mr Gruber's letter would now give Stella the freedom to deal directly with GUBSE.

I was gobsmacked. So was the mediation lawyer. It was hard to believe that GUBSE would be naïve and imprudent enough to write such a letter. Their actions were – yet again – clearly ruled by ego rather than reason. Providing Stella with that statement put all the power into Stella's hands. Stella was well aware that GUBSE had a very low-level risk disposition, opening the doors for Stella to pull the strings with little and rather predictable resistance. The slightest 'threat' would have GUBSE falter and act as they were told. GUBSE evidently had no idea that Stella had been playing us off against each other all along. It was all about the bottom line and Stella was stopping at nothing to accomplish their mission – one that had been 'served' to them by GUBSE. I have to say, however, kudos to Stella for being bold enough to even *think* that GUBSE would certify that they had failed in delivering a functional trust-accounting system. Not only would this deed put an existing multi-million-dollar contract as well as GUBSE's reputation in jeopardy, it could also potentially have them face a fragile legal position with *essense*. It appeared that Stella was playing poker in GUBSE's name.

We made it clear to Stella's lawyers that we would be fighting the case. There was more than sufficient evidence that the trust module was working and if I had to take Stella to court then I was prepared to do so. After several more discussions – in separate rooms – between each of the parties and the mediation lawyer, the meeting was concluded with the scheduling of a second mediation in five weeks' time. Stella had eventually come up with an offer to either keep working with *essense* or to pay a substantial amount of money to *essense* to be released from the contracts. That option two was on the table showed how low GUBSE must have been willing to go to make it worthwhile for Stella to pay us out. (Due to the nature of mediation I'm in no position to disclose details as to the particulars discussed; however, I could have lived with option two, especially bearing in mind that it was GUBSE that I now had to take legal action against.)

Mr Gruber's letter that Stella had produced during mediation turned out to have further significant implications. Stella owed *essense* $279,000 for the final instalment of the licence fee of their SIHOT Central Reservations System delivered a year and a half earlier. Due to GUBSE's masterstroke where Mr Gruber had gone behind my back to offer Stella better payment conditions, the final payment was now tied to 'a successful trust-pilot'. According to the corresponding clause in the contract, the final instalment of the payment for the Central Reservation System would only be 'due within 12 months from the date that is immediately after two successful month's-end rollovers of the SIHOT PMS pilot'. How unreasonable and intricate can payment conditions possibly get? Stella had been successfully using their fully customised CRS since November 2007 and full payment would now only be due in July 2009, 20 months later. I still shake my head at the imbecility of it all. This was the one clause that Mr Gruber could proudly call *his* accomplishment. And it was this clause, combined with the letter that Mr Gruber had voluntarily handed Stella, that now gave Stella enough ammunition to refuse payment of the $279,000, while at the same time happily using the system.

Following mediation, several more emails and letters – in large part regarding Stella's refusal to pay the outstanding amount for the licence of their Central Reservation System – were exchanged between our respective lawyers. Stella stopped paying their monthly support invoices altogether and my company's income had more or less come to a halt. The software support for all our clients continued on a 24/7 basis but, with all installations and associated services for Stella cancelled and our relationship with GUBSE in tatters, the monthly expenses far outweighed the income. With a continuous proactive sales approach to acquire new clients for SIHOT out of the question, it was also a challenging time for my staff and it wasn't long before the first two of my employees left of their own accord.

Chapter 13

New momentum

Over the years *essense* had managed to create a name and reputation for itself within the industry and I wasn't going to let my differences with GUBSE ruin the business as a whole. It seemed that on the outside no one had caught on to what was happening with SIHOT and Stella and, while the legal issues were unfolding behind closed doors, I decided to push forward with a new product. Our existing portfolio – the Reservation Assistant (RA) spa management software and the Smart cost control system we had been selling on the back of SIHOT – aside, we had to bring another flagship product on board.

After a fair bit of research, the pick of the draw was the ONEvision in-room entertainment system that promised to provide the latest technology in movies, entertainment, internet and guest communication for hotels. With the Australian market not having proven the right playing ground to solely focus on the RA and Smart systems, the latest developments in in-room technology seemed to make the timing perfect for introducing ONEvision to this part of the world. The ONEvision people had been behind the RA system before selling to its co-owners. I had always had a lot of respect for the RA company and its core team and I felt confident that I was making the right move. The crucial part now was to paint a picture of growth for *essense*, rather than one of a desperate grasp for a lifebuoy. Together with the remainder of my team and Russell, the Managing Director of a – at the time – small marketing company called OMC Connect, we set out to reinvent *essense*. While Russell's creative mind seemed to be doing continuous somersaults, his infectious enthusiasm and positive, fast-paced energy got us all excited again about the future. He was without doubt the best thing that could have happened to me – and *essense* – during a most stressful and challenging time.

Several meetings and brainstorming sessions into our redefining exercise, we eventually came up with a new concept. Rather than limiting ourselves to the sale, supply, installation, training and support of software, we were going to extend the business to offer a more holistic approach. Our vision now was to help meet *all* of our clients' technology needs, including general IT services and consulting, as well as the supply of hardware. In the past we had been asked by clients to help with the other requirements outside of our competencies, which would have spared the client the effort of going through multiple companies. And now was the time to react and respond to these requests. Our new mission statement – in line with one of our tags '*essense – the essence of your business*' – now was 'to help the hospitality and leisure industry improve their business outcomes and their customers' experiences through the leveraging of technology, people and processes'. So this was it; this was the road forward for *essense*.

I had almost all the right talent in my team and, together with the help of close present and future partnerships to fill any gaps, we were confident we could deliver on our promises. My remaining staff had come on board with the best attitude I could have wished for and as hard as it was to let go of SIHOT and Stella and all the effort and passion we all had put into both, they seemed to embrace the changes in a positive manner. While I was fighting for justice on two fronts – during the day against Stella and, during the night, against GUBSE in Germany, liaising with my German lawyer, Michael, who had joined soon after Damian – the show had to go on. There was no time to waste – the yearly industry trade show at the beginning of July was fast approaching. This was 'fake it til you make it – take II' and among all the doom and gloom of the financial crisis we now had to appear like the blooming exception. And oh, were we on a mission! If only the legal disputes with Stella and GUBSE weren't putting a big strain on the financial side of things.

I had always been one of the first to commit to a trade show in order to get the choice of stand location. That year, again, we had managed to secure the prime spot at the show. This was our chance to shine second time round. We had our brochures and stationery redesigned and, in line with our new, much grander and more sophisticated-looking website, we had also significantly changed our trade show display. The investment didn't stop there. I had to bring a new team member on board, Lee – who came with substantial experience relevant to our new flagship product ONEvision – and had to send both James and Lee to Europe to receive training in the new system. There was also the specific hardware for demonstrations, and an actual room to conduct these presentations, thus forcing us to move to bigger premises. By the time the trade show came around I was forced to go on penny watch, limiting any additional expense to the absolutely necessary.

The second mediation between Stella and *essense* was set for 2 June 2009, at which we would hear what Stella had decided between the two options. I very much doubted that Stella would have thought it sustainable and wise to keep working with *essense*. After everything that had happened between our companies over the previous months it would have been difficult to re-establish the relationship. The bigger challenge, however, would be to fix the strained relationship with GUBSE, not to mention the trust that had been lost. All ifs and buts aside, whatever Stella's verdict was to be, it meant that money would be flowing back into *essense*'s pockets in the foreseeable future.

So I thought. We entered the mediation lawyer's premises with an expectant and positive attitude, just to realise that the position we found ourselves in this time was a very different one to that five weeks earlier. The mediation lawyer's attitude appeared to have done 'a 180' – God only knows what communication had taken place – and Stella quickly made it clear that neither of the previously discussed options were on the table. Instead, we were offered a ridiculously low, unacceptable amount of money in exchange for an all-clear and a go-ahead for a direct relationship with GUBSE. Stella's lawyers argued that the letter Mr Gruber had handed Stella during our first mediation clearly proved that the trust module was not working and, as such, Stella no longer had any obligations towards *essense*. The mediation lawyer had no intention and made no effort to reason with Stella. Instead he bluntly suggested that we accept Stella's offer. We all – the two parties as well as the mediator – were very much aware that the letter was a blatant subterfuge, but for the purpose of the mediation Damian and I were outnumbered and overpowered and left with no choice but to end the get-together – one certainly couldn't call it mediation – with a notice that we would commence legal proceedings against Stella.

Chapter 14

One chapter closes

At the time when the relationship between Stella and *essense* had begun to sour, TV ads were dominated by slogans such as: 'Are you affected by the financial downturn? Get in contact with us – we are here to help.' One of those offers was repeatedly screened by the Australian Ministry of Small Business. Following Stella's first attempts to rid themselves of the middle-man, it appeared a good time to take the Ministry of Small Business up on its offer and see if the Australian government was in fact prepared to walk its talk. If nothing else, it seemed like an interesting exercise. I made an appointment with David, the Manager of the Sydney BAS – the Small Business Advisory Service – who acts on behalf of the government. During our meeting David very much sympathised with my story and eventually concluded our long conversation with the strong suggestion to contact the ACCC (the Australian Competition and Consumer Commission, who look after consumers as well as small businesses) and to also get the Federal Minister of Small Business involved. David had pointed out a clause relating to 'unconscionable conduct' and as long as I could prove that my issues with Stella fell into that category I evidently had a valid case. I wasn't sure what a valid case would actually 'give' me, but I was happy to find out.

I drafted a letter addressed to the ACCC, detailing Stella's conduct and requesting intervention and/or support. A brief meeting followed but it quickly became clear that the ACCC had no interest in my case, regardless of the fact that I had ticked all the criteria for their 'unconscionable conduct' category. To the contrary, the person allocated to my case seemed rather rude and determined to defend Stella to a point that was irrational and absurd. There was obviously a lot of politics – literally and figuratively – involved and I quickly understood that pressing the subject any further would be a waste of my time. So much for 'The ACCC is here to help you resolve problems …'.

My letter to the Federal Minister of Small Business was similar to the one I had sent to the ACCC. As expected, there was no response. I called the office a couple of weeks later and was informed that the letter had been received and would be reviewed by the minister in the near future. Over the following months, whenever I called the ministry, I was told that 'the issue' had been passed on to a different department, then that it had been passed back to the original department, then the department was on summer break, or another such excuse. Whoever I talked to at the time was aware of the existence of my letter – if nothing else, at least administration within the ministry seemed to be efficient – and although my actual letter had in the meantime become irrelevant, I continued to follow up out of sheer amusement. In the end I received communication from the ministry, many months after I had posted the letter and long after I had stopped bothering them. It read something along the lines of:

> … we hope that in the meantime you managed to sort out your legal issues with the Stella Group and wish you all the very best with the future of your business.
>
> Signed,
>
> The Federal Minister of Small Business

By the time I had received the response, the buck had been passed several times and I doubt that anyone actually knew whose responsibility it was supposed to be. It might have been a good idea to figure that out before putting an ad on TV.

My lawyer, Damian, was as much aware of my financial situation as I was and although the settlement that Stella had offered during mediation second time round would have helped my case, it was largely unjust and I was not prepared to give up without a fight. We continued to push our case regarding the outstanding CRS invoice and the $279,000 that Stella owed, but to no avail. Following mediation we had sent a letter to Stella's lawyers, announcing – again – that we were going to take the case to court, in response to which Stella had played their one trump card, stating that if I were to sue them they would request a security (in case *essense* lost the lawsuit) which, according to Damian, could have been up to $100,000 or more. There was no point in pretending that, after all those months without significant income through the SIHOT suite of products, *essense* had a truckload of money so we limited our comeback to a suggestion that we would fight the request for security. As a result, Stella marginally exceeded the offer they had put to us at mediation. We retorted with a counter offer that was still way too low for my liking but at least slightly more appropriate. Several more letters from both sides followed until my financial situation started to scorch and I was left no choice but to accept what I would be given. The final amount that we eventually agreed on was only a tad higher than Stella's original offer but at least it was going to take the pressure off the business for a while. In the course of our negotiations with Stella we had also tried to involve GUBSE in the settlement but they had happily declined, assuming that my threats to sue them were just as empty as they had – obviously – been with Stella. Once we had agreed on the settlement amount, it took another month and many more letters between our lawyers to reach agreement about the terms of the settlement, one of which dealt with the subject of protecting our rights to take legal action against GUBSE.

In the meantime, while I was heavily engaged with the settlement negotiations on the one hand and the preparations to sue GUBSE on the other, it was business as usual in the *essense* office. The guys were working hard on learning the ins and outs of our new systems – which now included ONEvision, ONEspeed (a hospitality-specific broadband solution) and ONEsignage (digital signage), while at the same time supporting our existing SIHOT clients. Our distributor agreement with GUBSE was still ongoing and we were determined to keep our issues with GUBSE behind closed doors and away from our clients.

The trade show at the beginning of June had been a great success and our new products, together with our brushed-up image, seemed to have woken significant interest among clients and the industry alike. With the details mostly still under wraps, word had got out that GUBSE had taken the SIHOT reins off *essense*. Over the course of the trade show I was approached by several suppliers suggesting I take on their products. Among the contenders was one of my – or SIHOT's – main competitors. Irrespective of the fact that I was still in dispute with GUBSE and legally in no position to add another property management system to our portfolio, I had no intention of going down the same path again. Yet I'd be lying if I said this wasn't balsam for the ego. All in all it very much appeared that our marketing exercise and our efforts of the months preceding the trade show were paying off. We had received more than a few positive comments on our stand and admiring queries on how it was possible that *essense* was doing so well and seemingly growing its business at a time of a financial downturn when the rest of the industry seemed to be struggling. To top it all off, I was even asked to talk about the ONEvision technology at an industry conference in Bangkok in a couple of months' time. All this while I spent my nights sleepless, sitting on a rock outside my home in Cremorne Point staring across the dark Sydney Harbour for hours at a time, hoping that our suppliers would take their time in sending their invoices.

We eventually signed our settlement agreement with Stella on Monday 31 August 2009. The week leading up to it was frantic, involving endless emails and phone calls, during which we desperately tried to sort out the final couple of clauses on which we and Stella still had different views. With basically not much more than a penny to my name by then and my flight to Bangkok (for the conference that I had been invited to) booked for 1 September, the pressure was on. I had urgent bills to pay and I could not afford for any gossip to spread that *essense* was insolvent. The first instalment of the settlement was paid on the day the agreement was signed. As chance would have it Stella, Damian (who first had to deduct his share) and *essense* all banked with the same financial institution and by 7pm that Monday – the night before I left for Bangkok – the money had gone through two accounts and reached the *essense* account. The relief I felt at the sight of a healthy bank account, I cannot describe. It had been six months since Damian sent the first letter to Stella. Well aware that this was only the start of a steep road ahead – both in my battle for justice and business-wise – I was incredibly proud of how, with everyone's hard work and dedication, we had managed to restructure *essense* in such a short period of time and were now in a position to fight our way back.

Once I saw the money from the settlement hit my bank account, it was a matter of first things first. I went to get takeaway dinner and, most importantly, a small bottle of champagne. With the scene set, I made myself comfortable back at my desk to finally face the three piles of invoices that had been sitting there for way too long. The piles were marked extremely urgent, urgent and kind of urgent. I eventually got home at 2am and by the time I had packed my bags and fallen into bed it wasn't long before the alarm went off and I had to get ready to catch my flight.

I will never forget the moment I sat on the train to the airport that morning, finally having time to gather my thoughts. Reflecting on the previous months, I had this incredible feeling of peace come over me. Although the money I had received from Stella wasn't a big win by any means, I still had – contrary to my first lawyer's predictions – taken a stance against the unethical conduct of a multi-billion-dollar company and walked away with compensation of sorts. One stressful chapter was closed, which would allow me to look onwards and upwards.

Chapter 15

Legal marathon

This was not the time to sit back and relax, however. The next challenge was ready and waiting in Bangkok. While I knew a fair bit about ONEvision, I was by no means a technical expert and never had been. My role in Bangkok was to sit on a panel with 'fellow IT experts', talk about our respective subjects, answer questions from the audience and partake in a discussion at the end. The tricky part was that the audience consisted of around 60 CIOs – Chief Information (technology) Officers – of hotels from the Asia Pacific region and beyond. To say that I was way out of my comfort zone would be a huge understatement.

I was well aware that I was about the only general manager of a company supplying IT systems who actually didn't know much about IT as such, and I had always been happy to keep it that way. I saw my main responsibility as running and growing the business and it wasn't without purpose that I kept myself from getting too involved in the technical side of things. (The fact that I was a perfectionist meant it was to everyone's benefit if I stayed out of at least one area of the business.) Upon arrival in Bangkok, I locked myself in my hotel room for the following day and a half and went through all the documentation from my IT team. I also conducted my fair share of research online and by the time I sat on that panel I felt like half an expert, as long as no one asked me any questions that hadn't been part of my learner's pack. When I had first been asked to present at the conference and talk to a group of CIOs I naturally had suggested that James, Mark or Lee from my office go to Bangkok instead but in view of the high profile of attendees Erik, the organiser, had insisted it be me, as the owner of the company. In the end, I got through the session without major embarrassment, but I sure didn't stand out like a shining star.

Back in Sydney, it was now full focus on '*essense* – take II'. What had got me through the previous months without wasting too much time contemplating the injustice inflicted on me and wallowing in self-pity had been the myriad inspiring biographies and business-related books I had read over the years. Almost every success story seemed to have started in someone's garage or kitchen and at some stage had – or almost had – hit a point where everything had been lost, only for the second or third attempt to eventually deliver the rewards; I was obviously on the right track. When I had first received the 'goodbye email' from Stella, my thoughts had turned straight to Richard Branson's dispute with British Airways and its so-called 'dirty tricks' campaign against Virgin Atlantic. Although on a completely different scale, Richard Branson's story had still inspired me to fight for my rights. Another person who had played a big part had been Damian. From the moment I had met him he had believed in my case and had given me his full support. Whenever I felt even the slightest doubt, Damian always provided me with the right arguments and encouragement to help keep it positive.

So, while putting as much energy as possible into *essense* and its new direction during the day, I was spending my nights talking to my German lawyer, Michael, and gathering all the information for our lawsuit against GUBSE. This was a major undertaking. We were going to sue GUBSE for compensation for loss and damage. Naturally, every penny we sued them for had to be justified and documented, including our investment in introducing SIHOT to the Australian market, our expenses in acquiring the Stella Group contract and last but not least the substantial loss of income due to GUBSE's unlawful interference in our relationship with Stella. It took more than three months for me to communicate the facts and details and for Michael to attach those to the relevant legal clauses, and, on 20 January 2010, we eventually filed a 31-page lawsuit in the German courts, together with damning evidence of significant scale.

GUBSE had always counted on our notice to sue being an empty threat. At one stage, just before Christmas 2009, they had thought it time to put an end to our 'differences' and offered to 'settle', with their idea of a fair settlement being that we distance ourselves from the dispute and that they, in return, would carry their own legal costs accumulated thus far. Interesting concept. I would have liked to be a fly on Mr Gruber's wall when he received the lawsuit to the amount of AUD 3,108,075 for compensation for loss and damages plus an at-the-time undefined amount for commission, including past commission that they had failed to pay me.

According to German law, one has to pay the court fees at the time of submitting the lawsuit. *'essense* – take II' still required significant investment and it was clear that the break-even point was still a fair way off. Gary, an old friend of mine who had been showing interest in *essense* for a while now, stepped in and offered to pay for the court costs in return for a 5 percent share in the company as well as a share of the monies received from the lawsuit. I kept being told that it could take up to two years to settle the suit but I was positive that this estimate wasn't going to apply to *my* case; after all we were dealing with the *German* courts. However, I was quickly proven wrong. Due to several delays on the part of the court, as well as requests from GUBSE for extensions of the due date for their pleading in response to the suit, it wasn't until late September – eight months after we had filed the lawsuit – that we received a copy of GUBSE's response. Their brief read like a full-bluff, all-in call at a poker game, without provision of evidence to substantiate any of their claims. Going through the document, my initial anxiety quickly turned into a frown followed by a smirk as their arguments were nothing but ludicrous. What they had presented us with was a blatant lie from start to end in an obvious desperate effort to have the lawsuit dismissed. So, for example, it was supposedly GUBSE who had prepared the cumbersome response to the Stella tender as *essense* was simply incapable; and it was GUBSE's product presentations and meetings with Stella on location that led to Stella signing the deal. They even chose to make it personal with an attempt to portray me as a nutcase, claiming that Stella, as a result of my uncontrollable temper, simply refused to deal with me. GUBSE was clearly counting on a lack of evidence from my side to crush their fabrications. They had sorely underestimated my memory and organisational skills. I had emails and documents at my disposal that were to prove each of their bogus statements wrong.

What followed were several writs from either side and another attempt from GUBSE to settle, but it seemed that their pride stood in their way of putting a *serious* offer on the table. In January 2011, a year after the lawsuit had been filed, we were finally advised that the first court hearing in Saarbruecken, Germany, was likely to take place in March. Anticipation from all parts was short-lived, however, as the potential date was put on hold due to the referring judge entering retirement. There was no replacement judge in sight and eventually a new date was set for the end of May. I booked my flights and accommodation as soon as I found out, just to be informed a couple of weeks before the actual hearing that the judge who had supposedly taken over would not proceed. The scenario repeated itself a month later, only this time around all parties involved decided I should still get on the plane and organise for court mediation instead.

The date for mediation was set for 21 June 2011. The months leading up to it can easily be described as the most challenging in my life thus far. The stress of the previous two years, fighting two legal cases against two companies whose sole aim had been to bust me while at the same time starting afresh and building up what could essentially be classified as a new business, had finally taken its toll. Truth be told, already a year earlier I was getting close to reaching my limit but the belief that an end to the legal dispute with GUBSE was in sight had given me just enough energy to keep pushing on. Giving up had never been an option; the question was how long my body – and mind – would hold up.

Back in late 2006, during the intense contract negotiations with Stella – in particular with Sunny – and at a crucial time for *essense* in general, a friend and I had been training very hard for the famed Coast to Coast race in New Zealand. We would spend every spare minute on our bikes, in a kayak or at boot camps. I had a lot of energy and pushing myself to exhaustion during exercise always gave me a real kick. However, I failed to give my body a chance to recover. I was running on adrenaline almost 24/7 – if not in the business, then while doing sports. Until one day, during a boot-camp session, I collapsed. The eventual diagnosis was stage-two adrenal fatigue. Each morning I woke up feeling like I had just run a marathon. Everything I had previously done with ease or that had only required little effort was turning into an exhausting and draining chore. I went on a strict diet, cutting out stimulants including coffee, sweets, alcohol and processed foods. I did everything I was told to do, with the one exception – take time off and avoid any kind of stress. This 'strong suggestion' was simply impossible to follow at that point in my life.

It is said that it takes up to two years for adrenals to recover – if one allows for the time to recover. Whereas over the months following my physical collapse I had steadily started to feel better, the events that eventually unfolded with GUBSE and Stella brought a very unwelcome setback. I was living as healthy a lifestyle as I possibly could but there was no time and space for considering my body, which kept screaming for attention. After two years of fighting on every front, not much sleep and a struggle to keep the business viable – finding money to cover the monthly costs had turned into an almost full-time job in itself by then – I was in desperate need of a positive change. If not on the phone to my lawyer in Germany, I would spend many sleepless nights on 'my' rock above the ocean in Cremorne Point, at times just sitting there empty of thoughts while on some occasions crying my eyes out in despair until two or three in the morning. And then, a few hours later, I would find myself back in the office, putting on a brave face and a smile, ready to keep pushing forward. I was mentally and physically exhausted. There was promising movement within the business with exciting times around a couple of large contracts in close reach, but it was all taking longer than what I could afford – physically, emotionally and financially.

One morning, on my way to the office after yet another night spent in tribulation, I had a sudden string of sentiments hit me. While driving over the Harbour Bridge, I was thinking who I would rather be or what I would rather be doing and was stunned by the fact that I couldn't think of anyone or anything. I loved my life and

I loved my business and, although I was probably at my lowest low at the time, I felt that *it was okay*. A strong sense of peace came over me and, believing that everything happened for a reason, I reminded myself that in the end things always worked out the way they should. I wasn't the first or only person to go through difficult times; this phase in my life was teaching me a fair bit and it would eventually pass. I knew I could handle the challenge and as long as I felt that I did whatever I could and the best I could, I would – in the end – be okay with the outcome. It was kind of an epiphany; one that I kept referring back to in my mind, especially over the weeks that were to follow.

Chapter 16
Bracing for mediation

With the legal issues dragging on much longer than I had ever believed possible and the sales-cycle of our new flagship product turning out to be quite lengthy, it was time to pull the budget strings. I had never held back when it came to the marketing budget and the way the company presented itself to the outside world, but I had always made sure I avoided unnecessary expenses. While the staff got to choose their own laptops, my PC was still the same one that I had bought when I had first started the business all those years ago. (After all, my requirements were comparatively limited.). Our internal phone system was second hand – not that anyone could tell – and the office rent, phone, internet and other fixed costs had always been thoroughly researched and negotiated. Although I had a bookkeeper who'd come into the office once a month, I now decided to double-check our recurring bills; at a time where every dollar counted, I had to find ways to reduce our costs.

As my investigations eventually showed, I was being taken for a ride by each company I put under the microscope. Over time my bank had been charging me the same fees twice; on a quarterly basis and, again, at the end of each year. When I called them on the issue, the department I was referred to tried to dispose of me by repeatedly telling me that the fees in question were not the same but two completely different kinds of charges. Once it had become clear that I couldn't be fooled, their customer service team worked very hard on making the process of complaint as cumbersome and time-consuming as possible, in the hope that I would eventually put it all into the too-hard basket. In the end, weeks of emails, phone calls and hours of time on hold later, I eventually received a refund of several thousand dollars. My car insurance company, too, had been charging an incorrect premium that was about 25 percent higher than what I was meant to pay, basing the premium on a suburb that in no way corresponded with the information I had provided them with. And when I requested an itemised bill from my tax accountant, I noticed that – among other things – it contained charges for a marketing email that they had sent to me; one of the accountants I had been dealing with had forwarded a mass email, alerting clients that the latest version for the accounting system MYOB would now be available through their office. Did they really make me pay for their time to try and sell me something I had no interest in? The example to beat them all was Energy Australia, who eventually admitted to wrongly invoicing me for almost a year for services that had never been mine. The first energy bill I received when we moved into our new premises had shown an amount that any layman could have identified as irrational. After several conversations with the building manager as well as Energy Australia, I was still being told that the usage shown on the monthly bills was correct, until one day they admitted that I had been paying for the lighting and air-conditioning for the whole office floor. This refund, too, was worth several thousand dollars. I don't even want to know how many millions of fraudulent dollars each of those companies are making on a monthly basis through people who don't take the time to check their bills or who don't have the endurance to deal with their – what seem to be purposeful – lengthy processes for complaints and refunds.

Although by that time – mid-2011 – I had kind of put my differences with Stella behind me, it still bothered me that Bob, the former CEO of the hospitality arm of the Stella Group (who had since been promoted to the Group CEO) and the one person I had always had a lot of respect for, had never had the courage to communicate with me directly since the first signs of 'unrest' had emerged. Bob had always put a human shield in front of himself. Several attempts to contact him at the time by phone or email had remained unsuccessful. While I believed that it was not Bob himself who was the driving force behind 'the plot' but rather his middle management, it was still him I had spent hours communicating with, after Sunny had left the scene. And, most significantly, it was his signature on the contracts.

One day, during a high-profile industry conference in Sydney where Bob had been asked to join a small team of keynote speakers, I spotted him sitting by himself in the hotel bar of the venue. This was going to be my chance to finally talk to him. Bob seemed lost in thought and busy with his phone when I approached him. His initial reaction was a friendly hello, quickly followed by a surprised: 'Oh! Hello.' He asked how I was and commented that it appeared that *essense* was doing well, to which I responded, calm and friendly, that yes, things were starting to look up again. I then continued by clarifying that my purpose in approaching him wasn't to revisit past issues – which I had largely put behind me – but rather that it had been my objective to let him know that I had always held him in high regard and that I was truly disappointed as I had seen him as someone who would do business more ethically. Bob's response was an uneasy 'Sabine, look, there were several factors … '. I had obviously put him in an uncomfortable situation and there was no need for me to dig further. We concluded our brief chat with Bob saying that he was sorry about the way things had panned out and, wishing each other all the best, I walked off. I don't exactly know why this conversation was so important to me, but it gave me a sense of closure. Now I could, indeed, leave it behind me, at least as far as Stella was concerned.

Since our official launch of the ONEvision system a year and a half earlier, we had managed to attract serious interest within the industry. Compared to SIHOT, the competition was limited to a couple of dominant players, yet a client's investment in the system was to be much greater. With an outlay of several-hundred thousand dollars for a medium-sized hotel we had had to up our profile, meaning further investment, including sponsorship of the yearly industry trade show where we had ONEvision on display in the 'Hotel Room of the Future' – a display hotel room showcasing the latest technology – and our digital signage system spread across the venue. By early 2011 we had managed to receive the verbal go-ahead from a major hotel group, while a couple of months later we found ourselves in a highly favourable position to win the contract for another potentially multi-million-dollar project. We were so close, yet so far. In May 2011 I was invited by *at-visions* – the Austrian creators and suppliers of the ONEvision system – to attend a conference and exhibition in Hong Kong. It was a successful event and, with *at-visions* well aware of the latest developments in Australia, we were all very excited about the future. But first a hurdle had to be jumped – to reach settlement with GUBSE in the upcoming mediation.

The couple of weeks prior to mediation I was very much on edge. I was going to leave Sydney on 16 June and spend a day or two with Michael, my lawyer, in his Munich office to go through all the details and possible scenarios before D-day. It had been over two years since I had first contacted Michael; we had spent hours on the phone and I felt like I had known him for a lifetime. Yet this was the first time we'd meet in person and there was a lot to discuss in regards to strategy and tactics.

I was booked on an A380 flight with Qantas to Singapore from where I'd continue with an affiliate airline to Munich. Upon arrival in Singapore, having had a seat right in the back of the plane, it took what seemed like ages to disembark. For some reason, back in Sydney the check-in staff had been unable to issue boarding passes for all legs of my flight and I was advised to get one for my connecting flight at the gate in Singapore. This was the first time that I wished I was on a smaller plane. By the time I finally made my way into the airport, my connecting flight was already being called. I ran as fast as I could to the other end of the extensive terminal to reach the departure gate, just to be told that my boarding pass had to be printed at the airline information desk half-way back from where I had just come. I freaked, but had the steward's promise that they would wait for me. I sprinted back to the information desk where I was then told that the flight had been closed on their system a couple of minutes earlier so they could no longer print my boarding pass. I begged the airline staff, offered them money, told them how desperately I needed to get onto that flight to attend a court mediation, but to no avail.

There was no other flight that night and no guarantee I could get on a flight the following day or the day after. And while I could have tried a different airline it would have involved a ridiculous amount of money and, again, there was no guarantee. It was peak season and all flights to Europe were full. The undeniable fact was that I had to get onto *my* flight that night so that I could spend time with my lawyer to prepare for mediation and, just as important, to get some serious sleep and a chance to recover from jetlag. A clear and fresh head would be crucial. After much ado, I eventually got to talk to an airport supervisor but all he could offer was confirmation that it would not be possible to re-open the system. There would be too many people involved in the process, including tarmac security and, unless there was an emergency, this was not a procedure that could possibly be followed. I stood there, tears slowly running down my face; this was the tip of the iceberg and more than I could take. Could someone please give me a break?!

And then, seemingly out of nowhere, this airline employee – the steward who had earlier given me his word that they would wait for me – appeared, grabbing my carry-on bag and shouting to me to run. I had two of his colleagues follow me, one carrying my jacket that I dropped along the way and the other telling me to run faster. With a big dash through the gate – the airline staff had taken my handbag and carry-on off me in order to run it through the security check – I literally ran onto the plane with a ground hostess calling the seat number out to me while I flew past her. A couple of minutes later, my belongings – my jacket, handbag and carry-on – were delivered to my seat and, with a big smile on his face, the gentleman who had initiated the dash wished me a good flight. The doors of the plane closed and a minute later we rolled off. Here I was on the plane, puffing like there was no tomorrow, with a face like a tomato, and without an official boarding pass. An act of kindness and benevolence that will stick with me for a long time.

I arrived in Munich on Friday 17 June. My hotel was right around the corner from Michael's office. I dropped off my luggage, had a quick shower and, within a couple of hours of landing at the airport, was ready for our first meeting. Michael's initial comments were that he had expected to look into the eyes of a train wreck and that instead I looked surprisingly fresh and healthy. I evidently appeared the opposite to the voice of despair he had come to know so well, especially over the past couple of months. I had been stressed out of my head before I left Sydney; then in Singapore I had some more spice added to my anxiety, followed by another long-haul flight with no sleep. It's amazing how the human body functions; how you can pull yourself together when you have to. For some reason, I felt fitter, mentally and physically, than I had in months. It had all been coming to a peak and this was it.

Relieved to see me in such a relaxed state, Michael stressed the importance of appearing unfazed during court mediation. On the day, when it would be my turn to summarise my side of the story, it would have to be a short, calm and clear recount of facts. We did a practice run and already with the first take I had hit the nail on the head; I was to repeat my story in the exact same way at court. Done deal. Michael made himself available for another two half days over the weekend, followed by a seven-hour train ride to Saarbruecken – in the far west of Germany – on Monday. Mediation was set for 11am on Tuesday morning.

I hadn't seen anyone from GUBSE's camp since Mr Gruber had left my office in Sydney 16 months earlier. In the hours leading up to mediation Michael had managed to keep me calm and composed – we had arrived at court unfashionably early – but as soon as the doors opened and Mr Gruber and his lawyer, Mr Fischer (not the real name), walked in, my whole body started to shake. It was no longer going to be an easy task to look those bastards in the eye and stay cool and collected. By the time it came to my actual 'recital', my words erupted into an emotional waterfall – far from what Michael and I had agreed on. I spoke a lot faster and included much more information than necessary; even a few whispers and kicks under the table from Michael couldn't slow me down. And once it was GUBSE's turn to recount their version of events, my whole focus was on breathing deeply, trying hard to return to a more confident state.

GUBSE's lawyer proved to be just as uncongenial as I had envisioned him to be. His suit was way too big and his appearance and laughter resembled Gargamel (the evil wizard from *The Smurfs*). It quickly became obvious that GUBSE's strategy was to derail me. They even used the odd term of abuse to describe me, to the point where the mediation judge threw a questioning look in my direction, inviting me to react and not let them talk to me in such a way. It didn't bother me. I was more than happy for GUBSE to keep going – it was testament to their character. Not long into the meeting, GUBSE was asked to put their first offer on the table and, although my hopes had been kept within bounds, I had certainly expected a much more reasonable starting position. Now, however, we faced yet another ridiculous and undoubtedly unacceptable proposal. My initial reaction was utter disbelief and I suggested ending mediation right there and then without further wasting anyone's time. If GUBSE seriously believed that theirs was an offer genuine enough to have me fly in from Australia, there was no point in continuing. I asked the mediator for a word in private to which he countered that it should be GUBSE who he should have a word with instead. Michael and I left the room and once we re-entered, we had a more acceptable point of departure and eventually came to an agreement, but not without the judge having one or two stern words with GUBSE in between. The final settlement agreement contained a two-week cooling period to give Mr Gruber a chance to discuss the outcome with his fellow board members and his son Andreas. I wasn't happy with the result – the agreed settlement amount as well as the payment terms greatly varied from what I had had in mind. It was far from fair but it was acceptable in a sense that it would allow me to keep the business alive. At the end of mediation, the judge enquired about the procedures that should be put in place in case either party decided to withdraw the settlement: '... would mediation be deemed to have failed or would we meet again to re-negotiate?' to which I responded that under no circumstances would I be open to further negotiations. If GUBSE decided to withdraw their offer, then mediation had failed. I was not prepared to go any lower than I already had and let GUBSE screw me once again. There was a limit, and we had reached it.

Straight after mediation Michael and I returned to Munich where I thanked him for all his help and efforts over the past couple of years and then stepped onto another train to Salzburg, Austria, to see my family. A long chapter had – just about – been closed and it was time to re-energise and move on. While I tried hard to feel the relief I had been awaiting with so much anticipation, the nature of the outcome didn't quite allow for it. If I hadn't been under the immense financial pressure I found myself in, there was no way I would have agreed to that settlement and I kept wondering if I had made the right decision.

After a few days in Austria, dividing my time between my parents, siblings, nephews and a couple of friends who still lived in Salzburg, I accompanied my mum to Spain for a week on the beach. It was high time for a holiday. Mum and I had always been very close and she was one of the few people who seemed to have the ability to forever say the right thing at the right time. There had never been much commiseration from Mum towards me but rather encouragement and assurance that everything would be all right in the end. Although I had kept a lot of the details to myself while I went through my toughest weeks, Mum still managed to make me feel better every time I talked to her. It was nice to go away together and relax, while Dad was happy to stay at home and hold the fort – or leave 'the girls' to themselves; Mum and I sure could talk a lot!

Four days into our time on the island of Mallorca, I received a phone call from Michael, advising me that GUBSE had withdrawn the settlement and put another offer on the table. I can only say that I'm glad that at the time I had no idea what was yet to come.

Chapter 17

Groundhog Day

GUBSE had evidently been well aware of my financial situation and had counted on me accepting their new offer in an act of desperation. As had previously been the case, however, their plan did not come off and we rejected their bid graciously. Although initially shocked, I took the news with relative calm. It was now time for plan B – one that was yet to be devised. Going by Mr Gruber's aversion to risk, I had not anticipated GUBSE being prepared to take a chance on the case now being heard at court. I still didn't think that GUBSE was actually prepared for such a scenario; rather, that they were counting on getting away with a cheaper result. In any case, I now had an emergency on my hands and had to come up with an alternative resolution. My budget had totally dried out and three days after I was scheduled to arrive back in Australia, the wages as well as office rent were due.

The only reasonable solution at hand – one that in fact could provide a mutually beneficial outcome – involved *at-visions*. Back at the industry conference in Hong Kong a month earlier, their executive team appeared to have been in full appreciation of *essense*'s progress in its region; after all, in regards to their ONEvision system, we had two major deals within reach. Although not easy on the ego to invite an investor into the business so close to a big break-through, taking into consideration past experience with GUBSE, it seemed like a smart idea to hand our main suppliers a share in the business. I had always trusted *at-visions* but there must have been something I had learned from my lesson with GUBSE. With my business relationship with *at-visions'* top management already going back six years, this should prove a good move in many ways. I contacted Frank (not the real name), one of top executives of *at-visions* and organised a meeting in Vienna for the day after I returned from Spain. With the weekend in between, leaving Spain early would have made no difference, and a bit more sun and ocean could only help to clear my spinning head.

Once back in Austria, the events of the previous weeks – or rather years – started to take their toll on me. While my time in Spain had offered a welcome change of scenery it was little more than a drop in the ocean. The surge of energy I had felt upon arriving in Munich just over two weeks earlier had long dissipated and it was now being replaced by utter mental and physical exhaustion. My meeting with Frank was going to determine the future of *essense* and with my engine running on empty, facing yet another two highly developed egos – Frank and his protégé Thomas (not the real name) – at that stage was not something I trusted myself to be equipped for. There was no point in hiding the fact that my situation was a desperate one – the clock was ticking – and I felt like a lamb to the slaughter. I needed help. I had introduced Frank to my brother Heiner years earlier when Heiner was looking for a customised IT solution for his business. They were both very successful businessmen, which had given them a common ground for respect. I required Heiner's support now, and he was quick to step in.

To create an amicable atmosphere, we chose to hold our meeting with *at-visions* over dinner in a sophisticated restaurant in the centre of Vienna, not too far from *at-visions'* office and a three-hour drive from Salzburg. Back in Hong Kong I'd already had various discussions with Frank and Thomas that had given them substantial insight into *essense*. They were also well aware of my issues with GUBSE, whose actions they had always classified as rather dumb and short-sighted. And they had now been fully informed about the settlement and GUBSE's subsequent withdrawal of the same.

Our meeting in Vienna didn't go as smoothly as I hoped. With my drained brain well on display, it was only a matter of minutes before I had to hand the game over to my brother. I was an emotional wreck and the best I could do at that stage was to shut up and try not to drop a tear. As expected, Frank played his cards well and although his offer was in our eyes ethically unacceptable, I was in no position to refuse. Frank knew of *essense*'s extensive investment in their product suite in Australia (like GUBSE, *at-visions* and its products were largely unheard of in the Asia-Pacific market at the time) and was fully appreciative of the impressive sales that were on the table, some of which were at highly advanced stages. Nonetheless, my meeting with *at-visions* was a last-minute dash and clearly had not presented me in the most favourable position, making my situation an easy target for exploitation.

I was due to depart for Australia a few days after my meeting with Frank and Thomas. The procedure we agreed on in the end was that, upon my return to the office, I would forward a formal proposal to Frank, including certain financial data. If all was well – which we both anticipated to be the case – Frank would authorise an initial transfer of funds the following Monday, allowing me to pay the wages and office rent in time and continue operating the business.

I arrived back in Sydney at 6am on Thursday 14 July 2011, and by 9am I was at my desk – at home – retrieving the required data and putting together the said proposal, ensuring that Frank would have it in his inbox at the start of his workday. Once that task was completed, all that was left for me to do was to sit back and await Frank's confirmation of 'the transaction'. That night I stayed up until all hours until eventually, after several failed attempts to reach Frank, or even Thomas, I could no longer stay awake and collapsed into bed.

There was no point in going into the office the following day without knowing what to tell the staff. I had sent an email to James straight after mediation to inform him that all was well and that I had settled the case with GUBSE, but I was yet to let them all know of the latest developments. I called the office to tell the staff that, although back, I was going to take the day off. While on the phone, Romana, a fellow Austrian who I had sponsored for a work visa a year and a half earlier, gave me a brief update and filled me in on the fact that Jack (not the real name), our sales manager at the time, had been acting weird over the previous couple of days and had alluded, among other things, that he was going to leave the company.

Slowly, alarm bells started to go off in my head. I had never before had any problems getting hold of 'the big boys' from *at-visions*. They were always on their mobiles and, if busy, they would call back as soon as they could. During our meeting in Austria we had all conceded the urgency of a formal acceptance of the draft proposal upon my return to Australia, followed by an immediate transfer of funds. The fact that Frank had seemingly chosen to ignore my emails and phone calls had me already suspecting inconsistency. To now hear that Jack – who had been my 'one rotten egg' in the company for quite a while, but who I simply had not had the energy, time and patience to deal with – had hinted at resigning made me wonder if I was in the process of getting screwed a second time around. I waited a few more hours until the sun had risen in Austria before I resumed my attempts to get hold of Frank. Again, to no avail. My suspicions were then confirmed the following morning, Saturday, with an email from Jack, officially resigning from *essense*, followed by an aggressive phone call advising me that he had heard that the company had no money to pay wages (his source obviously being *at-visions*) and requesting I transfer what was 'rightfully his' straight away – never mind that pay day wasn't until Monday.

My biggest nightmare had come true. Behind my back seemed to be Frank being practical. He must have figured that rather than investing in *essense*, it would be much cheaper and more efficient to let *essense* 'go under' which, I can only assume, he would have anticipated to happen if I didn't receive funds by Monday to keep the company going. In this situation, he could take over for free. All that would be required was Jack – he had access to all necessary information and, as the sales manager would be 'the key' to *essense*' clients. It was a simple and basic calculation and one that would allow *at-visions* to walk away without even remotely looking like they had done anything wrong. I had shivers running down my spine. No words can describe what went through my mind. Not in my wildest dreams had I thought this could happen to me yet again, least of all with *at-visions*. Wasn't I just six weeks earlier sitting with their team – including Frank and Thomas – at a table in Hong Kong, laughing and joking and drinking wine? But this must have been where it all started. The position of the highly paid CEO of their Singapore office, Oliver, probably had to be justified and what better way than to take over a market that seemed so close to a breakthrough. *at-visions* had obviously come to understand the potential of the Australian market and a direct move into Australia to put it all under one umbrella would make sense. This was it. I had had enough. But not only that, mentally and emotionally I could take no more. No matter what other solution there could have possibly been to replace *at-visions* as an investor, there was no way I could keep working with *at-visions* under such circumstances, let alone stay sane while at it. Here I was, looking at Groundhog Day.

Chapter 18

Threats and promises

On Friday afternoon, when I still hadn't had word from *at-visions*, I had already decided to get in contact with Prashant, the CEO of a Japanese hospitality IT company. I had had several meetings with Prashant earlier in the year to discuss a potential collaboration based on obvious synergies and, having shown significant interest in *essense* from when we had first met, I now asked him if he was available to meet at his earliest convenience. By pure fluke, Prashant was in Sydney at the time and, responding to the urgency of my call, he suggested meeting for lunch on Sunday. There was only one goal I now had in mind: to sell *essense*. There was no time to get emotional; the only way to save what I had built up over the previous nine years – and to not let my staff and clients down – was to hand over the business to someone else. It was time to let go, not only for the obvious financial reason, but also for the sake of my sanity.

Prashant had always been very approachable so it was easy to have an open, sincere conversation. I recounted my situation and the events of the previous weeks in detail and told him straight out that *essense* was on the market, asking if he was interested in buying the company. Expressing his sympathy and regret that I was to let go of *essense*, Prashant responded that my offer would definitely be one worth considering. He was, in actual fact, interested in taking over *essense* but it would naturally require time to discuss the details. To keep the company going in the meantime, however, he was happy to provide me with the required funds, which he would transfer first thing the following morning. I returned home that night in utter disbelief at the events of the previous days and weeks and the prospect of closing the door to *essense* behind me; an almost unconceivable thought that had never before entered my mind.

That same night I sent a friendly email to Frank, advising him that since I hadn't had word from him I had no choice but to bring on board another investor and that it was 'business as usual'. The next challenge I faced was Jack. I had employed Jack just over a year earlier out of desperation after Lee, our sales manager at the time and a much-valued member of the *essense* team, had announced that he was moving back to England. I was in the midst of my legal battles with GUBSE, the industry trade show we were sponsoring in Melbourne was around the corner and any attempt to find an experienced salesperson with an understanding of IPTV (Internet Protocol Television) and hospitality technology in general had failed. Up until then my employees had always found their way to *essense* by word of mouth and/or recommendation but with time running out before the fair, I was left with no choice but to involve a recruitment agency; and this is how Jack had joined our team. Although Jack had managed to impress us to a certain degree during the trade fair, it wasn't long before my instincts told me that he wasn't the real deal. Out of plain self-protection, I kept convincing myself that he was doing a good job. Until one day I found out that, all along, Jack had been spending a big part of his time in the office focusing on non-company related matters.

Frank and *at-visions* were well aware of my strained relationship with Jack. And while everyone knew that it was only a matter of time before we would part ways, Jack had now taken the burden off me and resigned. His impulse to resign, however, had been sparked by *at-visions* and the prospect of new employment. Yet what he had not counted on was *at-visions*' plan of taking over *essense* not eventuating. The day after I had sent my email to the CEO of *at-visions* advising him that it would be 'business as usual' at *essense*, Jack started terrorising the office with raging phone calls to the point that James and Romana refused to pick up the phone altogether. His deal with *at-visions* had obviously fallen through and I was the culprit. At the same time, I also had word from several clients advising that they had been contacted by Jack, who had suggested they refrain from doing business with *essense,* and to sign with *at-visions* directly. Jack was obviously hoping that he could help make a takeover by *at-visions* still happen.

As soon as I returned to the office from my trip overseas I updated James and Romana on the latest developments in regards to the failed settlement with GUBSE as well as the fact that I was in the process of bringing in an 'investor'. At the time we were also working on a large and significant Response for Proposal. With everything that was happening it required rigorous containment and, above all, incredible effort to keep myself as well as the shrinking team motivated. Prashant had left for Japan the day after our meeting and we had been in contact on an almost daily basis since – mostly late at night – to discuss the details of the takeover. Then, on 28 July, a Thursday night 11 days after our meeting, I received confirmation from Prashant that he was happy to proceed and acquire *essense*. Before any deals could be signed, however, the future of *essense* had to be discussed with my staff. The following morning, Friday, I informed James and Romana that unfortunately I was left with no choice but to sell the business and that Prashant would be stepping in as the new owner of the company. I would be available on a consulting basis for another couple of months but, other than that, James – if he was to agree – was now going to be in charge. My announcement was then followed up with a conference call between Prashant and the three of us.

As I had become so used to in the past, events took an unexpected sharp turn and by Monday morning I was, once again, faced with a completely different scenario. Whereas on Friday I had left the office with a to-do list regarding the transfer of the company, I woke up on Monday to a message from Prashant informing me that unfortunately things had changed and he no longer felt comfortable taking over *essense*, asking me to call him.

Over the weekend Prashant had had a conversation with Oliver, the CEO of *at-visions* Asia and had been advised that if he were to take over *essense*, the two significant leads that *essense* appeared to be close to signing would become the responsibility of *at-visions*

175

Asia, and that he, Prashant, would not be receiving any support whatsoever from *at-visions*. Prashant concluded our conversation by saying, 'Look, Sabine, I am well aware that this is legal hogwash, but I would obviously never be able to work with them on such a basis, let alone trust them'.

I was completely numb. I no longer knew *what* to think. I paced around the house in a trance. The situation had turned incomprehensible. This was it. This was the end of it all. I had just received the death sentence for my beloved company. The only thing left for me to do was to go to the office and tell James and Romana that – after nine years of hard work and total commitment from everyone involved – it was over. *essense* had to close its doors.

Chapter 19

A series of goodbyes

For me *essense* had never been about the money. It was *my baby* that, with the support of several amazing people around me, I had built up from scratch and that, against all odds and predictions, we had made into a respectable and successful company. An internationally recognised industry consultant once said to me that if there were an award for persistence and determination, he would give it to me. He was one of many who, when I had first started off, hadn't given me more than a year, or a couple of years at most.

I had fought until the end. There was nothing else I could possibly do. I had loved my business with utmost conviction; every time that I had walked through those office doors, I walked through them with pride and a big smile on my face. I had also always cared about our clients and, above all, my staff and it broke my heart to tell James and Romana that this was the end. They had stood by me and supported the business more than I could have asked for. I had always been sad to see any of the guys go. This, however, was going to be a very different goodbye under circumstances I would never in my wildest dreams thought possible. It was one of those situations that you hear of happening to other people but that you most certainly never envision happening to you.

James and Romana took the news with characteristic grace – as much as such a situation could allow – and they both offered to stay in the office for another week. Our existing clients still had to be looked after until we were in a position to make the news official; and the two of them were a much-cherished support while I started to wind down the business. There was also another challenge that I now had on my hands. I had to remove my lawsuit against GUBSE before placing *essense* into voluntary liquidation, meaning that the news of *essense* shutting down had to be kept under wraps for the time being. I could not risk GUBSE finding out and interfering with the process in any way. The lawsuit had been filed under the company name, *essense*, and if the company were wound down then the lawsuit would also cease to exist. My German lawyer, Michael, advised that due to the case not having been heard in court as yet I had the option of selling the lawsuit to another entity who could then fight it on my behalf. I had no idea about the procedures involved to facilitate a transfer of the lawsuit and finding out wasn't going to be an easy task, as I was quick to learn. Once you mention the word 'liquidation', people waste no time distancing themselves from you, including my long-time accountant. If you can't pay for advice, you won't get it. Michael was only in a position to help as far as German law was concerned and liquidation law was not one of my Australian lawyer's areas of expertise. I did not have much time or money up my sleeve. Apart from the legal implications of keeping a company running when insolvent, it was also not easy to live in pretense (about the status of the company) and not something I could comfortably ask of James and Romana either. I was in urgent need of professional advice but I didn't have the funds to pay for it. There was no way I was going to ask my family for another penny. Each of them had already been extremely supportive in the lead-up to mediation in Germany (which had always been my reference point for easier times ahead), and my brother Heiner had already agreed to buy the lawsuit off *essense*, the proceeds of which were to cover the fees of the liquidator.

After running in circles for a couple of days, I eventually heard of a government service that offered free legal consultation for certain cases and circumstances. I called to apply but getting through to a real person was a major challenge that involved yet another half day of my time and patience, both of which I did not – by any means – have readily available. Fortunately, in the end the complete process was quicker than expected and my meeting with a liquidation lawyer eventually took place on 4 August 2011, three days after the fate of the company had been sealed. In the meantime, Michael had supplied me with an 'Agreement of transfer of claims' that listed the conditions under which *essense* would assign the legal claims against GUBSE to my brother's company. It was now only a matter of the liquidation lawyer reviewing the document and confirming that it adhered to Australian liquidation law. This was a crucial step as any slight oversight could have meant the potential risk of forfeiture of the lawsuit.

Happy with what we presented and requesting only a couple of small changes, the liquidation lawyer recommended a liquidator – a friend of his – who offered to handle the winding up of the company for $8000. Mine was an easy liquidation; I had few creditors and being a software company – the ONEvision specific hardware aside – there were hardly any assets. My first meeting with the liquidator, Domenic, occurred the following Monday. Domenic, too, was happy with the conditions of the transfer of the claims – a certain percentage of the proceeds of the lawsuit were to be paid to the liquidator and eventually distributed to the creditors – and *essense* was now officially in liquidation.

The following day I personally called all our existing clients, explaining the situation and apologising for the very unfortunate inconvenience (GUBSE would now also be taking over the support of all our clients outside of Stella). This wasn't an easy thing to do and getting through all the calls involved several tear-filled breaks. Then it was time to finally send a goodbye email to our ONEvision prospects and everyone else in the industry that we had formed a relationship with over the years. Again, this was difficult. I had to remain professional while at the same time – for the sake of my own sanity – put at least some kind of doubt in the minds of our potential ONEvision clients. I could not let myself get screwed a second time. It was *essense* who had taken ONEvision to the Australian market and who had invested a significant amount of time and money into the sales and marketing of the *at-visions* products. I could not sit back now and watch *at-visions* take over for free where we had left off. The email read as follows:

Dear All,

We are very sad to inform you that due to insurmountable differences with the ONEvision head office, *essense* no longer feels comfortable representing ONEvision and other *at-visions* products in Australia.

Unfortunately this decision has also resulted in *essense* having to close its doors.

After nine years filled with passion for and commitment to the hospitality industry, this is a very difficult announcement to make and we sincerely apologise for any inconvenience this may cause.

Thank you very much for your support over the past years.

Best wishes from all of us at *essense*. We hope that our paths will cross again in the future.

Sabine

PS: Please note that the F&B division of *essense* hospitality will continue to trade under new ownership.

I later heard that the project manager of one of the two major prospects we had been working with supposedly refused to deal with *at-visions* directly; he was no longer interested in the ONEvision system if *essense* ceased to be involved. The second lead also went quiet and another client, with whom we had already entered the project-planning stage, decided to pull out too. To my knowledge *at-visions* never managed to make inroads into the Australian market, at least not within the following couple of years. It was yet another case of greed and ego taking over reason.

During the previous weeks while looking at all my options to save *essense*, I got in contact with a small company in Melbourne who had been interested in collaborating with us in regards to the food and beverage arm of *essense*. We had started to build on that side of the business over the previous year and a half, but had never had the chance to take it to its full potential. What I now suggested to the owner of the Melbourne company was that they take over *essense* without the *at-visions* products and make it a purely F&B-centric company. He was only just starting up and we could provide him with a reputable corporate identity, including all the marketing material. I would have been happy to accept whatever he could have afforded to pay. I just wanted to see *essense* stay alive. All our marketing material, including our trade show stand and displays, were of the highest quality and the *essense* website was sophisticated. I would have liked to hand it all over to someone rather than to see it all go to waste.

However, it was quite simply time for *essense* to disappear. The gentleman from Melbourne I had been talking to and who had appeared interested in my offer was facing a personal challenge that unexpectedly put our deal on hold. The plan was then to park that part of the business and transfer the relevant tangible and intangible assets to the new owner whenever he was ready. The course of action had been discussed with the liquidator and the transfer could have been executed even after *essense* had been placed into liquidation. In the end, however, it never came to that.

A couple of days after my first meeting with the liquidator, two of his staff came to the office to confiscate what had been my life and my passion for so many years. They took all of the folders, laptops, printers and whatever else they could find of value. Standing there watching them load up their trolley evoked a feeling I will never forget. It was *my* stuff they were taking away and that I had worked so hard for and yet they made me feel like a criminal. And while I would have loved to finally just let go and break down right then and there, there was still no time to get emotional. With a great deal to organise in very little time, I had to pull myself together once again, be rational and simply keep functioning.

The day I realised that I had to wind down the business, my first thought had been, *I have to get out of here*. I didn't have much more than a penny to my name and I would no longer be able to afford to live in Sydney, apart from the fact that a change of scenery was now crucial. To avoid falling into a hole, I had to go somewhere positive, somewhere cheap and cheerful – anywhere that would provide a warm, sunny and happy environment. My initial idea had been someplace in Asia but, then again, considering the state I was in, there would have been the danger of ending up dope-smoking on a beach in Thailand or similar. The most logical destination that was kind of close and wouldn't remove me too far from the western world seemed to be Hawaii. I could stay at a backpacker's hostel and do some waitressing work until I figured out the next step. I searched for the date and the airline that offered the cheapest airfare and the result was a $350 flight with Jetstar on Sunday 21 August, 12 days after my first meeting with the liquidator. Advising Domenic of my impending departure, I requested that the creditors meeting be scheduled within a week and all the paperwork be completed by 19 August.

I hadn't slept in weeks and what now followed was a very rational and structured schedule. My to-do list was long enough to fill at least a month of time, but knowing that in less than two weeks I could fall into a coma and sleep for days on end, I pressed the already very familiar 'button' and made myself function like a well-oiled machine. My days were filled with trips to the internet café – I no longer had a laptop or a printer, let alone a smart phone – to finish off several tasks and attend to all kinds of paperwork that was still to be completed: meetings with the liquidator, banks or business associates; attempts to sub-lease the office for the duration of my contract and, whenever I had a spare minute, clearing out the office. My nights were spent packing up my personal life and the place that had been my beloved home for 11 years.

Back at the office the phone system had been left behind by the liquidator and needed to be deinstalled, a task that required an expert. Prashant had offered to help wherever he could and one night sent a couple of acquaintances to help remove the remaining systems and to take with them whatever else there was still sitting around requiring a new home. Watching Prashant's men eventually leave the office building via the underground carpark with several shopping trolleys full of stuff in the middle of the night – their van was parked in a dark alley at the back of the building – for once made me laugh. It must have looked like a midnight hush-hush operation on the office building's security cameras. To me, this unusual scenario carried the air of a heist and kind of made up for having been treated like a criminal a week earlier.

At home, friends helped me organise a garage sale where I sold whatever I could, providing me with much-needed cash for my interim adventure. While cleaning out a household was a good exercise, it took up most of my nights, leaving me, still, with next-to-no sleep. On Saturday 20 August, the day before I left for Hawaii, the removalists arrived at my place at 10am. I was still packing while they started moving boxes into their van to take to a storage facility; and still cleaning by the time the real estate agent arrived for the final inspection. Every move had literally been timed to the minute.

Sunday was departure day. I had spent my final night at a friend's place and, finishing packing my luggage an hour later than planned, followed by a final dash to the storage facility, I just about managed to fit in what was now a very rushed goodbye lunch with friends. By the time we left for the airport, I was already running late but still had to drop off my car – which had been on a company lease – at the car dealer's along the way. I had been told that 'breaking a lease' would take two weeks to process but as I hadn't had that amount of time up my sleeve, I had suggested I drop off the car, rather than having the dealership collect it from me. And while the car dealer should have been aware of the company liquidation – I had re-confirmed the drop off the previous day – when I walked in to hand over the keys, no one knew about anything. I had no time for a lengthy explanation. Instead I left their sales manager with my name and email address and asked him to get in contact should there be any questions. This poor guy just stood there, not knowing what on earth was going on. I must have looked like I was high on drugs, sprinting into the showroom, mumbling some words at impossible speed and, on my dash back to my friend's car, shouting that I was sorry but I had a plane to catch. All I could hear on my way out was a concerned 'You *have* to leave the country?' It didn't sound like he was worried about the car and what was going to happen, but rather like sympathy and disbelief for my situation.

During a phone call with my brother several days earlier, I had told him I was going to Hawaii to clear my head and figure out the next steps. Up until that stage, I hadn't had a second to give that subject even the slightest thought. Two minutes into my conversation with Heiner, he told me that he had a friend in Hawaii, Niki, who owned a guesthouse on the island of Oahu and also looked after a couple of beach houses that he rented out to tourists; he would give Niki a call to see if he could do with some help. An hour later I had Niki on the phone, suggesting that I come and stay at his guesthouse. He had a couple of Austrian guys running the show and if I didn't mind simple accommodation, I would be welcome to share the caretaker area with them for as long as I wanted. This was fantastic news. Staying at Niki's for a week or two would give me the opportunity to breathe while allowing me to take my time finding a cheap, more long-term room, and hopefully also a job that would pay my expenses. The plan was – as much as there had been such a thing – to give myself a couple of months to recover, before returning to Sydney to start afresh.

At the airport, I was one of the final passengers to check in, followed by an almost straight walk onto the plane. Once in the air, I sighed with relief. I would finally have time to process the trials of the past weeks and months. It was an overnight flight – nine and a half hours – but I failed to doze off for even a minute. Utterly sleep-deprived, I had obviously reached a stage where I no longer felt tired. Slowly drifting into a contemplative state I still felt like I was watching a movie. Everything had happened so quickly and it was hard to comprehend that this was my reality. My company was gone, I had moved out of my home and I was on a plane to Hawaii with not much more than a thousand dollars in my pocket and no idea about what was going to happen next. I was neither worried nor excited; I just sat in my seat and stared out of the window in a trance.

PART III

'It's good to have an end to journey toward; but it is the journey,
that matters in the end'
– Ursula K Le Guin

Chapter 20

Tears and recovery

Following touchdown in Honolulu, I rented a cheap car and drove myself to the address I had been sent by my brother's friend Niki. I had never heard of the town I was heading to nor had much of a clue where it was. Two days earlier when a friend had asked me whereabouts in Oahu I would be 'pitching my tent', I had answered with a shrug; I couldn't have cared less. Upon my arrival at the guesthouse, I was greeted by Daniel, one of the two resident caretakers. When Niki had mentioned 'the guys' that were looking after the place, I had created an image in my mind of two 18-year-old boys, who would have just finished high school and were taking a gap year in Hawaii before moving on to university. Instead, they were two mature but at the same time cool and funny 29-year-olds who had graduated from university several years earlier and had both won the green-card lottery. They were now heralding the start of their new lives in the US by taking it easy for a few months in Hawaii. This was a welcome surprise; the reduced age gap allowed me to relax considerably, no longer feeling like an unwelcome mum intruding on 'the boys' camp'.

The guesthouse (The Mansion) was located in Waimanalo Beach, a local, non-touristy town about 35 minutes from famous Waikiki, with the crystal-clear ocean framed by the most beautiful white sandy beach a mere two-minute walk away. I couldn't believe my luck; I had landed in paradise! After a brief hello and an introduction to Chris, Daniel's partner in crime, as well as another

Austrian who was visiting for a couple of weeks, I had a quick shower and took off to Kailua, the closest town that would offer more than just a supermarket. Even with no sleep whatsoever, I was still on fire. I took my road bike, which I had brought with me from Australia, to a bike shop to have it reassembled and bought myself a $350 laptop, before taking a brief tour of Kailua. Daniel had told me that Kailua Beach was one of the best on the island for kite surfing, a sport I had taken up several years earlier. Full of enthusiasm, I had bought all my own gear at the time but the onset of the business challenges soon after, together with my decreasing health and energy, had denied me the chance of fully pursuing the sport. I had packed my kite without even knowing if Oahu had the right conditions for a beginner and, here I was, looking at a kite-surfing beach out of a picture book, just around the corner from where I was staying.

Once I returned to The Mansion, I joined the guys on the *lanai* – a Hawaiian verandah – where we ended up talking until all hours of the night. By the time I finally went to bed I must have been up for about 50 hours straight and I still didn't feel overly tired. The following morning I awoke pretty early and decided that it was time for a walk and a cry on the beach. I had had to let go of everything that had filled my life for so many years and it was now time to grieve. I sat on the beach, not a soul in sight, and started to play back the events of the previous weeks and months in minute detail, but I found that I couldn't even shed one tear. There were no emotions whatsoever. It was bizarre. I tried so hard to be upset, to get angry and to burst into tears, but ... nothing. How was this possible? I wanted to cry so badly but no matter how much effort I put into it and how much I attempted to travel back in time and see myself in the many desperate and heartrending situations, I remained totally indifferent. This was scary. I felt like I had turned into a cold, heartless monster. What came to my mind then was the story of an English backpacker who had been killed in the Australian outback years earlier and his girlfriend had become a suspect. I was one of many who had agreed that his girlfriend must have been guilty, considering her total lack of emotion at the time. My first thought now was that I would never be so quick to judge again.

With what seemed to be a lack of need to grieve, I returned to Kailua to pick up my bike and went on an hour-long cycle up and down the hills. I hadn't been doing much exercise over the previous years and, although I was puffing my lungs out, I thoroughly enjoyed getting my heart rate up again, especially as for once it wasn't out of agitation and worry. Back at The Mansion I had been allocated a basic, tiny room within the caretaker area. The hot water tap in the communal shower required pliers to turn it on and the whole area reminded me of the various field trips we had embarked on with school during my teenage years, but I couldn't have been happier. This was just what I needed – feeling young and carefree again.

Niki was overseas when I arrived and wasn't going to be back for another couple of months. He offered for me to stay as long as I wanted and whereas initially I had thought that my time at The Mansion wasn't going to be more than a fleeting visit, from day one I felt so happy and right at home there that I couldn't see myself leaving anytime soon. I very gratefully accepted Niki's offer. Several days into my stay Daniel then showed me what would become my home for the following couple of months or however long I chose to hang about. It was a very spacious guestroom with its own living area, located next to the main lanai. We were just moving into low season and according to the booking forecast at the time, the room – one of five within the guesthouse – was going to be free for a while. This was too good to be true! Sitting around, not doing anything while watching everyone else complete their chores, wasn't something I felt comfortable with and I soon suggested that the guys make me part of their cleaning troupe. Apart from perceiving the act of cleaning in itself as a therapeutic exercise that would give my brain a much-needed break, I couldn't possibly complain about cleaning rooms, folding sheets and making beds with two hot guys that looked like they were right out of *Vogue* magazine!

I had the time of my life in Hawaii and especially at The Mansion. Soon after I had arrived, Daniel's brother Paddy and another friend, Nerma, came for a visit and together we toured the island in the resident 'surf-bus', an old van equipped with surfboards, a cool box, a portable barbeque and a guitar. We hiked through dense bush to hidden waterfalls, climbed steep crater trails for views to die for, watched several surfing competitions on the famous North Shore, jumped out of a plane for Paddy's 25th birthday and relaxed on various beautiful beaches with a cool beer in our hands while watching the sun disappear. It was hard to believe the 180 that my life had taken in such a short time. I had gone from a business life with its final months marked by utter stress to a carefree, simple but extremely cheerful existence filled with joy and laughter. I couldn't have wished for a better group of people around me and I certainly didn't let the fact that I was at least 10 years older than everyone else stand in my way. Instead, it made me feel like I was 30 again myself, a refreshing sentiment after having aged 10 years within the previous two.

My younger sister Bettina had always been a big moral support and we regularly talked on the phone. One day when her eldest son, Raffael, who was about seven at the time, picked up the phone, he asked me, in a very concerned tone, where I was living now that I had lost my home, and, with my business gone too, what was I going to do for work? Not long after that conversation, my parents told me that Raffael was spending the afternoon with them the previous day and was allowed 'a little something'. He asked for a lottery ticket so that if he won, 'Sabine could buy a house'. In his eyes, it was so very sad that I no longer had a permanent home. I was so touched.

One night during my first week in Hawaii, we had an Austrian Night, cooking Wiener schnitzel and drinking the famous Opa-Schnapps that Daniel had brought from Austria, singing and dancing until all hours. The following morning – or rather afternoon – I awoke with a pretty bad hangover and decided to call one of my best friends in Sydney. I told her about the fun night we had had and how lucky I had been to have soft-landed in this amazing place. However, the response I received from her wasn't quite what I had expected; in a rather accusatory tone she stated: 'You know, when people ask me how you are, I tell them that you are in Hawaii, partying ...' I could see how it would have been hard to understand how I could possibly be having fun after putting my business through liquidation – I couldn't quite comprehend my happy and carefree frame of mind myself! – but I found it disconcerting that a close friend, who had witnessed me struggling for the previous couple of years, wasn't happy for me. It would have been one thing if her reaction had been one of concern but instead it was the judgmental tone that had me stunned.

It was now over a month since I had arrived in Hawaii and I still hadn't shed a tear, let alone felt overly sad about what had happened. One day, a local friend suggested that I go and see Ling (not the real name), a well-known psychic and resident of the island. While I wasn't keen to find out what was going to happen in my future – regardless of whether I believed what was said or not, I considered 'knowing' about my future rather restricting – I could certainly have done with some direction. Cleaning rooms wasn't something I was going to do for the rest of my life and I slowly had to start thinking about the next step. To make an appointment with Ling, one had to show up first thing in the morning, leave a phone number and first name with the secretary and be put on a waitlist for the day. There was no guarantee if and when one would get to actually see the psychic. But to be in with a chance we had to stay within 20 minutes of her rooms for the day to be around to receive the go-ahead. I had heard of people waiting for hours on end or even having to go back three days in a row. Supposedly the order that Ling chose her clients was according to whoever she felt needed it the most.

By 9am that day, it was my turn. Although I had heard a fair bit about this particular psychic by then, I had no expectations. I walked into the room and before I had a chance to introduce myself, she did it for me. She told me that I lived in Sydney, had two sisters and a brother and, after many more details about me and my family, she even gave me the first names of my lawyer in Germany and the one representing the other party. I was gobsmacked. Without going into detail, what I can say is that once I left the room I felt extremely calm and confident. I had asked Ling not to tell me any intrinsic details about what lay ahead and that I, as a matter of fact, wasn't entirely sure why I was there to see her, but I walked away with an affirmation that I was going to be all right, which was the only thing that I needed to hear at that stage.

191

The same night I had a call from my mum and I burst into tears for the first time since leaving Sydney. I sobbed on the phone like there was no tomorrow; it was such a relief that I could finally cry and let it all out. With the crying also came a physical breakdown. I suddenly felt utterly exhausted, hardly even able to make it up the stairs to my room. Each time the announcement was made that a room had to be cleaned or that one of the beach houses required our attention, I had to hold back tears. I simply didn't have the energy to attend to even the smallest of tasks; I had no physical strength whatsoever. My whole system appeared to have shut down. At times, even when someone just approached me for a chat, I would tear up seemingly out of nowhere. It felt like a big, heavy bubble was drifting to the surface and I had no control over it. I tried to hide my emotions – and the fact that cleaning had now turned into a major strain – as much as I could, but it wasn't hard to tell that I had finally hit the wall. All the caretakers at The Mansion (by then there were on average about five or six of us at any given time) were aware of my history and they each turned out to be extremely understanding and caring. I couldn't have found myself in a better place at that time. I was finally grieving and I started to spend a much larger part of my day by myself, sitting on the beach, lying in my hammock or just hanging out in my room. While during my first month in Hawaii I was riding up and down the hills into Waikiki on my bike, hiking up steep trails and kite surfing – and crashing – in strong winds, my daily exercise was now reduced to a slow walk along the beach, with plenty of rest in between.

I had expected the court hearing in Germany to be scheduled for some time in October or November that year, but soon Michael informed me that the date had been set for 4 October the *following* year. Keen to put it all behind me, initially I was upset but then became very grateful that I wouldn't have to deal with any legal issues for another year. Rather than taking two or three months off, as had been the plan initially, I now decided to give myself a full year to recover and regain my energy and strength. I could do odd jobs to support myself and only once I was fit again would I throw myself into the next big thing. The thousand dollars in my bank account that I left Sydney with was bolstered by the bond from my apartment. It was enough to last me a little longer but soon I would have to try to find a part-time job.

One day, not long after reality had finally caught up and forced me to slow down, my brother called to check on me. I told him how my system had shut down and how my highest priority was to regain my health. Heiner urged me to take my situation seriously and, in order to be able to take as much time out as necessary to recover, without having to worry about a job or how I would survive financially, he offered to help out – and this, without me even mentioning a word about my finances. He suggested that I think about my monthly expenses and let him know how much I would require to survive. I had handed him my inheritance – on the basis of a loan – years earlier so that he could invest it in his business, and he was now happy to reciprocate.

This was a huge relief. It was mind-boggling how everything was – and had been – falling into place without even the slightest effort from my side ever since I had let go of the business. Yet the aspect that I loved most was how utterly grateful I was now that none of the business deals with *at-visions*, Prashant or even the gentleman in Melbourne had gone through. I'm positive that had there been even the slightest opportunity to keep pushing myself, I would have cracked in the near future and been left with the responsibilities of running a business rather than the comfort of a white sandy beach, crystal-clear waters and a hammock in the best possible environment. This is not to say that having had to liquidate the business and put my staff out of work wasn't a heavy load on my shoulders. Yet, knowing that I had fought until the end and had done whatever was in my power to save the business, it was now very comforting to realise that – on a personal level – in the end everything had worked out for the best. Limiting my possessions to the basics and coming to Hawaii stripped bare had presented me with a very special experience, a very humbling and, above all, liberating one. I would have missed out on so much had I had the funds for a 'normal' holiday. Considering the state I was in – mentally and physically – being well-off financially (in the event that the sale of the business had gone ahead) would have been much more of a hindrance than a support. I would, undoubtedly, have put significantly more pressure on myself to sort out my life and move on, rather than giving myself the time and space required to recuperate and to find out what it was that I really wanted to do down the track. I'm convinced that arriving in Hawaii with a healthy bank account would, in my case and circumstances, have easily led to depression.

I knew that time would be important for my recovery but bearing in mind the level of exhaustion I had reached – having been diagnosed with stage-two adrenal fatigue several years earlier, my adrenals would surely be completely fried by now – it was time to call upon the help of a doctor/naturopath. It was swiftly established that I had severe hypothyroidism and I was handed natural thyroid pills to fix the issue. Within no time I began to feel my energy returning; my whole system seemed to slowly balance itself. I was like a dried-out plant that steadily started to lift its head again. I had forgotten how it actually felt to have energy and be able to do simple tasks – like walking and even talking – with *no* effort; and even reached the stage where I felt strong enough to exercise again. This was so exciting; I was getting my life back!

Unfortunately, however, the enthusiasm about my much-improved level of wellbeing was short-lived and, almost as quickly as I had felt better, I reverted to feeling sicker by the day. As revealed during an eventual visit to the emergency ward of the local hospital, I had gone from extreme *hypo*thyroidism to extreme *hyper*thyroidism. I had completely overdosed on the medication and was now feeling worse than ever. There was no quick fix other than to stop taking the pills and wait until my thyroid recovered from the shock, and to follow Niki's recommendation of seeing Uncle Alva. Uncle, as he was generally called, was a traditional Hawaiian healer, with an open-air practice in a stunning bush setting in the back of Waimanalo town. Seeing Uncle – and his protégé, Pomai – turned out to be a very special experience over and over; one that, after each visit, made me feel like I was glowing in the dark. It undoubtedly contributed to my gradual recovery.

Health issues aside, my time in Hawaii was one that I will cherish forever. I don't think that I had ever – continually – laughed as much. I could write a whole book recounting the exhilarating stories and incidents relating to life at The Mansion alone. Soon after Paddy and Nerma returned to Austria, two other Austrians had joined the Ehukai-Gang – the sobriquet we had come to be known by: Marina, a 26-year-old who had just finished her law degree and was a judge in the making; and Georgie, a 20-year-old guy who could be best described as an old soul in a young body. They both were vivacious, joyful and amusing characters – and the perfect additions to the crew. A few months into our time at The Mansion, Marina and I became involved in the marketing side of an Austrian business of Niki's. We complemented each other perfectly with our skills and it was a good interim project that allowed me to feel at least a bit less like a leech that one couldn't get rid of. Niki was an extremely welcoming and fun-loving guy and never once gave me the impression I'd overstayed my welcome. But all good things come to an end and when, six months down the track, the 'old gang' started to dissolve and the caretaker crew was being replaced by newcomers who brought a much younger vibe to The Mansion, it was finally time to leave. One day, while sitting on the beach with Marina, looking out at the ocean and reminiscing, Marina asked where my journey would take me next and if I was planning on going back to Australia. And all I could say was that no, I wasn't ready to go back and I didn't have a clue about the next step either; but something would come up, of that I was sure.

Two days after that episode on the beach, I had an email from an old friend in Austria, Constanze, asking if I would be interested in living in Cape Town for a while. She and her partner, Mario, had moved to South Africa a couple of years earlier and had started an inbound tourism business. They could use some help. Constanze and I hadn't been in contact in a long time and I'm sure she hadn't expected a 'yes' as quickly as she received it.

Chapter 21

Across the Indian Ocean

The cheapest possible option for my flight to Cape Town was via Sydney and then Bangkok and Dubai with a total flying time – not including the layovers – of 35 hours; quite a drag, considering that from Sydney it would have been an almost perfectly straight flight across Australia and the Indian Ocean. The cost of the ticket – although comparatively inexpensive – was an unwelcome attack on my budget but it was going to be made up for by the much lower living costs awaiting me in South Africa. I arrived in Cape Town on 16 March 2012 and spent my first week at my friend Liezl's house in Claremont, about 10 kilometres south of the city.

Liezl had been my partner-in-crime in Sydney before she had to leave the country due to her immigration lawyer submitting the papers a day late. We had always stayed in contact but this was the first time in over 12 years that we had actually seen each other. Staying with my friend and her housemate, Will, in an outer suburb allowed me to experience Cape Town in a different way to when I had lived there 18 years earlier. I loved taking the various local minibuses into the city; there was always a great atmosphere, with the almost exclusively black passengers more often than not singing, telling jokes or laughing for reasons I didn't quite get.

One day on my way into town, I walked with Lissie – Liezl and Will's maid – to the main street to catch such a minibus. When I asked her about her family, she told me she had had two brothers who both died when they were in their 20s; one had been stabbed, the other had cancer. She also had a twin sister, whose two sons had been killed as well. One (an 11-year-old) was stabbed; his brother had died in a car accident (at the age of 28). Lissie's husband had died 10 years earlier from cancer. When I told Will Lissie's tragic story and how two people in her family had been stabbed, he simply said: 'Look, for us this is nothing out of the ordinary, we are used to that.' Will then continued by saying that things had changed over the past few years, that black and white people worked so well together these days and for them – at least for his and the younger generation – there was no longer any difference between the races. It sounded like there was hope.

Eight days into my time in South Africa, Liezl and Will moved out of their house and into their own individual places in town and I went to stay with Constanze and Mario, who lived in a beautiful house more or less right on a long, wide beach with the most stunning view of Table Mountain. Over the following couple of weeks, I helped my friends with some business projects and although I enjoyed what I was doing, I felt I wasn't quite fit enough to commit myself to much. There was no pressure whatsoever from my friends – to the contrary – but I didn't feel comfortable hanging around their house barely contributing, especially considering that the purpose of my visit was to be an asset rather than a liability. My thyroid was playing up again – it seemed indecisive as to whether it wanted to be over- or under-active – and where one day I would feel well and strong, the next I would hardly function. So one day when Will asked if I was interested in house-sitting his sister Jean Marie's home in Camps Bay – my favourite suburb from all those years back – for a couple of weeks, I jumped at the opportunity. Will's sister's house was a stunning property on a hill behind the main street of Camps Bay and came with a swimming pool and two beautiful dogs. This was the perfect place to hang around and not do much other than go for walks with the dogs along the beach. The day that Jean-Marie and her partner returned from their holidays, Will left town for a couple of weeks and I went on to house- and dog-sit his place; a great little abode in Hout Bay, a small fishing village suburb of Cape Town, not far from Camps Bay.

Several weeks into my time in South Africa, Mum came for an impromptu visit. She was in her early 70s then and as cool, easy-going and adventurous as ever. Dad, seven years Mum's senior, had the fitness level of a 50-year-old, but having had done his fair share of travelling before he got married he was now happy to stay home and keep racing around Salzburg on his bicycle. While I was at Will's place, which was just big enough for one person and two pony-sized dogs, Mum stayed at an apartment in Camps Bay. We rented a car for the duration of her stay and had the best time touring Cape Town and its stunning surroundings. It was comforting to think that as much grief as I had caused Mum over the previous couple of years, at least she now got to embark on new adventures, visiting me in exotic places.

While Constanze repeatedly suggested that I move back to their home at the end of my house-sitting stints, I wasn't ready to leave Hout Bay. I had fallen in love with its flair the minute I got there. My plan now was to stay in South Africa – namely Hout Bay – until the end of May before moving on to tick off a long-standing point on my 'to-do' list: another summer in Italy. This would be followed by the court hearing in Germany at the beginning of October. The living costs in South Africa – as an overall average in regards to food and transport – were about a quarter of those in Sydney, and Italy was going to be somewhere in between. Bumming around the Mediterranean wasn't going to be an option, and it was now crucial to use the time I had left in Cape Town to do whatever I could to regain my energy and be fit enough to take up a job in Italy.

It had been more than eight months since I had packed up my life in Sydney and had left the stresses behind me. I had had the most amazing time since and I could not comprehend why I was still feeling so unfit; eight months of a most relaxing lifestyle should have sorted me out by now. Unfortunately, this wasn't quite the case and once again my health started to deteriorate. One day, while I was sitting on the bus on my way to see a holistic doctor, I felt that my whole system was about to shut down. It is hard to describe the sensation but I imagined that this would be how one must feel just before 'one's light is turned off'. My bus stop was only a couple of stops away and I had no idea how I was going to manage; I had no energy whatsoever to lift myself off the seat and get out. Somehow I did manage and with very slow steps I dragged myself to the doctor.

His diagnosis was that my intestines were in such a bad shape, my body could no longer absorb energy of any kind. The high-concentrate vitamin drip I had been given a couple of days earlier by a general practitioner had been a shock to my system and contributed to me feeling completely out of sorts, with my whole body trembling from head to toe. I had also been taking significant amounts of the so called 'superfoods' including maca powder, hemp protein, chia seeds and goji berries to help get my mojo back, but rather than boosting my energy, it had all been too much and had, instead, fried my system. On my way home from the doctor, my mum called. I told her about how screwed up my body was and how, eight months down the track, I was feeling worse than ever, which frustrated me incredibly.

The following day I received a call from my brother telling me that he had talked to his doctor, a well-known personality in the world of functional and energy medicine, and consulted him about my health issues. The outcome was a strong suggestion that I spend three weeks at the Haus der Gesundheit (House of Health), a holistic clinic in the south of Austria that specialised in gastro-intestinal issues and burnout syndrome. The thought of spending three weeks at an inpatient clinic freaked me out. In my head this was something retirees would do, not me. I was in my early 40s. I tried to negotiate the length of stay – my pride had obviously taken over reason – but eventually agreed to the suggestion. It was clear that I wouldn't be able to afford the stay at the clinic, let alone the treatments but that discussion never even arose, with Heiner stating straight up that it wouldn't be my place to worry about the costs. I must have done something right in my previous life!

The earliest possible start date for my three-week stint at the clinic was 31 May. This was perfect timing, as I wasn't ready to leave South Africa just then. It was now a matter of finding a place to live once Will returned. My budget was limited – I was still living off a loan from my brother – so my first thought was to check at the backpackers down the road to see whether they would take on long-term residents. As it turned out, the backpackers was booked to its last bed for the following 10 days, after which date the lessees would be moving their business to new and larger premises. They were not sure what was going to become of the place once they relocated and I was handed the phone number of the owners of the building – Clive and Anthea – with the suggestion to give them a call and find out. It so happened that the owner's idea was to conduct some minor renovations and then re-open the doors as another backpackers. Communicating to Anthea that I was looking for a place from 3 May – literally a couple of days after they'd be taking over management – I asked if I could possibly move in then, suggesting I'd also be happy to help with the renovations. Anthea had to discuss my request with her husband and about an hour later I had the all-clear. By the time I showed up, most of the repairs had been done. The backpackers – a beautiful two-storey house full of character with a nice garden and swimming pool, all set in the best possible location – hadn't officially re-opened and was yet to be advertised under its new name. With no other bookings at that stage, the owners had removed the bunk beds of one of their rooms and made it into a beautiful single room for me, complete with my own en-suite. All that for $10.50 per day, which equalled the price of a bunk bed in a crowded dormitory. I basically had the entire downstairs area, together with a fully equipped kitchen and a beautiful African-style living area all to myself. The upstairs rooms were occupied by Shannon, a local guy in his mid-20s who was going to run the show and a lady my age who was kind of part of the inventory. I couldn't believe how the stars had aligned for me yet again. The thought of a packed hostel with what most probably would have been travellers half my age partying through the night had been a bit scary to start off with. Besides, had the 'old' backpackers continued trading at the same premises, there most likely wouldn't even have been a spare bed for me. As fate would have it, I was presented with yet another sanctuary.

My time at the backpackers was a most relaxing one and just 'what the doctor ordered'. The owners and staff treated me like family, we had barbeques and movie nights and I got to meet several locals and have great chats. Over time a few travellers came through, which, too, made for interesting company and conversations.

I had always felt very safe in Cape Town and not once had anyone ever even attempted to rip me off or cheat me. Over my weeks in Hout Bay I walked up and down its deserted sandy beach by myself on an almost daily basis, at times sitting on top of the sand dunes for hours, staring out to the harbour and its stunning backdrop. One afternoon, following my leisurely routine along the beach, I stopped at a small stream that had cut the beach in half and I decided that, rather than taking off my shoes and exposing my feet to the freezing water, I would walk through the sand dunes and cross the river via a bridge further back. It was a cold, windy afternoon; I was wearing a jacket with the hood pulled over my head and, listening to music on my iPod, I disappeared into my own little world. Wandering along in complete oblivion, all of a sudden I had a large hand appear on my left side in front of my face, forcefully grabbing hold of my mouth, while another hand reaching in from the right pulled my hood over my face and what seemed to be a third person pushed me to the ground.

I tried to scream but other than a little mumble no noise got through the strong hand. Well aware that I was right at the bottom and in between two sand dunes, I knew that most probably no one would hear me in any case. I still decided to keep trying to scream until the guy on my left briefly lifted my hood and waved a large knife in front of my face, followed by a second knife from his accomplice on the other side. I couldn't move; they were holding me down to the ground with a lot of force. Following a motion that suggested I would stop screaming, the guy on my left eventually let go of my mouth. The scariest part was the hood over my head and the darkness in front of my eyes; I had no idea who and how many guys I was dealing with and how bad my situation was.

Once my attackers realised they had scared and intimidated me enough to stop any attempt to react or fight back they finally let go of me and fully lifted my hood to reveal three black guys between around 15 and 20 years of age. While I was just sitting there in a trance, they emptied my pockets and took my bag off me. Still completely spaced out, I asked one of the guys who was holding my purse if I could please have my credit card back. He then opened my purse and handed me my credit card as well as my driver's license.

I continued asking to get stuff back; next in line was the SIM card from my phone. Again, they took the time to open the back of the phone, remove the battery and pull out the SIM card. I then went for the purse without its content, but I received a distinct 'no' to that one. Once they had gone through all my pockets, they again waved the knives in front of my face, warned me to not make a sound and ran off.

I must have sat there in the same spot not moving an inch for another few minutes. When I finally got up, it all of a sudden occurred to me that they had forgotten to hand me my SIM card. I had watched them take it out of the phone, but they never gave it to me! I was about to run after them but then came to my senses and started to walk towards the main road behind the sand dunes. I was totally numb. A couple of people walked past me, but I just kept going, without a direction in mind. At some stage I turned right to cross a car park. Walking down a laneway, I saw a couple in the distance. I began to run towards them but then stopped and continued to walk in a trance until I eventually entered a restaurant and sat down at a table out of sight of other guests. When the waiter handed me the menu, I – shaking from top to toe and tears running down my face – stuttered that I had just been mugged. A couple of minutes later, the owner came over and sat down next to me. She handed me a glass of sugar water and tried to calm me down. I was still in so much shock that I had difficulty speaking. Taking off my jacket, the SIM card rolled onto the table. I had no idea where it had come from or whether they had put it into my jacket or actually given it to me. Soon after, the police chief showed up. He went through his repertoire of questions and then took me to the police station where they made more notes and offered immediate victim trauma counselling.

The description of my offenders that I gave to one of the policemen was only very vague. As absurd as it might sound, I didn't want them to be traced and locked up. After all, they had turned out to be 'nice crooks'; they hadn't harmed me and had only kept what was valuable to them. All they got away with was the equivalent of $20, an old iPod that was half broken as well as a $20 old-school Nokia phone. In a lucky turn of events, my friend Lucy, who had lent me her old iPhone before I had left for Hawaii, had needed it. I had mailed it to her only two days earlier, replacing it with a cheap Nokia. I still couldn't believe that the young attackers had actually taken the time and effort to remove the SIM card from my phone. Their actions seemed to have been motivated by desperation and I blamed myself for waving a carrot in front of a donkey. In my eyes they were opportunists and I couldn't account for them being punished like criminals as the police chief had suggested; after all, one of them was still a kid. I thanked the police chief for his help, and he handed me his card with the request to contact him should further details come to mind.

I couldn't return to the beach for another three days; what used to be heaven for my regular mental escapes now evoked anxiety. However, the day before leaving Hout Bay, I had to go for a final walk along that beautiful bay. I felt that as long as I stayed in close proximity to other beach walkers – of whom there weren't many – I would be able to relax enough to actually enjoy it one last time. Just as I got to the edge of the water, a lady walked up to me and suggested that I turn back. She had been observing 'these five guys' who seemed to be hanging around the sand dunes for an awfully long time. The way they were walking up and down the beach close to the dunes had appeared dubious to her. As soon as I turned around, I noticed the bright yellow sweatshirt of the guy who had grabbed my mouth. I asked the lady to walk a little closer with me so that I could make sure that three of them were in fact the same guys. And yes, they were. It was a sad realisation. I had obviously been such an easy target for them that they had identified mugging as a worthwhile pastime. I now had no choice but to call the police chief to check on them. They had to be stopped before they turned into full-blown criminals.

I spent my final three nights in South Africa at Constanze and Mario's place. They made sure to send me off in style before I was going to be stuck in a strict regime. As grateful as I was to be given an opportunity to put my health into the hands of professionals, it was not quite something I was looking forward to. The thought of going to Austria at that stage of my life wasn't sitting easily with me; Austria was too close to reality, which I wasn't ready to face. Spending time in foreign countries where people didn't know me – apart from a close friend or two – was one thing, but it was a completely different story to go back to your birth place where it was likely that everyone would want to hear the details of the present, past and future. I had no clue what I was going to do with my life. This, at that point in time, was absolutely fine with me, but having to explain my situation and probably justify my movements to extended family, friends and acquaintances was not something I was keen to be confronted with. As always, however, my family was very understanding and happily agreed to my skipping a trip home to Salzburg and Bad Gastein, and to visit me at the health clinic in the south of Austria instead.

My three weeks spent at the clinic was the best thing that could have happened to me at the time. The House of Health classified itself as a 'Centre of competence for an acute regeneration by means of a holistic health approach'; and that's exactly what it was. The main focus was on my gastro-intestinal health and the reactivation of blocked endogenous healing systems. I was put on a restricted, personalised diet that would support an inner cleanse and detoxification, together with regular checkups by the doctor and a therapy plan that included treatments such as special belly massages, energetic therapies, vitamin and mineral drips and haematogenous oxidation therapy. The health centre itself was a small and simple yet well-equipped inpatient retreat in a beautiful, tranquil setting that never accommodated more than 15 patients at a time, at least half of whom were my age or younger. The personal attention I received was heartwarming; I wasn't just a number, rather an individual who each of the employees seemed to care about. At any given time, everyone appeared to know the smallest details of the progress I made or new challenges that I faced. By the time I left the health retreat I felt like a newborn. I hadn't quite regained my previous levels of energy and strength but I could finally function like a 'normal' human being again; there was a spring back in my step.

Chapter 22
A slice of paradise

It was now 21 June and, if I was to spend a summer in Italy, I had to get myself down to that peninsula as soon as possible. The season would already be in full swing and each day closer to July made it harder to find a job, let alone affordable long-term accommodation. From the retreat I headed straight to Innsbruck in the east of Austria to undergo a final checkup by the referring doctor, the specialist who had originally recommended to my brother that I spend a few weeks at the House of Health. My appointment had been scheduled for late afternoon on the day I left the clinic. The doctor's office was in Lans, a small town in the mountains above Innsbruck. The plan was to stay overnight in Lans, then take a train to Italy the following morning; the only catch was that I hadn't yet decided which Italian town or city I was going to call home for the summer.

Someone had once told me about a place called Diamante in the south of Italy. As I had liked the sound of it, up until that morning that was where I was going to go. However, during a brief conversation with my mum while waving me goodbye at Salzburg station where my train to Innsbruck was passing through, I found out that my auntie had spent a few days in Diamante the previous year and from what Mum had heard she thought that it might not quite be what I was looking for and that opportunities to find a seasonal job there might be limited. Later that night, sitting in my room in Lans, I went online to figure out my next destination. I looked at several towns that had come to mind until I decided that the island of Capri, off the coast of Napoli in the south of Italy, would be the go. I had spent a few days on Capri almost 20 years earlier and I had nothing but great memories attached to it.

Next on the agenda was to book accommodation for my first couple of days on the island. On a prominent online site I filled in the various categories to narrow down my search, including the price: 'Euro 0–50'. I scrolled through my options and within a minute my attention was caught by a place called Agritourismo L'Olivara, an olive farm that rented out rooms. I was sold straight away and already saw myself sitting in trees picking olives for the summer and learning how to cook real Italian farm food. Only once I had booked and paid for the room did I realise that the olive farm wasn't actually on Capri, but in Piano di Sorrento, a small coastal town on the mainland across from Capri. As it turned out, over the years Capri had become so exclusive and expensive that my search for accommodation in the range of Euro 0–50 had returned no results for Capri and instead had suggested options in the vicinity. I had to laugh. I had been so taken by the olive farm that I had failed to check the details. Either way, I was happy with my choice.

The following morning I took a bus back to Innsbruck and headed straight to the train station to purchase my ticket to Napoli from where I'd then catch a bus or local train to Piano di Sorrento. It's no secret that Italians like to go on strike and this was such a day. When I inquired about the next train to Napoli, the man behind the counter told me that the best he could do at that stage was to issue me a ticket to Bolzano in the north of Italy. The staff of *Train Italia* were on strike and with no further details available, he had no idea about how long that strike was going to last. Bolzano wasn't quite what I had had in mind, but it was a good start that would at least get me across the border and in front of a glass of excellent red wine.

Upon my arrival in Bolzano I was told that the strike was apparently going to end at 9pm that night and my overnight train to Napoli, scheduled to leave just after 9pm, should be leaving on time. With a big grin on my face I got my ticket, deposited my luggage with the staff behind the counter and headed out. With three hours to spare I now had plenty of time to walk around town and, most importantly, buy new sneakers to replace the ones I was wearing, which were about to fall apart – who knew how far from 'civilisation' the olive farm was going to be! Bolzano was strewn with beautiful shops and, within no time, the task was ticked off. I kept wandering around the streets for a while until my blissful state was interrupted by the realisation that I had lost my purse. I freaked. Trying to retrace my steps in full panic, I ran back to the shop where I had bought the sneakers, but nothing. Never before had I lost my purse and not in a very long time had I carried that much money on me either. Back in Austria Dad had slipped me 500 Euros as we had hugged goodbye. This was a lot of money, especially considering my circumstances. Extremely upset, I went straight to the next bar for a glass of prosecco to calm myself down – at least I carried my credit and bank cards in a different purse so it was only cash that had been lost.

As I was sitting in my chair gazing into space, utterly annoyed with myself, the owner of the bar came over and asked if I was alright. Embarrassed by his question, I briefly recounted my mishap, to which he responded by advising the waiter that the glass of prosecco he had just served was on the house. Soon after, I also had a tiramisu and a chamomile tea put in front of me, courtesy of the restaurant. When I went to say goodbye and thank the owner for his kind gesture, both he and the waiter gave me a broad smile and sent me off with well wishes and a suggestion to drop in again on my way back to Austria. I very quickly returned to see the world in a different light. Welcome to Italy!

Upon my arrival in Napoli the following morning, it didn't take much to realise that I was now in the *south* of Italy. All the escalators at the train station were out of order, as was the elevator. Struggling with my heavy luggage I asked a young local where I could possibly catch a train or bus to Piano di Sorrento. He then showed me the way by helping me carry my bag to the train, onto the train, an hour and a half later off the train and uphill to the main piazza of the town where he bought me a cappuccino and a croissant only to then return to the station to take a train back to where he was meant to go in the first place, which was several stops before Piano di Sorrento. Once the young gentleman had left, I called the owner of the olive farm to announce my arrival at the piazza, from where I was to be collected. Twenty minutes later I found myself in the car next to Antonella, *La Mama* of the farm, driving up through the hills with the smile on my face becoming bigger and the scenery more spectacular with every bend. By the time we turned into the property gates my jaw had dropped. This was the exact image I had been dreaming of ever since I decided I needed another summer in Italy. I had been to the north of Italy many times but, other than a few hours in Napoli and a short holiday in Capri, I had never made it past Rome. The setting of the farm, with its view across the hills and over the Gulf of Napoli and Mount Vesuvius, was stunning. The old farmhouse was right in front of the olive trees, surrounded by flowering bushes, lush lemon trees and big, ripe vegetables that sprouted from the ground in all colours. My room was in a small tower on top of the farm house and featured a cute little balcony that provided an even more spectacular view.

A mother of two teenage kids, La Mama started to treat me like the grown-up daughter from the minute I sat next to her in the car. I later found out that she had guessed my age at around the 25-year mark. I attributed this to my being an unmarried woman with no children travelling by herself with no specific plans whatsoever. A backpack with a yoga mat dangling from its side was not quite something a woman in her 40s would usually carry, let alone in Italy. On Sunday, the day after I arrived, I was invited to join the family for lunch underneath the lemon trees, indulging in homemade pasta with freshly picked herbs and homemade olive oil, followed by a very fresh salad straight from the garden, plus the obligatory glass of local wine. I was in heaven. Later that day I walked down to Piano di Sorrento and took the bus to Sorrento, a neighbouring town, to watch Italy play England in the European Soccer Championships. Sorrento wasn't far from Piano and with its large piazza it seemed like the perfect place to watch the game; it was the quarter-finals and every bar, café and restaurant had at least one big screen. The only challenge was the lack of a bus to take me back up into the hills later that night. With my 'adoptive parents' concerned about my safety, they suggested I give them a call once

I had arrived at a certain bus stop on my way back from Sorrento and they would come and pick me up, no matter what time of the night. So when I did, indeed, call them just before midnight, I even *felt* like a teenager. Thankfully en route home we also collected their 'other kids' from the various locations, easing my guilt over getting them out of bed in the middle of the night.

Italy ended up beating England 4–2 in a penalty shootout and the atmosphere was electric. As we drove through the small streets, every vehicle was tooting and people were dancing on cars and in the streets. That's what I had come to see that night and that's what I loved so much about Italy. Yes, Australians are a very sports-focused nation and know how to celebrate after a win, as do most other countries, but Italians sure master the art of rejoicing like no one else. A few days later, Italy beat Germany in the semi-finals 2–1, a win that no one had foreseen. Germany had been expected to dominate Italy but as a German commentator put it – as relayed to me by my sister – the biggest issue for the Germans had been that the Italians were so unpredictable and 'all over the place' that for a team like Germany, who played with structure and precision, they were simply too hard to figure out. In a few words, this perfectly summed up the two nations – and it's the passion that comes with the chaos that makes Italy and its people so endearing.

Needless to say, the celebrations that followed the semi-finals were like nothing I had ever witnessed before. It was pure joy to watch. The Sorrentine police seemed ignorant of any rules that night. They were still around, but perhaps for the purpose of participating in the celebrations rather than to interfere. Masses of people were hanging from even the smallest cars with the Fiat 500s all of a sudden having a capacity of 10 people, half of whom were squeezing through the open rooftops. Cars, trucks and motorbikes were driving in circles on the piazza, in between crowds of people and against one-way traffic. Fireworks were going off from all directions and everyone was cheering and dancing in the streets as if Italy had just won the war. And this was only the semi-final. In the end Spain triumphed over Italy in the final but they still went ahead with the fireworks and the celebrations. They had been so happy to make it to the final that the loss couldn't dampen their mood.

On Monday morning, two days into my stay in Italy, I set out on a mission to find a job and accommodation and settle in for the summer. As much as I would have loved to stay at the farm, my vision of offering a helping hand in exchange for free room and board had quickly been abandoned by the realisation that the farm was way too small for needing an extra hand – and it was way before harvesting season. When I first arrived, I had taken myself on a discovery tour of the area. Following a small road down the hill from the farm I walked through beautiful scenery until I reached a small village called Sant'Agnello, nestled between Piano di Sorrento and Sorrento. In search of the ocean I was all of a sudden hit with a huge surprise when I reached the end of a road and found myself standing on top of a cliff, overlooking the most magnificent coastline with a view straight across to Mount Vesuvius. Back in Austria, once I had found out that L'Olivara wasn't quite on the island of Capri but somewhere around Sorrento, I hadn't bothered looking up the region on the internet. Sorrento had sounded familiar and for some reason I had this image of a not-very-attractive industrial harbour. With the accommodation already booked, I saw no sense in dampening my spirits by further research.

What I was staring at now was the polar opposite. I was speechless. While gazing with amazement, my eyes kept fixing on a terrace across from where I was standing; it was the most beautiful space reaching right to the edge of the cliff. Exceptionally maintained, it appeared to be part of an exclusive establishment but it seemed abandoned. I continued walking along the road, passing the terrace shielded by a big gate and a wall partly covered with vegetation. I walked around the wall until I ended up at the driveway of a hotel further down the road. Following a path that seemed to be leading to the cliff face I eventually found myself on a huge patio with an outdoor restaurant that clearly belonged to the hotel, which turned out to be the renowned Grand Hotel Cocumella. With no one else about, I set forth for a peek around and spotted access to the empty terrace that had caught my eye. It seemed separate from the hotel, closed off by a row of potted trees. There were a few chairs and tables and a white tent – or rather a few poles that held a simple white roof – but it all looked deserted. I couldn't quite comprehend how one could leave that prime space unused.

Now that it was time to look for a job, I returned straight to that oceanfront at Sant'Agnello. At the time I had also spotted a smallish, less grand hotel along the way, at which I thought to make my first inquiry. Once I stood in front of its entrance, however, I changed my mind. I didn't want to work in a hotel; I was after a much more casual job in a café or bar. Continuing along the road I had taken two days earlier, I again passed the Grand Hotel Cocumella and couldn't help but wander back down to that terrace to investigate. On my way back up the path towards the main road, I noticed a guy on a bicycle not far behind me. I wondered if I should stop and ask if he knew of a place that might need staff but then decided against it. Instead, and in stark contrast to my intentions, I pulled into the hotel entrance and all of a sudden found myself in front of the concierge asking for a job. This was bizarre as the last place I had wanted to work at was a stiff five-star hotel. Many luxury hotels in Italy are very old-school luxury, a fact that I adore, but this was not a place where I aspired to spend precious time during my 'gap year'. In a rather casual tone and annoyed to have put myself into a situation that was pointless, I told the concierge – who had the demeanour equal to that of a hotel manager in Australia – that I was looking for a job and asked if by any chance they had any vacancies. He glared at me with skepticism and to his question as to what kind of job I was looking for, I responded with an ignorant 'It doesn't matter, anything'. I didn't want a yes, I just wanted to get out of there. He then asked for my résumé and I responded, rather bluntly, that I didn't have one. Handing me someone's card, the concierge then suggested I drop off a résumé over the next couple of days, a gesture that was clearly courteous rather than sincere.

Okay, this was awkward. It is one thing to walk in off the street, unprepared and indifferent and ask for a job in a casual three-star property or a restaurant, but my entrance and attitude was not the order of the day at hotels such as the Grand Hotel Cocumella. For a second I felt embarrassed but then I had to laugh. I didn't know what the hell had come over me to have crossed the steps of that hotel and I certainly had no intention putting together a résumé, let alone dropping one off. I decided to continue my walk down the road towards Sorrento, which was bubbling over with small cafés and restaurants; I'd just have to try my luck there. As I was meandering along deep in thought, a guy on his bicycle appeared from behind and stopped me. It was the same guy I had seen on the path as I was walking back from the ocean front. Apparently he had overheard my conversation with the concierge and proceeded to tell me that the restaurant and bar he was working at was looking for someone for three to four nights a week. He gave me the name of his manager – Roberto – and suggested I be there at 6pm that night, and to refer to him, Nello, as a friend from years back. I didn't quite get where this place – called Coku – was meant to be but I figured I'd find it when I returned that night.

So this sounded pretty promising. There was no sense checking other places for work before speaking to Roberto, and it was now a matter of shifting my mission to finding a home. From Sant'Agnello it was only about a 15-minute walk to Sorrento, which I had decided was going to be the place I lived for the summer. With no clue as to where to start my search, I walked into the local tourist office and asked if they knew of any long-term rentals. The office was very busy with tourists and the receptionist advised that it would be very difficult to find a place at this time of the year but if I wouldn't mind waiting a while, she could have a look when she had time. She eventually returned to tell me that unfortunately she couldn't help but a colleague of hers supposedly had something in mind. That colleague then briefly appeared to inquire about my budget and, a mere 10 minutes later, he offered to show me a place owned by a friend of his. It was his lunch break and he was happy to take me there.

Another 20 minutes later, I had a home for the summer that was way beyond anything that I could have hoped for, let alone imagined. All I had expected I would get for my limited budget during peak season was a small, simple room, most probably in a shared house. What I ended up with was a place resembling something in a movie. Right in the middle of a lemon grove, at the back of a small apartment block at the end of a laneway less than a 10-minute stroll from the main piazza, was a container on wheels painted green with a pitched roof. It had been given a couple of new windows and a door leading out to a bamboo terrace attached to the 'container'. The inside walls and floor had been covered with bright wood; there was a small bathroom, a kitchenette, a queen-sized bed, a small table and chair, a wardrobe and chest of drawers. I even had a TV and air conditioning. But best of all, I could pick lemons and grapefruits from the trees simply by reaching through any of the windows. This place had so much character; it was simply a classic, one that I wouldn't have traded for anything. And as I was later shown, there was also a veggie patch in the far back of the property from which the owner of my home suggested I get my freshly grown organic zucchini, eggplants, tomatoes, potatoes, basil, etc.

At 5pm I made my way back to Sant'Agnello to find the restaurant and bar where Nello was working. I walked around the area for a bit and eventually asked a passerby if he knew where I could find the Coku bar. He directed me towards the terrace I had been so taken by. A fully functional high-end bar and restaurant had appeared seemingly out of nowhere in that exact spot. Only hours earlier the space had seemed abandoned, yet now it was one of the coolest places I had ever seen. It was as if someone had waved a magic wand: 'You want a cool bar on that stunning terrace? Well, here you go – take this!' As it turned out, the bar had been closed over the winter months – with the furniture stored away – and due to delays of some kind had only opened that night for the summer season. It was an outdoor-only restaurant and the white open structure I had noticed earlier had now turned into a cocktail bar and a small yet well-equipped kitchen. By the time I arrived for my interview, chefs and waiters were swirling around and ready to go as if this was just another night at an establishment that had been trading all along. Once I managed to close my jaw, I had a brief conversation with Roberto and he suggested I show up for a couple of trial shifts, starting Wednesday, in two days' time.

That same Wednesday morning I moved into my new home and, as soon as I had settled in, I emptied my kitchen drawers and piled up on my forearms whatever I could find. It had been 12 years since I had last worked at a café or restaurant and I had to make sure that I was prepared for the night. Using my laptop as a tray, I then did several laps around my lemon-tree cottage with wine and water glasses that I had filled to the top. Eventually I came to the conclusion that I still had what it took. I started my first shift at 6pm. The restaurant was only open at night and the first guests that walked in were 'mine'. Under the eye of Roberto, Nello – the bar manager – and the hotel manager from next door who had just shown up for a visit, I had to serve an expensive bottle of wine. Feeling all stares on me, I sure enough broke the cork as I tried to open the wine, not a very smart move in a venue of that standard. Within a second, Roberto appeared next to me to take over. Thankfully, that little slip of mine wasn't met with much scrutiny and I ended up making the cut.

The Coku terrace was in the running for one of the 10 most beautiful terraces in Italy and with the sun setting right in front of us each night, I couldn't have wished for a better workplace. Roberto had assigned me four shifts per week and I walked to work in joyful anticipation every time. I never thought I could take that much pleasure in waitressing. The nights could get very full-on and at times we were running our butts off until all hours of the morning, but in general we would close by around 1am and more often than not conclude the night with a glass of wine, chill-out music and good conversations, and – in my case – a lift home on the back of someone's Vespa.

What I love most about Italy is that the people seem to be living their lives with so much more passion than most other Western nations. One day I dropped off a dress at a tailor; when I returned to pick it up a couple of days later, the owner, who must have been at least in his 70s, wouldn't let me pay, simply saying, '*Le donne non pagano*' – women don't pay. His was a tiny shop but obviously it brought him more joy to flirt with women of any age than to make a few dollars more. At my favourite café I loved observing the waiters, especially one elderly man. Moving around with grace, no matter how busy it was, he would always make the time in between taking orders to puff his cigarette that was resting in an ashtray in the corner, while still keeping his section under perfect control. Impeccably dressed and visibly enjoying being a gentleman and delivering good service, he was a pleasure to watch. Even so, unfortunately these days there is another side to the story. On more than one occasion, locals and customers from various parts of the country alike kept asking me – with kind of a sarcastic undercurrent – how I was enjoying my time in Italy, expecting me to rant about how chaotic and unorganised their country was. I kept responding that I found it very refreshing to experience *'la dolce vita'* and the fact that there was more to life than money and a rigid lifestyle.

As much as I loved Sydney, I still felt that there were way too many rules and regulations and that way too many people hated their jobs. Yes, rush hour might start at 4pm and on Fridays the pubs might start to fill at lunchtime, but it still seemed such a waste to spend two-thirds of the week doing something you hated. I was naturally well aware of Italy's economic situation but I wished to urge an argument that the grass was always greener on the other side. My point, however, never found appeal. That the Italian government was rather screwed up was a valid fact, but the value of the true Italian spirit was another and it was sad – although understandable – to see how a population who used to be so proud of their country was now becoming frustrated and disillusioned.

During my stint in South Africa I had quickly learned to avoid mentioning that I had been calling Australia home. As one local had put it: 'We don't like Australia; too many of our compatriots took the easy way out and 'defected' to Australia after the elections in 1994.' Yet in Italy the mention of Australia made me everyone's best friend. It was deemed the new land of opportunity, the Holy Grail of escape destinations.

With Sorrento posing as the gateway for the famed and stunningly beautiful Amalfi Coast as well as the Island of Capri, there was also plenty to explore. Through local friends I was shown the most secluded and hidden swimming spots, the best restaurants and cafés with views to die for, as well as local treasures that as a tourist I wouldn't have known existed. We went on several boat rides to various destinations along the coast as well as a daytrip to Capri and on an overnight outing to Napoli. My friend Vicky – an English girl who I met soon after my arrival – had been dating a guy from a neighbouring town whose family owned one of the main bars on the piazza in Sorrento and whenever we caught up at that bar we got treated like royalty. In general, with a constant stream of *ciaos* and waving hands from every corner, the locals had a way of making you feel welcome and at home. It had been my intention to write a book while in Italy – something that had been on my bucket list for quite a while – but I only managed the first few pages. Sorrento was simply not the right place; the distractions were way too many.

At the beginning of September my parents came to visit for a couple of weeks. It was especially nice to have my dad come along too. He was just about to turn 80 but was more easy-going, fit, relaxed and flexible in his attitude than ever and, together with Mum's adventurous spirit, we had a very special time touring the coast and exploring the area. Another great surprise was a brief impromptu visit by my older sister Evelyn and my seven-year-old nephew. Having lived in Australia for so long, one forgets about the convenience of the proximity of the various countries within Europe.

Saying goodbye to Sorrento wasn't something I looked forward to but I had to go back to Austria to prepare for the court hearing on 4 October. Over the whole summer I had barely wasted a thought on the legal case and had made sure to drag out that period of no worries for as long as I could. In the end I gave myself just over a week to prepare for the big day.

It had been 13 months since I had left Australia and the only way I could sum up my time since having had to close the business and move out of my beautiful flat was by quoting Janis Joplin: 'Freedom's just another word for nothing left to lose.' The couple of years and especially the months leading up to the liquidation of my company had been by far the toughest, most challenging years in my life. On the contrary, the past 13 months had been the most valuable and among the best of my life. I had met the most amazing people along the way and made many new friends, not to mention the great experiences and unforgettable times I had. Yes, I had cried my eyes out in between and faced a major challenge health-wise – even after all this time my whole system still felt rather weak and fragile at times – but if I were given the choice, I wouldn't want it any other way. As the saying goes, it's the hard times that make you stronger and in the end it's the experiences that count. On no account had that past year been planned the way it eventually panned out; I was still travelling with the same backpack I had left Sydney with over a year earlier and that had been packed with the intention to take time out in Hawaii before returning to Sydney to start afresh a couple of months later. Everything had fallen into place and doors had opened way beyond what I could have imagined or wished for. I can say with absolute conviction that I will cherish that time forever.

Chapter 23

The court hearing

Back in Austria, however, it was time to face reality. *essense* had sold the lawsuit to my brother's company and Heiner would now be representing the suing party, whereas I would assume the role of a witness. Part of GUBSE's strategy in withdrawing the settlement in June of the previous year had been to follow up their initial 'bid' with a ridiculously low offer, based on the strong assumption that *essense* would have no choice but to accept, due to the company urgently requiring funds. If I was to reject their offer then they could always draw on plan B, which was to request a security from *essense*, following Stella's line of attack at the time.

The only reason GUBSE could have requested such a security was that the suing party was registered outside of Europe. The amount involved would have been in the tens of thousands of dollars at least, likely more. Well aware that I was in no position to come up with such funds, I can only assume that they had counted on the lawsuit eventually being dismissed. What they had not counted on, however, was the transfer of the lawsuit to a European entity. So, to their dismay, plan B failed, and to top the bad news, I had now moved from the position of suing party to becoming a witness, giving my word much heavier weight. The downside for me was that although my lawyer, Michael, was very familiar with the ins and outs of the case, I, as the sole bearer of all the intrinsic details, would no longer be sharing the court bench with him.

My anxiety over the days leading up to the hearing reached its peak a couple of days prior but, by the time we walked up the stairs to the court house, the calm had set back in. Once inside the rather sterile courtroom, I received the obligatory handshake from both Mr Gruber and Walter Schmidt, but neither of them looked very pleased, and Walter could not look me in the eye. I had – against their every expectation – dared to take legal action, and they had underestimated the operational consequences of taking on a project the size of Stella's almost 10,000 miles from their head office. It had put a significant strain on their business and, as proved to be the case further down the track, their reputation. Whereas GUBSE, in their first response to the suit back in September 2010, had claimed that Stella was no longer going to go ahead with the rollout of their SIHOT system – trying to deny us a basis for a claim – the said rollout was already in full swing at the time that same written plea was being drawn up.

As I later found out, from the outset GUBSE had major staffing issues and as a result had soon run into an uprising from within Stella. Several initial installations of their system into the various Stella hotels had gone badly (apparently due to poor training and project management) with the issues eventually coming to a peak with a Facebook 'hate' page set up by hotel staff dedicated to SIHOT. To top it all off, over the first six or so months, GUBSE's 24-hour support still had to go through their office in Germany, causing major delays in responding to support issues, while during the German summer holidays the rollout had to be put on hold altogether. GUBSE had obviously not thought ahead prior to making the far-reaching decision to shift *essense* or, rather, they hadn't considered the implications of refusal by *essense* to play along with their preposterous offer to subcontract *essense* to undertake the installations, training and support while they would be building up their own team.

As soon as the hearing had commenced and the judge had concluded the introduction, Mr Fischer, GUBSE's legal representative, requested that I leave the room. This was to be expected, considering it would be much easier to swerve from the truth without me present. The judge, however, countered that he had no intention to hear me as a witness that day and thus was happy for me to stay. It had been almost three years since we had formally sued GUBSE yet it appeared that the judge had barely read through the file relating to our case. In the end the hearing turned out to be no more than an attempt by the judge to intimidate us – the suing party – and coax us to settle out of court. An understandable strategy. But we had already settled previously and GUBSE's withdrawal of the earlier settlement had sent my company into liquidation. We could only assume that the judge had gone by the feedback received from his colleague mediating the case between our two parties in June the previous year, at which time *essense* had been far more prepared to divert from its initial proposal to settle than had been the case with GUBSE. As such, a repeat of the exact scenario would have – in the eyes of the judge, we presumed – been achievable and the easiest and quickest approach to rid himself of a complex case. If, from the onset, the judge gave us the impression that our chances for a high award in court were pretty low then hopefully we would debase ourselves and take whatever GUBSE were prepared to offer. This was our interpretation of his actions.

The conclusion of the hearing was such that the judge requested we provide evidence that the trust module that had been developed by GUBSE in line with Stella's specific requirements had indeed been working. His request was referring to our claim – one of several – that GUBSE's assertion, in the form of a written statement addressed to Stella that 'the trust pilot had been deemed unsuccessful', had been unjust and unlawful. The judge seemed to make any chance for compensation dependent on that one subject. Although we felt we had already provided enough evidence in our original suit as well as the various submissions that followed, the judge believed our arguments had not been convincing. What he seemed to be after was proof in the form of a statement by an expert witness who would have to formulate a detailed overview of the status of the software at the time that the trust pilot had been deemed unsuccessful. It didn't take a genius to understand that with GUBSE as the developers and the owners of the software code, it would be almost impossible for us to champion our position.

Michael, who himself was rather stunned by the proceedings, concluded the course of events with the statement that – if nothing else – we at least now knew what the judge was after. Our attention could now be focused on the one point, and Michael was positive that this would be an obstacle we could overcome. Feeling victorious, GUBSE left the courtroom with an air of confidence and arrogance. Interestingly enough, I was neither majorly concerned nor worried. Instead I had a strong feeling that justice would prevail. The judge's position appeared to be so farfetched that I had a hard time taking him seriously at that stage and already I saw the case ending up at the court of appeal.

Chapter 24

A testing return to Australia

Following the court hearing I spent another couple of weeks with my family in Austria and eventually returned to Australia on 17 October 2012. It had been 14 months since I had left the country and, although I hadn't missed Sydney one bit, I now had to go back to see how I would feel about living there again. Above all, I had to make sure that I would not let the legal issues and the loss of my business stand in the way of a life lived happily in Australia.

My homecoming was an interesting exercise that ended up presenting me with plenty of opportunities for personal growth, to put it nicely. Up to that stage I had rarely pondered how I might feel once I was back and facing reality; there was no use in wasting my energy over guesswork. Time would tell. Yet the fact that I would be returning to a different scenario and lifestyle than what I was used to was staring me in the face. Not only had I lost my business, most of my possessions and my health, but also most of my friends had disappeared over the previous year.

It is interesting how when you go through difficult times, especially when a liquidation or bankruptcy is involved, society expects you to go into hiding, get depressed and/or feel ashamed for an *appropriate* period of time following the event – the natural and logical progression in many people's eyes. However, I wonder what good it does anybody to follow that scenario. For me, the only way out and up – and to avoid falling into a hole – had been time away in a positive environment that would allow me to process the events, gain back perspective and eventually move on. As a result of the liquidation, I was left with debt. Although the company's debts in general were quite limited and assessable – and would at least in part be covered by the eventual settlement of my legal case with GUBSE (of which the liquidator was to receive a certain percentage) – I could only see myself being in a position to make reparations once I was fit enough, mentally and physically, to re-enter the business world. And to get there, I had to sort myself out.

The liquidator as well as the few creditors had always been informed of my whereabouts and as much as they had understood that I could no longer afford to live in Sydney and that leaving the country had been a reasonable option, many of my 'friends' seemingly hadn't. I can only assume that if I had moved to an outer Sydney suburb, holed myself up in a small room and succumbed to suggestions to go on antidepressants, they'd still be my friends. Flying to Hawaii or 'living the dolce vita' in Italy apparently wasn't appropriate.

We had been a close group of eight girlfriends who, over the years, regularly caught up for Friday night drinks, long lunches at nice restaurants or a girls' weekend away. By the time I returned to Sydney, out of that group of friends only one remained – my dear friend Sybi, a German girl. Working a high profile 60-hour job, Sybi still made it her mission to offer support in every possible way. The rest of the group had either turned nasty over time or silently dropped off. None of them had found it worthwhile to confront me with their perceived issues. You would think that, after many years of close friendships, people would actually care. They had seen me struggling for two years before I eventually had to admit defeat and yet it seemed that they couldn't handle the fact that, rather than falling into a hole, I went to Hawaii and dared to have a good time, regardless of the fact that I was cleaning rooms in exchange for free accommodation. In the absence of individual explanations, this was the only reason for their conduct I had managed to come up with. That experience was another big lesson in life. Most of the people I had thought to be my closest friends absconded while others, who I hadn't seen nearly as much of over the years, turned out to be among the most caring.

To support my fresh start in Sydney, I opted for a change of scenery and decided to settle in the Eastern Suburbs, the 'dark' side of the bridge. There had always been a bit of a rivalry between the so-called 'snobby' North Shore and the 'cool' Eastern Suburbs, separated by the Sydney Harbour Bridge. This was now the time to 'defect' to the other side. With neither the funds nor the furniture – apart from my bed I had sold almost everything before I had left Sydney – to rent a place on my own, it was now a matter of looking for shared accommodation, a concept that only a couple of years earlier would have been unthinkable. During my year away, I had come to appreciate sharing a house with various people and it now didn't concern me. On the contrary, I had been fully embracing my nomadic lifestyle and the freedom it brought. The less settled I got, the more it would allow me to keep doors open. A lease under my name was certainly not something I was eyeing at that stage, regardless of the fact that without a job or security of any kind, it probably wouldn't have been an option anyhow.

It is one thing to advertise yourself on any of the 'flatmate finder' portals when you are in your 20s, but it becomes a completely different story at the age of 42. It sure was an interesting exercise and in the end it took several weeks and many failed attempts before I finally found a place I could call home for the foreseeable future. After a brief interlude in a house that I shared with a slightly crazy mum and her son in Bondi Junction, I eventually moved into a large, stunning house in Bronte, complete with ocean views and a mere 10-minute walk to my favourite beach. My housemates were two brothers, slightly older than me, as well as the girlfriend of one of them. Four of us sharing the place made the rent affordable, especially considering the very expensive Sydney rental market.

Next on the agenda was a job. It had been 11 years since I had last updated my résumé and I was not looking forward to it. I had absolutely no idea what kind of job I was looking for, other than that it had to be something very different. Once word had got around that I had returned to Sydney I received a couple of offers for high-ranking positions as well as a business partnership, all within the hospitality IT industry but, as much as I appreciated the trust of the various former industry partners, I simply couldn't see myself returning to the same field. I had loved my business but my main passion had been in building something of my own. This was a new beginning and I felt that going back to the familiar would be a waste of an opportunity. So, rather than tormenting my brain to figure out what else I could be doing with my life, I handed my résumé to several large recruitment agencies to let them do the work for me. Naturally, they would be equipped with the right experience in that area. Aware of the kind of jobs out there – in the big, wide world (I was open for anything) – I envisioned the various agents scanning my résumé and instantly coming up with inspiring options. After all, having had my own business, I would surely be 'hot property'. However, rather than labelling me 'hot property', apparently I was a much better fit for the too-hard basket. Several recruitment agents agreed that yes, I had an 'interesting' résumé, but sorry, no company wants to employ someone who has had their own business. Ouch.

Reading the final version of my updated résumé again, I couldn't help but think to myself that the *one* company that it would fit would be the Virgin Group. Without question, my work history was unusual but with Virgin seemingly drawn to doing things differently, I felt that my background could be a good match. I had always had great admiration for Richard Branson and how he appeared to be motivated by screwing the rules and doing things his way. I searched the Virgin website and – bingo – there was a position advertised that sounded like one I could possibly identify with. I followed the links to the application criteria and process and within no time I had a feeling of anxiety creep up. What happened to the more flexible, less sterile, off-the-script selection process I had expected to encounter in true Virgin style? Instead, the instructions read just as rigidly as any other corporate job. Deciding to apply nevertheless – motivated solely by my 'no regrets' philosophy – at the same time I was hoping that I wouldn't make the cut. I was too old to fit into a box and it was not something to which I aspired. It didn't have anything to do with arrogance or a lack of flexibility, but authenticity. Needless to say, I received a 'thanks, but no thanks' response by return email.

My attempt to apply for a job with Virgin nonetheless acted as a catalyst for a lightbulb moment. I didn't actually want a high-profile job at that stage. I had enjoyed myself so much in Italy working at that cool restaurant and bar that the thought of it still made me smile. Who says that just because I had my own business I now had to hold a prestigious job title? Rather than falling into a trap, getting stuck in a rut doing something that I wouldn't enjoy, I decided to find a part-time waitressing job and use the remainder of the time to finally 'continue' writing my book, of which I had written just a couple of chapters. Along the way, I would figure out my true calling.

Again, my age proved a bit of a handicap, especially in a place like Sydney, where most waiters were young travellers or students. I wasn't after a senior position with responsibility; I just wanted a casual job in a cool place. After walking across town and receiving various rejections, I eventually found a French Bar and Brasserie in The Rocks quarter called Ananas – right across the street from the former Sydney Cove Providore, the home of my first job when I arrived in Sydney 14 years earlier. As soon as I walked through the doors of Ananas, I knew this was where I wanted to work. I was given the business card of the manager and, although I had been trying to avoid forwarding my résumé without a personal meet and greet, I managed to downgrade my work history well enough to get invited for an interview. I started my first shift the following week. Senior staff aside, the majority of my colleagues were about half my age. Mostly French, they were all extremely welcoming and fun, and the combination of French Mediterranean glamour and top-quality food made for a great atmosphere and happy customers. I ended up working four nights per week and, no matter how tired I was at the end of each shift, I would always leave the restaurant with a big smile on my face. The hospitality industry must have been in my blood after all; I couldn't help but enjoy it.

Once I had accepted the job, I was wondering how I would feel if one day a former client, employee or colleague from the industry walked in and spotted me in my waitressing uniform, let alone sat down at one of 'my' tables. While initially that thought had triggered an awkward sentiment, I assured myself that it wouldn't be an issue; I didn't have anything to prove and, as long as I did what I felt was right for me, no one's opinion or thoughts mattered. However, I was also aware that reality might well prove otherwise. My theory got a real chance to prove itself eventually when one night James, my former long-time employee – who by then thankfully was employed again in a suitable position – walked in. I was genuinely happy to see him. We had a good chat and then he disappeared to join friends in another section. I later walked up to his table to say hello to the rest of the group that I had also known for a long time. It was a great relief to realise that James seeing me in my waitressing job indeed hadn't bothered me at all; not for one second had I felt the slightest bit of embarrassment. I loved what I was doing and I was happy to stand by it.

Ananas seemed to be getting busier each night and at times we exerted ourselves for eight or nine hours nonstop, with hardly time for a sip of water. My system was still rather weak and in order to keep up with the strain on my body, I had to feed it lots of energy. The typical superfoods that would have come in handy now but that I had overdosed on back in South Africa still wouldn't agree with me, prompting me to go back to the good old green smoothie. I started each morning with a mix of organic kale, lemon, ginger and the occasional other green vegetable. It made me feel like Popeye, instantly giving me a boost. Soon one glass was no longer enough. If I could speed up my recovery process, then I might as well increase the dose and before long I was having three-quarters of a litre of green smoothie a day. It seemed to do the trick, until I started to feel unwell and my energy levels slowly but steadily began to drop yet again. It was now time to pull out my other trick, which was unpasteurised milk. A couple of years earlier, when my stress levels had started to approach dangerous heights, raw milk had been a big part of my life. After getting home each night, too exhausted to even move off the couch, I would have a glass of raw milk and instantly feel like a withered plant coming to life again. I had absolutely sworn by it.

The sale of raw milk for human consumption is illegal in Australia – one can only wonder why – and because it was hard to find I had totally forgotten about it. I knew where to get it though and, to make up for lost time and a lack of energy, I now quickly increased my daily intake to about half a litre per day. The phrase 'happy medium' had never been part of my vocabulary. It was always 'all or nothing'; if someone told me that a certain food, habit, exercise or whatever else was good for me, I would in general at least double the recommended amount. Why muck around if the process can be sped up? Needless to say, I soon became sick again. The fact that it could be due to yet another overdose of some sort – not that I had learned from my experience back in Cape Town – never occurred to me. Everyone was talking about the health benefits of green smoothies and there had been enough written about raw milk, apart from the fact that I had experienced its wonders first-hand. That I had gone from nothing to extreme amounts in no time, without giving my body even a chance to adjust to my new diet, had never struck me as a naïve and stupid idea, let alone absolutely idiotic. I felt that I was being the healthiest person around and simply could not understand why I was feeling so out of sorts. I eventually met with a doctor and underwent a series of blood tests. The test results were perfectly fine – I had through-the-roof levels of Vitamin B12 and folic acid, which according to the doctor, were of no concern whatsoever. However, I was advised to take antidepressants. That the actual source of my frustration was my continued health issues had no relevance. Several weeks later, my attempt to come upon a more sensible doctor (while at the same time dealing with a major cough – the restaurant's air conditioning hadn't helped my health) unfortunately failed and once again I found myself in a familiar situation. Barking like a dog, I was given an asthma spray, antibiotics and another recommendation to take antidepressants.

It seemed that both doctors, aware of my background and my previous stress levels following routine question-and-answer sessions, had made a diagnosis and put a stamp on me before they had even examined me: 'She lost her business, she has no 'proper' job, surely she has to be depressed.' Yes, returning to 'the real world' and finding myself among a mountain of uncertainty was – without doubt – challenging, but nothing I couldn't deal with and antidepressants certainly weren't going to give me the answers, especially not concerning my specific health issues.

Back at Ananas, when I first started to feel unwell I tried to push myself for a couple more weeks but eventually decided to resign. After several weeks in bed with a fever, a cough that kept getting worse, a trembling body and energy levels that couldn't have been much above zero, I eventually went to see an iridologist, Eli, hailed by some people as the best diagnostician in Sydney. Within two minutes Eli concluded that my hormones were all over the place (the actual diagnosis was in much more detail), that I had high-grade candida and a double chest infection. No wonder I had no energy. His findings were formed in the complete absence of knowledge of any of my historical or current health issues. I was handed several strong liquid herbal mixes and asked to return in about three weeks' time. Four days into taking his 'respiratory mix', my chest infection disappeared. This after two months of the worst cough – one that my local doctor had unsuccessfully tried to treat with an asthma spray and antibiotics.

As much as I had been impressed by Eli and his incredible skills, I felt that it wouldn't hurt to get another opinion on my hormone levels. This time round I decided to consult a specialist in that field, Dr Gary. Following a phone consultation and a first diagnosis based on my latest blood results that I forwarded to him, Dr Gary confirmed Eli's diagnosis, saying, 'Yes, your iridologist was right, but how he would have known is beyond my comprehension'. He wasn't happy with the test results of my thyroid and suggested that my adrenal levels were way too high at night. He basically validated what I had been trying to tell the previous two doctors, namely that my system was completely screwed up. If only they had looked at my blood results and managed to interpret them correctly prior to prescribing me antidepressants.

All in all I ended up spending about six weeks at home, feeling completely under the weather. Overdosing on the raw milk had obviously contributed to my chest infection and the ridiculous amounts of kale I consumed in my green smoothies would have contributed – at least to some extent – to my hormone imbalances. (Supposedly the only proven fix for one of my issues were pills consisting of cruciferous vegetables, of which kale is a part, and although it all didn't quite make sense, there seemed to be an obvious relation between kale and oestrogen.) Discontinuing the consumption of both the milk and the green smoothies, combined with another herbal mix from Eli (I had naturally declined the 'cruciferous pills' that Dr Gary had prescribed) I eventually started to get better.

Chapter 25

Meditating on a plan

With still no idea about what direction to take in my life and how I could possibly figure it out, one morning I suddenly thought about a chance encounter with a young Indian guy several months earlier. Full of enthusiasm he had, at the time, recounted his experience of a meditation course he had attended not far from Sydney. The place was a Vipassana Meditation centre and courses were being held regularly throughout the year. This might be just what I needed. Complete peace and quiet for an extended period of time would have to provide at least some kind of insight!

The Vipassana Meditation centre was in the Blue Mountains, one and a half hours from Sydney. The website described the course as 'a 10-day residential course with a qualified teacher where the student is free from distractions so that the reality within can be observed'. What this implied was that upon arrival one had to drop off any mobile phone, books, writing material and anything else that could potentially be distracting; it was a silent retreat, meaning that there was no talking for the duration of the course. The day started with meditation at 4am and ended with meditation at 9.30pm. Apart from breakfast, lunch and a couple of tea breaks during which we were also given time to walk around the beautiful grounds, the days were solely dedicated to meditation – either in a group or by oneself – as well as a nightly teacher's discourse. And while 10 days seemed like a long time, it wasn't until day eight that I finally succeeded in quietening the chatter in my mind for more than a few seconds and getting my fidgeting somewhat under control. Sitting in awkward positions for hours on end wasn't an easy task. But when the final hour of meditation concluded and we were allowed to speak again, I wasn't ready for it, wishing I had another couple of days.

Although certainly a challenge on more levels than one, the Vipassana course was a fantastic experience. I didn't quite manage to figure out my life purpose but I had several inspiring insights and returned to Sydney feeling like I was walking on clouds, very calm and refreshed. Deciding to go with the flow and give myself more time to recover, what I was after now was an easy Monday-to-Friday, nine-to-five job that would be interesting but not too demanding, or physical. Most importantly, it would have to be on a temporary basis. I had to keep my options open for when an epiphany finally hit.

Before too long, I managed to score a four-month assignment as the Executive Assistant to the Head of School of Optometry and Vision Science at the University of New South Wales. The job was exactly what I was looking for; it was going to be an interesting, completely new experience. And while in the end it turned out to be not quite the walk in the park that I had expected – working at the Faculty of Science meant that I was dealing with subjects and terms I could hardly even pronounce – by the time I left the campus at the beginning of October 2013, I was farewelled with a goodbye lunch and a big bunch of flowers.

Over the previous 12 months since the court hearing in October 2012, we'd had several pleadings going back and forth, each taking weeks to draft. In our eyes we had very much proven that the trust module had worked, but GUBSE kept coming back with reasons why this wasn't the case. GUBSE had also been trying to have the lawsuit dismissed due to ostensible legal inconsistencies regarding the transfer of the lawsuit to my brother's company. It appeared that they had never actually attentively read through the relating documents and in the end GUBSE was left with no choice but to accept that there was no way out. By mid-August 2013 we finally received notice for the next oral proceedings to be held on 17 December that year, 14 months after the first hearing.

Following my interlude at the university, it was now only two and a half months until my departure for Germany. I found myself, yet again, at a crossroads, facing what to do next. Since my early 20s, I had had a big vision of what my ultimate purpose might be and this was still sitting strong with me. It would require a significant amount of money and although I was positive that I'd get there eventually, I had to figure out the right path to set me on my way. I could feel the 'eureka moment' simmering, but the bubble was yet to burst. There was no sense in starting anything new so soon before my departure for Europe and it was now a case of deciding on an interim plan. Over time I had had a couple of people from within the hospitality-IT industry approach me to help with their various projects and the most obvious solution was to take up jobs on a consultancy or contract basis for the time being. I could rent a desk in a communal office and get started in no time. What I had to do first, however, was another 10-day Vipassana meditation retreat. It was unfinished business first time around and I had to go back; more quiet time might just give 'that bubble' that final push to the surface. And there was no better time than now.

My second round at Vipassana turned out to be an even more enlightening experience and, by the time I returned to Sydney, I knew what I had to do. First and foremost, I had to stop people asking me 'So, what's the plan?' and trying to push me in directions that didn't sit right. Although subconsciously aware of it, I had only now realised how much these outside influences had been affecting me. As much as I had always appreciated people caring and wanting to help, it was exhausting having to explain myself over and over, apart from the fact that anyone who wasn't a close friend didn't seem 'to get me' as it was. No one appeared to understand why, when I'd been offered a high profile job or a seemingly exciting business partnership, I would respond with a 'thanks, but no thanks'. I was fed up with being 'analysed' and told that my reaction could only be due to a loss of confidence or the like. I just wanted to be left to do my thing.

Another point that I had to put to rest was that certain things supposedly weren't possible or couldn't be done. I had to erase any negativity around me.

So what I now decided to do was to register a business called 'Dare the Impossible', in conjunction with a website with the domain name 'The Plan'. Not only would that hopefully put an end to people interrogating me and questioning my actions, it would also put a frame around everything I was doing at the time, that I had been doing over the previous couple of years and that I was going to do in the near future. It was all part of The Plan, the bigger vision. And with everything being part of The Plan, I could work towards my own goals and dreams, in my own time and manner, and people would no longer have to try and figure me out. It should stop the questions 'So, what's the plan?' and I doubted that anyone would still dare to tell me that whatever it was I wanted to do wasn't possible. On a psychological level I found this new outlook motivating, giving me a sense of 'being on my way'. I was still far from feeling fit and strong, but that was okay; at least I felt I was heading in *a* direction instead of beating myself up for being all over the place and not having yet managed to make something of myself.

The next step was to share my ideas with Russell from OMC Connect, my 'rock' during the *essense* reinvention stage. Russell actually 'got me' and it was, once again, a refreshing exercise to work with him. Without much ado, I had a sophisticated website to go with my new 'project'. I then updated my LinkedIn profile with the new details adding 'Co-founder' as a title. If there were more people involved in the 'new venture', it would be easier to respond to any queries with a simple 'It is too early to talk about'. Within no time the questions, offers and suggestions had stopped, which was such a relief. I felt as if a heavy weight had been lifted off my shoulders; I could now focus on living life and doing things my way, in my time and without having to answer to anybody, while at the same time not burning any bridges.

Upon my return from the meditation course, I attended the meetings I had arranged prior but immediately it became clear to me that working as a consultant or contractor in my old industry was no longer something I could get even slightly passionate about. My heart wasn't in it and it wouldn't have been fair to whoever was paying me. Although still not exactly sure about the next major steps, I knew they would be heading somewhere very different from anything that I had done before. For now, the biggest objective was to prepare myself for the upcoming court hearing.

The second court hearing took place on 17 December 2013. This time around, we had decided it would be better if I waited outside the courtroom; we assumed the case was going to end up in the court of appeal in which instance my absence from the various hearings would give my potential statements as a witness more credibility. However, for some reason the judge decided to call me – or rather the 'public' who were there to attend the hearing – into the courtroom as he was about to open the trial. (Having been the only member of the public, I thought that he could have referred to me directly.) I followed his instructions and entered the room to be greeted by nervous protests on GUBSE's part. Mr Fischer, GUBSE's legal representative, argued that they had left their witness at home, so could I please leave the courtroom too. Looking stunned, the judge stated he would be happy for me to stay, prompting an interesting comment from Mr Fischer somewhere along the lines of: 'But she knows all the details.' Confident that I had briefed Michael and my brother well enough for them to recognise any lies, I decided to leave the room.

The hearing was over within 45 minutes and, again, not much was covered. The judge felt that in their latest pleading GUBSE had submitted sufficient proof that the trust module had indeed *not* been working, thus their written confirmation addressed to the Stella Group during mediation back in April 2009 stating that the trust pilot had been unsuccessful could not be seen as unlawful. The suing party would, however, still have the opportunity to respond to GUBSE's latest arguments. The judge also agreed to our suggestion that – if required – it would be more reasonable to hear witnesses from within the Stella Hotel Group rather than a material witness (a subject matter expert). This was contrary to what GUBSE had in mind. They had long stopped offering witnesses from the ranks of Stella and whereas during the first court hearing 14 months earlier they had boasted that they were prepared to 'fly in half of Stella' as witnesses, it was now something that appeared to trigger a stress response in them. For whatever reason, GUBSE no longer seemed to receive full support from the Stella Group. From our standpoint, we welcomed Stella witnesses. I personally doubted that anyone from Stella would be prepared to lie in court.

All in all we felt that the outcome of the hearing wasn't all bad, even though the case had hardly progressed over all that time. As long as no expert witness was involved, we felt we could overcome the hurdles. In our eyes GUBSE's arguments as well as the judge's reasoning in regards to the trust module were again very far-fetched and we were confident that no judge from the court of appeal would accept such senseless lines of argument.

Chapter 26
Not quite home

After the court hearing I continued on to Austria with my brother where I spent Christmas and New Year with my family. It was the first time in 11 years that I was in Austria over the holidays and 11 years since I had seen snow. I couldn't wait to go back to Bad Gastein and ski down the slopes and visit the bars that had been a big part of my youth. It is funny how, at 42 years of age, I again felt like the teenage girl who had spent season after season in the snow, expecting to return to the same scenario. While still holding the mental image of being with my friends on the mountain or drinking Gluehwein at après-ski, I was shocked to realise how much everything had changed, from the infrastructure on the mountain to the pub-and-bar scene, and the atmosphere in town. It was a harsh realisation as to how much time had passed and how much I had aged.

I arrived back in Australia on 3 January 2014. It was great to be 'home'; summer was in full swing and I made sure to make the most of it. Health-wise I was also slowly starting to feel better and I began getting into a habit of ringing in my days with a walk along the beautiful Bronte to Bondi coastal path. No matter how often I strolled along that same path or sat on the same beach, I was always amazed at the beauty of it all. Yet there was a nagging voice that I couldn't seem to rid myself of. While my head kept telling me that it couldn't get any better, that there was no city more stunning than Sydney, no place that would offer a better lifestyle, etc, my heart was longing for a bit of chaos, more soul, fewer rules and more imperfections.

All its beauty aside, in some ways Sydney was losing its appeal and, no matter how much I tried to fight it, I simply no longer perceived the city in the same manner I used to. As much as I loved the fact that more and more trendy cafés, restaurants and wine bars kept popping up all around and that various suburbs had received serious upgrades, to me – after having lived in places like Hawaii, South Africa and Italy – it all somehow appeared a bit too polished. Clearly my personal situation was very different from a couple of years earlier and I had certainly changed too, but I couldn't fight the impression that Sydney was all about money and control these days – a sentiment that was also felt among many locals. Within two minutes of parking without a ticket, a parking attendant would jump out from behind a tree. (At least I never understood where else they could have appeared from in such a short time.) They'd hand you a ticket for $100+ (a no-stopping fine these days was $240!), even if you just wanted to do a quick drop-off. Bronte park, a beautiful place with fixed electric barbecues, had recently been turned into an alcohol-free zone. Yet isn't a barbie and a beer part of the Australian culture? And some of the beaches and parks these days had more prohibitory signs than people. It almost felt like councils were competing with each other to have the most control over its people. More recently I even came across an article in the paper suggesting that a Sydney resident could cop up to 10 fines a day without even realising they were breaking the rules. Some of the examples were: leaving your car unlocked or the window partially open when more than three metres away from the vehicle (each 'offence' entailing a $99 fine); beeping your car horn and waving hello to a friend (the illegal use of a warning device attracting a fine of $298); not to mention sticking your middle finger up at someone that, as per the article, could cost you another $298.

Since my time at the Vipassana retreat I had been trying to keep a regular meditation practice, which wasn't quite as easily done as planned. I was far from turning into a monk but I had certainly recognised the benefits of it. One day, when I was – once again – contemplating my future, I decided that it was time for some serious meditation. I sat down on my pillow and, just before I got started, sent a quick, 'Can you please give me a very clear sign of what I should be doing?!' to the universe. Later that afternoon I received a call from the real estate agent advising me that we had to move out of the house. I was completely beside myself. I had been living in that house for a year and absolutely loved the place; it was my new home – they surely couldn't just kick us out? My consternation lasted for about 10 minutes at which point I realised I had just received the answer to my lack of clarity about my future. How could I possibly ask for a clear sign and then get upset about it? I had to laugh. I obviously had to move. It was time to let go of the idea of happily ever after in Australia and move to a different country – at least for now. There was a reason why instinctively I had been so reluctant to settle in again.

The idea of packing my bags once more and setting out on another adventure quickly lifted my spirits; straight away I knew what I had to do. I had started writing that book of mine over a year and a half earlier but had never got past the first couple of chapters. It had been sitting in the back of my mind for a very long time now and – subconsciously – it had always stood in the way of any other possible future full-time project. I now knew with absolute certainty that before anything else, I had to write this book. There was no sense trying to make it a part-time project, as this clearly hadn't worked. I had been so attached to the house and the area I was living in that I had left no space for other options. What I had to do now was to move somewhere cheap and cheerful and dedicate my full attention to writing. The first place that popped into my head was Thailand; however, the idea of sitting in a hut on a beach surrounded by backpackers didn't quite resonate. I let it go and decided that the right destination would come to me in time. The following morning I concluded that another meditation might be the solution, and within five minutes of sitting in a lotus position, Bali popped into my head. I had already been to the small Indonesian island three times and, although I had always liked it, it wouldn't have been my first choice; Bali had become way too busy over the years and I hadn't really felt the need to go back. But now the thought of it lifted my spirit. Rather than settling somewhere close to the beach, I'd go inland where I could get inspired by the surrounding rice fields. At the same time it would be a good opportunity to sort out my health once and for all. Knowing now the source of my health issues and equipped with the correct remedies, it was just going to be a matter of time and patience, and an environment that encouraged yoga, meditation and a healthy lifestyle would sure complement the process perfectly. All of a sudden everything made so much sense. On top of that Bali was only a skip and a jump away.

Chapter 27

An intriguing offer

As soon as I had decided to move, I checked the date for the cheapest flight and, within 10 days of receiving notice regarding the house, I was on my way to Bali. Again, I didn't leave myself much time to pack up my life in Australia. I didn't actually have much to pack this time round, but expecting this now to be a more long-term goodbye, there were a great many things to sort out. I departed for Bali without much preparation. Arriving late, I spent my first night at a cheap hotel in Seminyak, a beach town not far from the airport. While I had no idea how long I was going to stay on the island, I assumed that it would be for at least several months. The following morning, just before jumping into a minibus heading to Ubud, I quickly booked myself into one of the first places I came across online that I felt drawn to, Michi Retreat. Not quite the typical Balinese-style place I had had in mind – it sounded much more intriguing than it looked (judging from the images) – it was only going to be for a couple of days while I searched for long-term accommodation. As a start, anything would do.

I arrived at Michi around lunchtime and as I was about to move into my room, a woman called Ambu – a rather eccentric Columbian in her 60s who was travelling the world running some kind of spiritual courses – introduced herself and started chatting to me. Two minutes into the conversation, she suggested that before I settled into my room, I should have a look 'at this other room'. I wasn't quite sure what she was going on about, especially considering that she was just another guest who was staying in the room adjacent to mine, but I followed her nevertheless. She led me to a very cool one-and-a-half-storey Greek-style semi-detached house. It was painted in blue and white, had a daybed on either side of the entrance and a stunning bathroom resembling Cleopatra's times. The best part, however, was its big patio overlooking a river and rice terraces. It had been given the name Nausicaa (a character in Homer's Greek epic *The Odyssey*). Ambu briefly told me about the retreat and how it needed a manager, eventually getting to why we were actually standing in that house; still not knowing anything about me other than that I was planning to live in Bali for a while, she asked if I might be interested in moving into Nausicaa to take over running the retreat.

I was absolutely stunned. I had only met Ambu a few minutes earlier and she didn't have the slightest idea what I had been doing in my life. She proceeded to tell me that the owner, simply called the Professor, had been looking for the right person for a very long time. There had been quite a few people interested in getting involved in the place, but he had rejected each of them. She then recounted a conversation she'd had with him a couple of nights earlier, when he had talked to her about an Italian woman he was considering for the job. At the sound of the news, Ambu's whole body had apparently started to shake uncontrollably; she had a bad feeling about the person he was considering and asked him to please not employ her as she, Ambu, had a vision that the perfect person was about to appear. As soon as Ambu spotted me when I arrived she knew that I was the subject of her vision. Overjoyed, regardless of the fact that I – while completely dumbfounded – told her I wasn't sure about this and had to think about it, Ambu went straight to the Professor and told him that The One had appeared. Apparently, the Professor was happy with what she had to say and wanted to meet with me straight away. Having just arrived, I certainly wasn't ready for such a conversation; I had to settle and take time to breathe.

What added to the utterly bizarre scenario was that only a few weeks earlier, while I was staying at the family hotel in the mountains back in Austria (now run by my sister Evelyn), I had been thinking to myself that it might be fun to manage a boutique hotel again. This thought had been simmering in the back of my head ever since. Not only that: since I had first come up with the idea of writing a book, I had been envisioning myself doing so seated among white and blue houses on the Greek island of Santorini. When Ambu opened the door to the Greek house, I was simply blown away; this was where I had to write my book! And when she proceeded to suggest that I manage the retreat, it all turned into a weird, 'What the hell is going on? Where is the hidden camera?' scenario.

Michi was in a small local village called Jukut Paku, 10 minutes south of Ubud. It was a stunning, rather extravagant place that looked like Spanish architect Antoni Gaudi had had his hands in its design. In need of serious renovation and maintenance, Michi seemed like the Balinese version of the Marigold Hotel from the movie *The Best Exotic Marigold Hotel*. One couldn't help but feel the urge to bring it back to its old glory. The only difference was that it wasn't even 20 years old. The morning following my conversation with Ambu I was led to the Professor's home, a couple of large rooms filled with thousands of books, with him living right among them. Not much space for furniture, just books, books and more books. Professor Kung was an 84-year-old Japanese-American history and sociology professor of Manchurian origin who had grown up in the States, travelled the world over and met and befriended some of the biggest names in the arts, architects, artists, composers and musicians alike. Once I actually sighted the Professor among all the books, I felt like I was looking straight into the eyes of Mr Miyagi, the wise old guy from the movie *Karate Kid*. Moving a few of his books out of the way so that I could actually sit on the chair and see him, the Professor didn't waste much time and proceeded to interrogate me about my life. Within about 10 minutes, he made an offer for me to 'Take over Michi, do with it whatever you want and make it your legacy'. I could consult with him if need be, but he needed the few years he had left to finish writing his books, which would be *his* legacy. I told the Professor that I had come to Bali to gain back strength and energy and, above all, write my own book, to which he simply responded that he had been looking for the right person for a very long time and that I should take as much time as I required to recover. He would be happy to wait; another couple of weeks – or months – would make no difference.

The Professor was unquestionably one of the most intriguing and knowledgeable people I had ever met. No matter what time in history, what continent or what subject matter, he had all the details. It's hard to portray the strangeness of my first 36 hours in Bali. I wish I could have taped the conversations and filmed the meetings we had. In the end I left the Professor with the suggestion that I would consider his offer over the following couple of weeks. I was still given the all-clear to move into the Greek house, no matter my eventual decision.

Nausicaa had been empty for several months and was in need of maintenance. Having fallen in love with my new abode at first sight, however, I was happy to live with any issues until fixed. Bearing in mind the relative mess the house was in, I suggested to the housekeeping staff that I help clean. The Balinese women were clearly not amused about having to fight their way through the dirt that had accumulated over time and within less than 10 minutes all the staff had deserted me with the excuse that they still had several other rooms to clean. Considering that their idea of clean – as I had come to learn – was very different to mine, losing the extra help wasn't much of an issue. If I was going to make the house my home for the foreseeable future then I might as well sort it out myself. After three days of scrubbing floors, walls, ceilings and every bit of furniture and fixture, I eventually settled into my new home. It rained on my head when I was sitting on the loo and I had to go to a different room to take a shower. The water supply to the shower and huge bath tub was yet to be fixed, and the geckos who kept dropping in through the ceiling tended to mistake one of my daybeds for a collective outhouse. But I loved it.

All in all it hadn't been the most gentle of starts to my new adventure. Bathed in a myriad of unusual events, my first few days on the island were challenging. I faced high expectations and pressure as well as negative energy from a couple of people who had been staying at Michi for an extended period of time and who had wanted to get involved in the running of the property, with the hope of getting included in the Professor's will (the Professor didn't have any descendents). I eventually told the Professor I'd be happy to help out when and where needed but that I was not prepared to commit to anything full-time, let alone long-term. My purpose of living in Bali for a while had been different and as difficult as it was to reject this intriguing offer handed to me seemingly out of nowhere, I had to put my gut instincts ahead of the 'this is obviously meant to be' thinking and get on with my life.

As tumultuous a launch into a next chapter it had been, however, I certainly wasn't one to complain. Back in Australia I had been longing for more chaos, and chaos I had certainly been given; it had been a long time since I had felt this alive! And without Ambu and her vision I wouldn't have ended up in my treasured Greek house.

Chapter 28

Among the Ubud expats

The Michi Art Village, as it was known among the various expats who felt drawn to use its special ambience and setting for their various events (including yoga and meditation classes, concerts and themed parties), attracted intriguing and interesting international visitors of all ages. At any given time it would be home to at least 10 to 15 long-term residents.

Over the course of my stay at Michi, I shared the space with a jeweller from Italy, a teacher and writer from South Africa, a French journalist, an American lawyer, a Czech writer, a German physicist, an American writer specialising in drafting degree dissertations for strangers, an Irish teacher who taught Aboriginal kids in the Australian Outback, an American who used to own a renowned candy shop in New York and was now making perfumes, a couple of American musicians; the list went on. Michi was the perfect place to enjoy peace and quiet and retire to your 'own little world' – a place I happily resided rather frequently. At the same time, company was about whenever one felt like a chat; there was always someone hanging around the open-air restaurant or the pool to have interesting conversations with.

With still no official manager to run the show, visitors from all walks of life who recognised the potential of the magical place kept getting actively engaged in its running and rehabilitation, either on their own account or with the Professor's approval. There was a constant flow of new faces taking charge and disappearing again not too much later. Take for example the two middle-aged women from Australia with a commitment to give Michi the attention it was screaming for. Investing all their time and energy they quickly managed to make a significant difference on various fronts – the swimming pool had never been as clean or the restaurant as organised, and I could actually lock the door to my house for the first time since I moved in. As it turned out, however, their obvious efficiency wasn't quite in line with the Balinese culture and when they decided to let go of a long-term employee (with the okay from the Professor), two-thirds of the staff responded with a walkout. To top it off, the resident maintenance guy came by Michi during that night and turned off the water supply to the whole property. And with most of the staff coming from the local village – and to avoid further retaliation – the *Kelian Banjar*, the leader of the village, eventually had to be consulted. Like many of their predecessors, the Australians eventually put it all into the too-hard basket and walked away, and the Balinese employees returned to work.

With the staff seemingly not too bothered about the condition of Michi – their pay apparently was very low – it was almost heartbreaking to watch the place fall apart. As per tradition, before long and within a week of the walkout, the next volunteers stepped in. Two of Michi's permanent tenants decided to take matters into their own hands and establish a 'core team' among the long-term residents that would share some of the responsibilities on a 'one for all, all for one' basis, rather than one or two people trying to do it all and fail, as in the past. So when the two musketeers – Ken, an American musician, and Gideon (not their real names), an Australian who had only arrived a couple of weeks earlier – asked for my help with the administrative side of things, I agreed.

While initially I found their vision inspiring, it quickly became clear that their intentions were more self-serving than anything. While Ken was an amazing musician, unfortunately his ambitions seemed to end there; all he appeared to be interested in was organising parties and getting free access to an on-site exhibition space that would allow him to showcase his handmade jewellery. On the other hand, Gideon was hoping that his new self-imposed title of Operations Coordinator would provide him with free room and board. Having recently decided to become a spiritual guru he had changed his name from John to Gideon and believed that everything in life could be achieved effortlessly, without money, as long as we all hugged each other, warmly, 10 times a day, for five minutes at a time. (At least this seemed part of his strategy.)

I would have fully supported his spiritual journey, if only he hadn't missed a few crucial steps along the way. So while the guys were planning parties and spreading love, I tried to be productive by getting at least some kind of a system happening, like, for example, the booking system, which up to that stage had been non-existent. I created a detailed booking sheet, as sophisticated as it could be with the sole use of Excel, and entered all current and future bookings that I could find noted in various places. The purpose of the exercise was to spare arriving guests the 'what-are-you-doing-here?' look. Apart from the fact that the reception at Michi was never attended, the staff was hardly ever aware of any comings and goings. In general, new arrivals who turned up and in fact got a room had to count themselves lucky – considering that at times guests had to be turned away and sent back into town or, if the Professor thought that certain newcomers were more interesting than someone who already had a room, he would use his walking stick to frantically knock on their door and kick them out in order to make space for the new, more important guests.

My enthusiasm about making a difference was short lived. Without any valuable support and contribution to 'the project' from either of the guys I couldn't help but feel like the resident idiot, putting all my energy into a situation that seemed pretty hopeless, and I eventually told Ken and Gideon that I'd take a step back for the time being. About a week later, immigration showed up and Gideon, who was reportedly checking his Facebook page in the office at the time, got deported for 'working' without a permit. Word had it that immigration had been tipped off; I can only assume that someone had been hugged a bit too much.

The real and sincere healers and spiritual teachers aside – local, and visiting from the various corners of the world – the typical Ubud scene wasn't quite my cup of tea. I met some wonderful people and had amazing experiences during my time in Bali, but with more self-proclaimed spiritual gurus than one could count, their emphasis on 'we are all one' seemed a bit hypocritical, considering the extreme self-centredness displayed by a great many of them. I can only assume that their 'oneness' would have been more geared towards the omnipresent cuddle-puddles – as endearingly called by a local improv-team – than its spiritual meaning. Like with Gideon, it appeared that a lot of the 'Western locals' felt that simply changing their name, appearance and vocabulary would make them an integral part of the community and lift their spirituality to a new level. Or, to quote one member from the Ubud community Facebook page: 'There are enough cool-crowd hippies. What we need is authenticity and people being prepared to walk their truth.' I obviously wasn't the only cynic. Once a month a large audience got treated to a show called Cosmic Comedy, a parody of the typical Ubud scene performed by a group of expats and guaranteed great entertainment.

The subject of expatriates in Bali in general was a rather complex one; the unofficial number of expatriates was supposedly 30,000 at the time and there appeared to be quite a divide between the 'old crowd' and the so-called 'superbules' (*bule* = foreigner in Balinese) who moved to Bali for the lifestyle. A lot had been written about Bali and how its rice fields were being traded for the construction of yet more villas. When asked how they felt about expats taking over Bali and, in particular, Ubud, most locals responded that they needed the tourists. Not everyone felt the same, however. One Balinese local erected huge letters across his rice paddies spelling out 'Not for Sale', reflecting a quote by the aforementioned local: 'Do not just think about what you can get from the earth in the short term, but what the earth does for you and your future generations. You cannot eat asphalt.'

My Greek house with its large terrace that provided one of the best views in Ubud was the perfect space to finally get stuck into that book of mine. Getting started on the writing required quite a bit of motivation on a daily basis. Usually within a few minutes of working hard on denying myself any distractions, I would disappear into a different sphere and get fully consumed for hours on end. I absolutely loved the process and, together with everything else the environment in and around Michi had to offer, I was in heaven. During my time in Bali I mostly kept to myself, contemplating life while watching the farmers work the rice paddies across from my abode or staring at the moon while swinging in my hammock. Whenever I needed a change of scenery, I would scooter into town and work out of Hubud (HUB in Ubud), a very cool communal office that was filled with 'digital nomads' of all ages from all over the world. When busy writing my book, I'd place myself at the café outside, feeling inspired by the scenery while sipping on a fresh coconut. Whenever I worked on yet another submission for the court, I'd find a desk indoors, where the atmosphere had a much more serious feel to it. Ubud was packed with great cafés and *warungs* (casual Balinese restaurants) and one certainly never faced the issue of getting bored. Yet what I cherished most was being able to get back to the peace and quiet of Jukut Pakut Village and Michi at the end of the day.

While experiencing several local rituals during my time in Bali, I was also lucky enough to witness a cremation ceremony that involved six adjacent communities. Families who can't afford individual cremations bury their dead relatives in a graveyard until they can share the financial burden with other families in and around their community at a later point in time. The Balinese invest enormous efforts in preparation for the cremation, which is viewed as an occasion for celebration, and only happens around every four to six years. One of these cremations was held in the local village. Having watched the arrangements coming to life over many weeks, my friend Joyce and I looked on as hundreds of people gathered in the pitch-black cemetery at 3am to dig out the bodies of their deceased family members.

Otherwise eerily dark and quiet, loud cheering and clapping could be heard each time a body, wrapped in a sheet, was 'found' in the glow of someone's torch. It was the most surreal sight. With the atmosphere akin to that of a treasure hunt, at the same time the scene resembled the set of a horror movie. Once the bundles had been lifted out of the graves, the bones of each skeleton were then lovingly washed and wrapped in a fresh white sheet (at one stage a young local remarked with a grin that this was 'the best lesson in anatomy'). The following day the bones were placed into a sarcophagus – in most cases resembling a large, beautifully decorated ox made out of wood and paper. The main event was then the simultaneous burning of the structures (the ox or similar) containing the deceased as well as myriad offerings; the fire is needed to liberate the spirit from the body and facilitate reincarnation.

Soon after I established some kind of a daily routine, I gave myself until the end of September to finish the first draft of my manuscript and move on. At the time I was unaware of the Ubud Writers and Readers Festival (Southeast Asia's largest literary event), which was being held at the beginning of October. In the end the festival was the perfect conclusion of yet another chapter along my journey. Thinking about the defining aspects of my life and re-living them again through writing was a fantastic exercise and a great way to digest the events of the previous years. I greatly cherished the freedom of scootering around town and through chaos on my motorbike, accompanied by very few rules and living my days accordingly. The countless hours of meditation, yoga, breath-work sessions and massages, combined with the plethora of organic food and fresh juices, while living among scores of like-minded people (the wannabe gurus aside) removed from the pressures of society, made for a very special and unforgettable time.

On the legal front, through the exchange of various documents between the court and the two parties, we seemed to have finally managed to convince the judge that the trust module had indeed been working and that GUBSE's preposterous claim that the trust-pilot site was unsuccessful had been fabricated solely with the simple purpose to checkmate *essense*. Meanwhile the court had also requested a written witness statement from the CFO of the Stella Group and the whole case seemed to be slowly but surely entering its final stages; that is, until Michael, who had been my lawyer and fighting the case for me for over five years, seemingly disappeared from the face of the earth. For weeks I desperately tried to get hold of him to find out about the outcome of the witness statement but despite a number of attempts to get in touch via email or phone, I received no response other than the occasional 'he promised that he will contact you' from his secretary.

Michael had been hugely overworked for months, if not years. Having experienced a serious burnout myself, and not wanting to push him to the limit, I tried to be as understanding as I possibly could without jeopardising the case. Eventually I was left no choice but to contact Michael's law firm and to bypass Michael to check for any updates. What I found out absolutely shocked me: the court had forwarded the written witness statement weeks earlier; the other party, in the meantime, had requested an extension and had since responded; and Michael had requested a further extension to our response, the deadline of which was only days away. All of this while I was under the impression that the court was still waiting for the requested witness statement from the Stella Hotel Group CFO. I freaked. We only had a few days left to present to the court our comments relating to the witness statement – which had turned out to be pretty much in our favour. On top of this we were yet to respond to another one of GUBSE's absurd pleadings that they had submitted three months earlier and that Michael had kept delaying due to time constraints.

What followed were further desperate attempts to get hold of Michael, again to no avail. I then had no option but to find a new lawyer, present him/her with a file the size of at least three large folders, provide updates on all the information not in the official files and request preparation of two documents for the court, all within three days. In view of the circumstances, Michael's law firm was eventually able to arrange for another extension of the due date through the court and, rather than three days, I was now dealing with a three-week reprieve. Within a couple of days a lawyer friend of my brother's came to my aid and provided me with a new contact. The case was back on a roll.

We submitted our documents in time – I'm still not sure how Alexander, my new lawyer, managed to get through all the files and produce a response that I was happy to give a nod to. (With all the emotions attached to the case, I sure wasn't always easy to please.) A couple of weeks later, in mid-August, we received notice from the court that the next hearing would be held on 9 December 2014, in four months' time.

This whole episode was a kick in the guts, especially considering the amount of understanding and insight the case required at that late stage. Yet no matter how hard I tried, I couldn't get angry at Michael. If it hadn't been for him, I doubt the legal case would have been alive and kicking at that stage. Once my finances had dried out, everyone else around me in the business world had been very quick to abandon me, yet Michael had kept going regardless of the circumstances. He had been a huge support during the most stressful of times and over the five years we'd worked together via countless emails and phone calls, we had developed a great understanding and appreciation of each other; I had trusted his decisions as much as he had appreciated and valued my input. The original lawsuit as well as the many writs that followed had been complex pieces of writing and Michael had always given the case his fullest attention, putting endless hours into it even while I had to delay his payment for a period of time. As disappointed as I was that he had 'abandoned' me, I had to wish him all the best.

Chapter 29

The US plan

Since living in Hawaii three years earlier, I had known that I would return at some stage. The island of Oahu had put a spell on me and a version of my ultimate goal at the time had been to create a life between California and Hawaii. I had no idea then how I was going to achieve that, and still had no idea while in Bali three years later, but I was sure that the right opportunity would present itself at the right time. In the back of my head I had the idea of eventually moving to Los Angeles. For people who knew me – myself included! – Los Angeles was an 'interesting' choice to say the least and one that had never before been on my radar. Still, for whatever reason I felt that some place in southern California would be the setting for the realisation of my ultimate dream. One day, while rocking in my hammock watching the Balinese farmers plough their fields, I decided to make Hawaii my next stop. I'd take it from there.

Once an idea hits my mind I generally don't waste much time analysing the decision. My only concern at that stage was not being able to afford a car. Public transport on Oahu can be a bit of a challenge, especially if one doesn't intend to live in or around Honolulu or isn't equipped with enough patience and toughness to spend an hour in a freezing bus for a distance that – in some cases – could possibly be covered faster on foot. Having reached my verdict regarding my next home, I gave my friend Katrin a call to let her know of my plans (we'd met in Hawaii and had stayed in contact).

We had been contemplating various business ideas over the years and this felt like a good time to revive them. Once I had her on the phone, I barely made it past 'hello' before Katrin offered me the use of her second car upon my arrival. I hadn't even mentioned the word 'car', nor was I aware that she even owned another car. I couldn't help but laugh and feel like I was on the right track; the only apprehension that I had about my decision of moving to Hawaii had been abolished within half an hour of it coming up.

The cheapest flight to Hawaii was via Sydney, a welcome 'best option' that provided me with a 10-hour stopover to run some errands and catch up for lunch with my friend Sybi before continuing on to Honolulu. Stepping off the plane in Honolulu put a big grin on my face, even after two nights on the plane and a full day rushing around Sydney in between. The sounds of the ukulele, the tall, swaying coconut trees and the sight of Hawaiian shirts everywhere made my heart sing.

The great aloha spirit, however, seemed to have bypassed the immigration officer who appeared determined to find a way to send me back to wherever I had just come from. Hugely sleep deprived, I assume that I would have looked like I was on drugs and having spent the previous ever-so-many months in Bali might not have helped my case either. Add to this that I had entered the word 'friend' under the 'address where you will be staying' on my arrival card, without bothering to add an actual address, and he kept questioning my motives by posing the weirdest questions. Not happy with my responses, the officer eventually pressed 'the button', setting off a large red light that prompted a solid-looking woman to lead me off and into the deportation room. At least that's what it felt like. Further interrogations by a gentleman with a much more approachable nature followed and eventually ended with a phone call to my friend Katrin to confirm my claims. With the stamp in my passport I was finally allowed to exhale. This experience scarred me for life; I will never walk through immigration the same way again.

From the minute Katrin picked me up from the airport, we started talking business. She and another business partner had been planning to open a restaurant/coffee-bar/deli in one of the coolest locations in town and she was keen for me to be part of the project and join them as a third partner. Considering my newly found passion for hospitality, it seemed like the perfect opportunity and a good stepping-stone. While spending my first few days at Katrin's place, finding decent long-term accommodation that would fit my budget turned out to be a bit of a challenge, especially after having been so spoilt in Bali. I was still living on a loan from my brother but with the next court hearing less than two months away – considering the direction that the legal case was taking – we were counting on GUBSE having entered desperation stage to settle and I anticipated finding myself in a more favourable financial position in the not-too-distant future. I wasn't after a luxury home, but I at least had to find a clean, reasonably maintained room in a shared house or studio or whatever other option was available. Lucky as I was, I eventually stumbled across the perfect home – a small, very cute and bright cottage on a family property in Portlock less than a minute from the ocean with the sun setting right in front, and close to my favourite spots on the island. It came fully furnished, with no set contract but with regular deliveries of fresh papayas, bananas, coconuts and mangos from the family's garden.

Once settled, I spent a substantial part of my days preparing for the court hearing, working hard on gaining credibility and trust from my new lawyers. I had forgotten about that perception that as a layperson – especially a female – one was expected to remain quiet and to simply accept and trust the advice of the professionals. After five years of dealing with the case, I had a fair understanding of at least some of the legal possibilities and the do's and don'ts, as well as the strategic path that might support a positive outcome. Yet it took a significant amount of effort and energy to be taken seriously and listened to. As much as I appreciated my new lawyers taking over this complex case at such short notice, I wasn't going to be content with the obvious minimum that the lawsuit might eventually award us (in regards to commission versus compensation). Not to mention the moral side of the case; justice had to be upheld. Several emails and phone calls into this still-new relationship I eventually managed to be heard and understood and in the end our final legal document before the hearing was submitted with everyone's approval.

My flight to Europe was booked for 1 December, giving me a week to recover from two nights on the plane and an 11-hour time difference before the court hearing on 9 December. I was all pumped and ready to go when, four days before I was meant to step onto the plane, I received an email from my lawyers informing me that the judge – well aware that I was residing somewhere on the other side of the world – had decided to postpone the hearing to March. The reason given was that due to personal circumstances he hadn't had enough time to prepare for the hearing, although he had set the date himself back in mid-August. My cynicism might be hypocritical and out of place considering our own delay of the case months earlier, but at least it had only involved the submission of a document, rather than the physical presence of people. Not only was my flight non-refundable without the option of a date change, I now had to do a three-day 'excursion' to Canada to renew my visitor visa for the US. In addition, my parents had changed their previous holiday plans to work around my visit to Austria.

Once my initial anger had subsided, I had to admit to being quietly relieved that the hearing had been postponed. Having arrived in Hawaii less than six weeks earlier, I had only just settled into my new place and I wasn't quite ready to leave again. I also managed to get the original flight refunded by my travel insurance and the extra weeks until my new departure date at the end of February presented a welcome window to get started on the review and edit of my manuscript. Furthermore, while still patiently waiting to see how the restaurant project was going to proceed – the contract with the owner of the premises was yet to be signed – this was also a good time to finally meet with an immigration lawyer to look at my options regarding a permanent visa for the US.

My short trip to Canada turned out to be not just a visa-renewal exercise but a very enjoyable three days spent in Vancouver with a daytrip to Whistler walking down memory lane. I stayed in a room that was being rented out by a very interesting artist/performer/actor couple, who were just as cool as their house, and helped to add to another great little adventure. To avoid yet another one-on-one with my special friend at immigration in Honolulu upon my re-entry into Hawaii, I decided to go for the next cheapest option, returning from Canada on a 12-hour journey via San Francisco instead of the five-and-a-half-hour direct flight. This paranoia was unusual for me, but it was worth the peace of mind. No questions were asked this time around and I was a happy camper for another couple of months, until I had to re-enter the country a third time upon returning from the court hearing. (As I later found out, a brief 'excursion' to Canada no longer counts as leaving the US. It was only by sheer luck that the immigration officer had added a fresh stamp to my passport upon my re-entry).

Chapter 30

The adjudgement

The third court hearing took place on 3 March 2015.

After an hour-long meeting with my new lawyers – Alexander and Michael, his superior – in their Munich office the night before the hearing, we spent six hours on the train to Saarbruecken the following day going through more essential details. In view of the circumstances, we decided it was important for me to join the hearing on this occasion and assist through the use of sign language from the back bench if need be.

This time around the focus of the oral proceedings appeared to be the date that GUBSE had terminated their distribution agreement with *essense*. During the year and a half after pushing out *essense* there had been a couple of desperate attempts from GUBSE to terminate its contract with *essense* without notice, with their reasons clearly based on dubious legal merits. It was officially terminated (in line with the terms of the agreement) in October 2010. The question relating to the duration of the distribution agreement should, however, have been void and of no relevance to the case. With Stella we were dealing with an 'apportioned contract', meaning that – our claim for compensation aside – GUBSE would have had to pay commission for their various earnings from their contract with Stella *to this day*, rather than until whatever date the distribution agreement proved to have been terminated. To our surprise the judge saw even this fact differently and the hearing was eventually concluded with the suggestion that we provide further proof as to why our contract with the Stella Group had been an apportioned contract rather than a simple framework agreement. Our pleading in that regards would be due on 7 April and a court adjudication would follow on 28 April.

I returned to Hawaii 10 days after the hearing and spent the following week gathering and summarising all the evidence to substantiate our point. In our eyes it was so very obvious that we were dealing with an apportioned contract. To start off with, the purpose of the Stella Hotel Group's request for tender at the time had been to implement one system across all their hotels and there was plenty of evidence confirming this. We were stunned that the judge could possibly have seen this otherwise. On the due date we submitted a pleading that we were confident provided very strong proof to champion our argument. We had approached the subject from every angle, attaching the relevant evidence to each of our points. Now we were waiting for a decision from the court as to what extent GUBSE would have to lay open their books to allow for a calculation of commission owed, following which the topic and scope of compensation could be dealt with. Instead on 28 April we received a full and final ruling purporting that the Stella deal had been based on a *framework* agreement and that GUBSE would have to disclose their earnings up until 30 September 2011 only. (The date by which GUBSE had validly terminated the contract with *essense*.). In regards to *essense*'s claim for compensation: the claim was unfounded and the lawsuit was dismissed by the court. The suing party had to carry the costs.

I was in shock. Although we had always counted on the case eventually ending up at the court of appeal, over the past five and a half years we had managed to prove – or so we thought – that the trust module had been working; the one witness statement requested by the court had turned out in *our* favour and we had also provided very strong evidence about the nature of the Stella contract. I had no idea how the judge could possibly have reached such a verdict. On the day of the verdict (at which we weren't physically present), we only received a copy of the tenor (the summary of the adjudgement). For the full verdict, including the reasoning, we had to wait for a postal delivery. My lawyers were positive that we were dealing with a false judgment but not much could be said until we received the complete file.

The adjudgement was a 53-page document. The various incorrect details contained within the Statement of Facts aside, we felt that the judge must have reached his verdict even before the most recent court hearing in March. There was no reference to any of our points from our latest pleading nor to GUBSE's response to it. Instead, the judge had spent several paragraphs dealing with a subject that had since become void. In regards to our claim for compensation, the dismissal of the lawsuit had been based on the court's understanding that there was no breach of contract on the part of GUBSE. The fact that the trust module – a completely new module that had been developed in collaboration with Stella to accommodate their specific requirements – had revealed several bugs during its pilot phase meant that GUBSE's written claim and confirmation that the module was not working was not unlawful. Their actions could not be seen as the foundation for Stella's stance that it no longer had any obligations towards *essense* in regards to installing SIHOT into its properties. Never mind that we had more than proven that neither of the so-called 'bugs' had been anywhere grave enough to prevent the system's classification as 'working'. The complete lack of communication from Stella at any time during the pilot phase suggesting that the trust module was not working had obviously left the judge unfazed. So too the irrefutable fact that only days prior to Stella deciding that their only chance to enter into a direct relationship with GUBSE was by way of de-installing the trust module from its pilot site (and with this branding it a fail) *essense* had been asked to install that same trust module at a couple of other Stella sites (a request that was eventually reversed in view of the bigger picture).

Naturally we appealed the ruling in its entirety.

Meanwhile in Hawaii, the restaurant project with my friend and the investor had been put on hold. The owner of the premises kept changing the contract terms and putting off commitment – a fact that in the end turned out a blessing in disguise; no matter how much I loved Hawaii, I could gradually feel the dreaded 'island fever' creeping in. While over the previous months my beloved sanctuary in Portlock had been posing as the perfect place to revise and edit my manuscript, I now knew that, once completed, it would be time to move on and follow the road towards my dream by letting fate take me to the next pit stop (and to start making money again).

Chapter 31

Another Italian summer

My mum's 75th birthday was around the corner and, based on her love for the beach and the ocean, the family planned to celebrate it in Sardinia, Italy. Following my sojourns in Asia and Hawaii, a touch of European culture seemed like a good choice. Why not make it another summer in Italy? With the legal case still ongoing, I was happy to preserve my brainpower for our pleading to the court of appeal (which was set to be another time- and energy-consuming exercise) and to keep my working life low-key for the time being. I consulted with my Italian friend Beatrice, whom I had met in Bali a year earlier, to see if she had any suggestions and by return email I received a link to a much talked about beach establishment in Fregene, a village just outside of Rome. I had always loved Rome – more often than not, when returning to Australia after visiting my family in Austria I would stopover in Rome – so without much deliberation I sent off my résumé. I never heard back but decided to make Fregene my next staging post nevertheless.

I couldn't leave the US without testing my previous sentiment of eventually settling in California, so for my flight to Italy I chose a connection that included a 10-hour layover in Los Angeles, allowing me to spend the day in Santa Monica (the exact setting of my mental picture). I rented a bike for a couple of hours and tried hard to get inspired by the beachfront city's vibes but returned to the airport satisfied that the idea of living in Santa Monica at some stage was a simple bubble that had just burst. After another night on the plane and a stopover in Istanbul, I eventually arrived in Fregene early evening on Saturday 6 June. I had booked a basic room for a couple of nights and pretty much fell into bed straight away.

The following morning I went for a stroll on the beach – an endless, wide stretch of sand lined by restaurants and bars. At one point I noticed a weak wifi signal coming from one of the restaurants. Moving closer as I was searching for a stronger signal, a *bagnino* (lifeguard) approached and asked if I was looking for something. He visibly belonged to the same establishment as the wifi signal, Onda Anomala. Too embarrassed to admit the truth, I responded, 'Ahhh, yes, I'm looking for a job.' It was only 10am, but, it being a Sunday morning, the place was already packed with Romans escaping the heat of the city. Of all days, this was certainly the most irrational one to be asking for a job. To my surprise the lifeguard suggested I come back at 1.30pm to meet with the owner, a friend of his who was due to return from a business trip to Kenya that day. I argued that I would rather arrange for a meeting the following day, Monday, when it would be less busy but he dismissed my concern. By the time I returned, the owner was already down at the beach, waiting for me. He led me inside to have a chat with his wife, Katia, who was running the place and 19 hours after touching down in Italy, I had a job. This was my personal best!

As usual, I now had to make sure that I was only settling for the finest, so following Katia's suggestion that I start my first shift in a couple of days, I walked up and down the beach examining the competition. And it was the finest. Onda Anomala was a very cool, rather large beach establishment with beautiful white sun-chairs and sofas spread out over a lawn that, at night, were complemented by white sheets in the sand to sit on and gaze at the ocean. It encompassed a café, restaurant and bar; my job was to look after events, of which there were many, and to help out at the café whenever needed. My favourite time of day was sunset, which each night was accompanied by the same most beautiful piece of music that the beachside DJ would tune into with the sun's first touch of the ocean and that ended in a dramatic finale (timed to the second) and a cheer from the crowd just as the last tip disappeared – it was truly magical, over and over again.

It was another very special summer. I moved into a great little granny-flat with my own outdoor area and garden, a stone's throw from the beach and a 15-minute bike ride along the beach to work. I appeared to be the only non-Roman around and people were wondering what, of all places, I was doing in Fregene – but I loved it. Mid-July I spent a couple of days in Sardinia with my family for Mum's birthday and whenever I was itching for city life, I went to Rome for the day.

One day, as I was just about to leave for work, my sister Evelyn called and asked for my help. About nine years earlier she and her husband, Ike, had bought a hotel in Bad Gastein, the Hotel Miramonte, which was at the time rather old-fashioned. In walking distance from Haus Hirt (the family hotel that they had taken over soon after they got married) it had undergone its last major renovation in the late 1950s. It was an exciting project for Ike, an architect. Over the years he had turned the Miramonte into a much talked about boutique hotel but after their general manager – who had run the Hotel during its first six years since reopening – left, they hadn't had much luck finding a suitable replacement. They were now in burning need of someone they could trust to get it back on track and bring back order into its day-to-day operation. Evelyn's call now was to enquire – with a sense of urgency – if I could be persuaded to move back and take over management of the hotel from the start of the winter season. My heart jumped straight to my throat. The thought of going back to my birthplace and work in a hotel, a career that I had vowed to stay away from (regardless of my converse notion a year earlier), freaked me, to say the least. As proud an Austrian I was, I no longer belonged there and in no way could I see myself back in Bad Gastein. I had had the most amazing childhood and fun-filled teenage years in those beautiful mountains but a lot of time had passed since. This was a tough one. With my mind going at 100 miles an hour and running late for work, I left Evelyn with the promise that I would have a think about it.

My immediate idea was that I had to find someone else who would fit the job. Maybe an old college friend, or a friend who might know of someone with the right credentials. But all such attempts turned out fruitless, leaving me to play the various scenarios in my mind, back to front and front to back, envisioning myself in my hometown, the hotel, dealing with staff, some of whom would have been there for years (and would actually know what they were doing as opposed to me, who hadn't worked in a hotel for 21 years). I eventually came to the conclusion that *yes*, things happen for a reason and I had to step up and support my sister.

Up to that juncture, my reference point for my next career move had always been the settlement of the court case. With my bigger vision ('The Plan') requiring considerable investment, it was first and foremost the legal – and with this the emotional – stresses that I had to rid myself of before I would be ready to commit to something more tangible. Subconsciously I think I had always been grateful that that point hadn't come around as yet. The years since closing the business had been providing me with the most amazing experiences and a feeling of freedom that I cherished to its core. I had come to embrace and love my nomadic lifestyle and the unknown that it brought with it more than anything. I simply and wholeheartedly enjoyed living life's adventures. Now that I had regained my strength mentally and physically, however, and keeping in mind the costs involved in taking the legal case to the court of appeal, I could no longer justify my current way of life. It was time to reexamine the word 'commitment', a challenge that didn't sit easily, especially not with my free spirit.

Only a few days prior to Evelyn's call I had booked a flight to Australia, ready to take the bull by the horns again. While I had no idea about the specifics of that next step, fate had now made the decision for me. My flight to Australia was non-refundable, so I decided to still step on the plane at the end of the summer, if for no other reason than to pick up warmer clothes for my upcoming months in the snow. There was also the chance that I – or one of the several people that I had contacted – might still come up with an alternative solution regarding a suitable manager for the Miramonte. I had six weeks up my sleeve before the start of the winter season in Austria and anything could happen in that time. Yet, as it turned out, much of that time would be consumed by working through a 90-page response to our pleading to the court of appeal, drafted by the other party's newly commissioned lawyer.

Back in Italy I had spent endless hours conversing with my lawyers (at least for once we found ourselves in the same time-zone). While they now suggested we limit our appeal to the part referring to my claim for commission and let go of the much more costly (in court fees) claim for compensation, I insisted that we appeal the judgment of the court of first instance in its entirety as we had previously agreed. As a layperson it is no easy feat to argue with your lawyers but I had to listen to my gut instinct and do what I felt was the right thing. Alexander and Michael, who had only come on board a year earlier, had been trying to convince me all along that the original suit should have been based on a claim for commission rather than compensation – an assessment that I had always seen differently, confident that my previous lawyer, (the other) Michael had followed the right path. Our claim for compensation was in the amount of AUD 3,108,075 and the court costs to appeal were going to be calculated as a percentage of that amount. To be able to go ahead I now had to take out a loan, for which my sister Evelyn volunteered to act as a guarantor. That additional financial pressure – and going against my lawyer's advice – counted for a lot of extra weight on my shoulders but it was a risk that I had to take. With the ridiculously large amount of time, money, energy and emotion that had already gone into the case – it had been five and a half years since we had sued GUBSE – I couldn't cower just before the finish line.

GUBSE's lengthy response to our appeal now meant another big dig into the pockets, having to respond to each of their still entirely unsubstantiated assertions. Within that pleading, their new lawyer, Prof Dr Anton had also included a cross-appeal. This attempted to take a different route and championed an idea regarding a fact that up to that point neither of the two parties nor the court of first instance had considered disputable. While initially unsettled, once I had read through the complete document I felt calm, dismissing their grand work, dominated by empty words and bombastic language, as a weak and desperate attempt to justify GUBSE's actions. This sentiment was shared by my lawyers.

Chapter 32

Hometown

I arrived in Austria on 19 November 2015 in time for my dad's birthday. After a couple of days with my family, most of whom now lived in Salzburg, I continued on to Bad Gastein to throw myself into what was undoubtedly going to be an intense endeavour. There was no denying that the Miramonte had a very special feel about it; located just at the bottom of a ski-hill, it was a hip place with the most magnificent view of the town and the surrounding mountains. Bad Gastein itself – once crowned the 'Monte Carlo of the Alps' – had an intriguing history. Frequented by European monarchs in the 19th century it was characterised by its Belle Époque grand hotels and villas that had been built into the steep slopes, with a massive waterfall running right through the middle of town.

When I was growing up, Bad Gastein's centre was a lively picture of well-dressed visitors (many of whom were spa guests who stayed for several weeks to bathe in the town's famous thermal springs) strolling through the streets, browsing the shops and listening to classical concerts on the village square – and to Liza Minnelli, who gave a concert one New Year's Eve. Over the years Bad Gastein's grand image had slowly dissipated, with a couple of its turn-of-the-century hotels shutting its doors and several businesses relocating to newer premises.

When in 1999 a Viennese investor (with no intention to invest) purchased five historic buildings that made up the majority of the centre, the heart of the town was transformed into an image of abandoned structures and empty shopfronts secured by wire fences. And it has remained like that ever since. A lot had been written about Bad Gastein over the previous decades and while for several years the headlines of most articles were talking about 'the downfall of Bad Gastein' or branding it a ghost town, in recent years it had undergone a major upsurge, turning it into a melting pot for creative people; the international media now heralded the town as *the* place to go: 'an extreme picture, a metropolitan splendour in the middle of the mountains'.

So here I was back in my hometown, all of a sudden looking at this place with fresh and very different eyes. My life had been rather surreal over the previous years and this was a perfect continuation of it. Rather than feeling stuck in a small town in the mountains, I felt like I was part of a movie set – from looking out at the magnificent backdrop of Bad Gastein (which unwittingly made one draw comparisons to the set of *The Grand Budapest Hotel*) right across the Miramonte to the town's morbid charm when strolling through its deserted centre. What I had perceived as depressing during a visit a couple of years earlier, I now found incredibly intriguing. One could literally feel the creative buzz and renewed enthusiasm for this magical place oozing out of its every pore.

As expected, once I was in this new position, I was facing a challenge on more than one level. From a lack of handover when I first started, and a team of which half were new, to guests and locals greeting me enthusiastically, at times hugging and kissing me hello, while I had no idea who they were. For some reason people kept mistaking me for my sister Evelyn or recognised me from when I was a child with the unfair advantage of having heard that I was back. Not to mention trying to communicate in German without constantly throwing in English words and sounding like a wannabe hipster.

My working week comprised an average of 90 hours but the hotel's cool and interesting clientele together with a mostly wonderful team made it an absolute joy to work. In fact, it rarely ever felt like work; I was in my element and just loved what I was doing. Several times during the day I would go outside and look at the extreme beauty that surrounded us: the snow-covered mountains in winter as much as the intensely green meadows in summer (we even had a farmer's sheep graze right next to the hotel). It was such a tranquil setting that it made me wonder how I deserved to grow up and now live in this blissful spot while the rest of the world was in so much turmoil.

I had committed to taking over the reign of the Miramonte for the winter season but come April, it was clear that I had to stay on; business-wise and on a personal level I wasn't ready to cut the ties. The summer season was dominated by events, from cultural and artistic in nature to conference gala dinners and weddings spanning several days. We had a couple of well-known brand names use the interior of the hotel and its backdrop as the setting for their new catalogues and even BMW had Bad Gastein feature in its Austrian ad-campaign for the 'Mini' with the protagonist proclaiming that he was *now going to check into his favourite hotel, The Miramonte* (during filming I tried to sneak in the hotel's logo whenever I had a chance, completely oblivious that we were going to be set into the scene in such grand fashion). By the end of summer I was so exhausted I was crawling on all-fours and while I knew that I was going to miss the Miramonte and Bad Gastein, it was time for my nomad soul to move on. Too tired to even think about the possible next move, I bought a one-way ticket to Thailand for some serious rest and relaxation.

Chapter 33

Ready to put it all behind me

Back in January that year we had submitted our response to GUBSE's pleading (and cross-appeal) and shortly after that had been advised of the date for the hearing at the court of appeal, namely 20 July. On 13 July we received a copy of yet another 69-page apologia from GUBSE. They had had six months to hand in further legal documents but had chosen to wait until the very last minute (the general rules state that submissions could be made up until seven days prior to a hearing). While an obvious strategic move to deny us any chance to respond and to rectify what was bound to be another stringing together of absurdities and incorrect assertions, I felt that GUBSE's conduct surely couldn't sit well with the appellate judges (the court of appeal has a three-judge panel). This wasn't just another hit at us but in my eyes also demonstrated complete ignorance and disrespect towards the court.

As it turned out, I wasn't far off with my assessment. The following day we received notification from the court that the hearing on 20 July had been annulled due to the majority of the exhibits having been presented in English where the language of the court was German; and 'the defendant party submitting a 69-page-long pleading just one [!] week prior to the hearing'. While we now had to have the various documents translated (a job that was going to be divided between the two parties), we were also given six weeks to respond to GUBSE's latest pleading. A new date for the hearing was going to be communicated in due time.

I booked myself into the 'Spa Village', part of the original and among travellers well-known Spa Resorts in Koh Samui, an island off the east coast of Thailand. This was the third time that I had signed up for a week-long fast there and I couldn't wait to get started. Although initially I wasn't sure if undergoing a fast when feeling worn out would be the right thing to do, it turned out be exactly what I needed. My days consisted of massages, meditation, yoga and the regular intake of detox drinks and special herbs – and all this in a basic yet beautifully serene setting. I cherished the peace and quiet. While in no rush to decide on my next destination, one night following a lengthy Skype chat with a friend talking about Australia, I all of a sudden had this strong sense come over me that it was time to go home.

It was now the end of November (2016) and keeping in mind that December was peak season in Australia and about the worst time to look for a place to live as well as a job, I thought it best to return to Sydney after the Christmas holidays. So, following a couple of weeks at the Spa Resort and a week at the beach on the neighbouring island of Koh Phangan, I happily accepted my friends Kathi and Martin's offer to come to Bali and stay with them during Christmas and New Year (I had met them in Bali almost three years earlier). It was exciting to be back in Ubud and to retrace my steps, but once I had caught up with old friends and assured myself that Michi, my beloved former home, was still operating – and the Professor was still happily residing among his books (although he was slightly more frail) – it was time to get down to business.

Sydney was going to be an expensive place to hang about and I'd have to start sorting out an income stream before I got there. I updated my résumé and prepared several versions of it (from downgrading my skills and experience for interim jobs to bring in the money, to listing my strengths and achievements in great detail for potentially exciting career opportunities). What I was not prepared to do, however, was to amend my résumé in a manner that would fit people's expectations of a successful career progression. While I could have easily claimed to have worked at the Miramonte or for a friend's or other family's business over the four years preceding my stint at the hotel, I noted all the various stops of my journey under a header 'Overseas Travel'. On occasion I had people offer advice as how to restructure my résumé to make it look more professional but I would always respond with defensiveness. I was who I was – and I was happy to stand by it.

This was a sensitive subject for me. I was well aware that I might be hitting a wall but I still believed that the right opportunity would present itself and that there would be someone out there who would appreciate my versatile background. Once ready to roll, I searched the various online job sites to get inspired and started sending my résumé and corresponding cover letters to any position advertised that I felt I could handle for the foreseeable future. At the same time I also put my feelers out for a place to live. Six days after arriving in Sydney I moved into my new abode with my own little first-floor terrace in a shared house in the best possible location in Surry Hills (a buzzing inner-city suburb known for its stylish cultural and café scene). However, on the job front I soon found myself sympathising with The Beatles, having to deal with rejection in a confidence-crushing manner. Well, I actually wasn't really rejected, I just never heard back from anyone – be it an agency or a direct employer. And every follow-up with a call turned out just the same.

While trying to stay positive, at times I got rather frustrated. I found it hard not to get affected by the sight of homeless people, often older than I, and I would wonder how they could ever get back on their feet if it was difficult for *me* to find a job. I couldn't help but think that if all those years back I hadn't had the help and support of my family, friends and the many amazing people that I met along the way, there would have been a good chance that I would be sitting on one of those street corners too. Considering how the stress had affected my health at the time – and with not more than 1000 dollars in my pocket – I would have been in real trouble had I been left on my own. That thought-process provoked something in me that had a good chance of finally pushing me into 'that hole'. My financial situation was not good; I was 46 and *no-one wanted me*. Focusing on homeless people and the 'what if's now gave my situation a dramatic edge that wasn't helping my case. Rather, it was very much counterproductive. I had to give myself a kick and look past it all, using that experience as nothing other than a motivation to make a difference at some point in the future, once I was in a position to do so.

What I needed right then was a good (self-) pep-talk and to flip that familiar switch in my brain. And, as always, it worked without fail. Before long I had two calls inviting me to attend interviews as well as a couple of written responses to further job applications. In the end I decided that a casual position would be the way forward for the time being and I accepted a job in Facilities Management at the new Sydney International Convention, Exhibition and Entertainment Precinct. If all went well, my bank account would soon be looking healthy and it would then be time to attend to that fiercely burning fire and do 'my own thing' again.

The new date for the hearing at the court of appeal was set for 29 March 2017. The court requested that a signatory of both parties be present at the hearing, signalling the likelihood of an attempt by the court to have the matter settled on the day. Over the previous months, and up until the very last minute, several more pleadings were submitted by either of the parties and the night before D-day my brother, Heiner, and his company's CFO, Josef, met with me at my lawyers' office in Munich – I had flown in from Sydney a couple of days earlier – to talk about our strategy and the minimum amount that we would be prepared to accept. Early the following day my lawyer, Alexander, Josef and I (to make it look less like a family affair we had decided that it would be better for Josef, rather than Heiner, to attend) embarked on our journey to the hearing.

Upon entering the higher regional court in Saarbruecken seven hours later, the first person we encountered was Walter Schmidt of GUBSE. Displaying a very relaxed and confident demeanour, Walter greeted us with a friendly nod and a slight grin on his face and proceeded to point out the direction of the in-house café, the bathrooms and the appointed courtroom. Rather stunned, I turned to Alexander and commented that something wasn't quite right. Considering Walter's hate-filled eyes and questionable behaviour during our previous encounters at court, his happy-go-lucky manner now was a somewhat unsettling sight – not least in view of what was at stake.

Once the hearing started and following routine questions directed at the legal representatives of either party, the presiding judge declared that he and his co-judges had already had a busy day and that rather than wasting too much time he would plainly read out the current assessment of the senate. (In Germany, the judges at the court of appeal discharge their judicial duties in senates, each of which consists of a presiding judge and further judges.) What followed was a very blunt assassination of each and every one of our claims, with the senate's main findings of the actual and legal considerations – as conveyed by the judge – all turning out in GUBSE's favour.

The scenario that we faced was beyond surreal. While GUBSE and their lawyer, Dr Anton, kept their facial expressions frozen, we were in absolute shock to the point that Alexander asked to leave the court room for 10 minutes (together with Josef and I). When we reentered the room, Alexander set out to prove why neither of the senate's assertions were correct. The presiding judge, in a rather condescending tone, kept interrupting him, sounding annoyed while looking at his watch. In regards to the question whether the SIHOT trust module had been functional at the time of installation (the substantial evidence that we had already submitted in that context aside) Alexander suggested that the court would at least have to hear a subject witness. The presiding judge simply looked at GUBSE and responded on their behalf that it surely wouldn't be possible to retrieve the relevant version of the software, would it?! There was no attempt to have the case settled and there was no reason whatsoever to have a signatory of either of the parties present – never mind that the CFO of my brother's company had travelled 550 kilometres to attend the hearing as previously requested by the court. It was so odd that it was hard to grasp.

The presiding judge was flanked by a female judge on either side, one of who took the occasional note while her colleague just kept staring into space (I couldn't help but wonder if she felt just as 'uncomfortable' as I did). In the end, the judge concluded that the final ruling would be delivered on 26 April, in a month's time. Alexander announced that we would be requesting a revision (for the judgment to be reviewed by the

Federal Supreme Court). We said our goodbyes to GUBSE and left the courtroom in utter bewilderment.

Once we had closed the heavy doors of the courthouse behind us, Alexander remarked that he had experienced a lot during his career as a lawyer, but this was certainly a first. We had our theories as to what may have happened, but that wasn't going to help our case. Alexander was convinced that several of the judge's assertions were legally incorrect and unlawful and what we had to do now – and prior to the announcement of the final judgment – was to submit yet another writ to the court outlining why the senate's view was flawed. Up to that juncture I had always been fully confident that I would walk away with compensation of some sort (I never once doubted that it would be in the seven-figures). The possibility of completely losing the whole case (and being liable for the legal fees of the other party) had never even entered our minds, regardless of the outcome at the district court. Ours was such an obvious case of deception and betrayal; every dollar that we had claimed had its justification and every assertion that we had made had been supported by substantial evidence. Not to mention the commission that I was owed in accordance with my contract with GUBSE. How a legal institution could disregard any or all of that was way beyond my comprehension.

I returned to Australia in a very different headspace to what I had envisioned. With the potential scenario of losing my long battle for justice looming, reality hit and despair and fear set in. The legal costs of the past few years and the loan from my brother, together with the business monies that I had been determined to repay, had added up to an overall mountain of debt. The thought of it made me choke. It wasn't just that the prospect of doing my 'own thing' again anytime soon was evaporating into thin air, but the vision of working a random permanent job and paying off my debts until I was too old to move now had me crumble under a big flood of tears.

In the end, the final verdict of the court of appeal reflected the senate's assessment at the hearing weeks earlier and our claim for both compensation and commission was dismissed. Regarding our request for revision, we were not granted the right to appeal.

(Interestingly enough, in order to take a case to the Federal Supreme Court, the relevant senate of the appellate court – the same senate whose judgment was at the bottom of the request for appeal – has to give the seal of approval.) Alexander and his superior now strongly suggested that we make use of the alternative relief of submitting a complaint to the Federal Supreme Court regarding the non-admission of our appeal. The prerequisites were evidently very high but they appeared to be met in our case: the reasoning provided within the adjudgement contained significant errors and legal misjudgments of the court, and the senate had infringed the prohibition of arbitrariness. These points would now have to be examined by a lawyer who was accredited to deal with the Federal Supreme Court (there are only 42 such specifically selected lawyers in Germany).

I had been so ready to put it all behind me and move on but I couldn't afford to, nor was Heiner prepared to (after all, the legal case was now under his company's name). There were going to be further significant costs involved and Heiner, once again, was going to step in. All I could do at that stage was to put my hand up for as many shifts as I could possibly get at the Convention Centre (including late nights and weekends to make use of the applicable penalty rates during these times) and to use the remainder of the time to sort out my head.

Chapter 34

What now?

I ended up working in facilities management (at the Convention Centre) for seven months. It was a completely new experience and a good 'interim project' that I quite enjoyed. Although on a casual basis, I worked an average of five days per week and used the remainder of my time to gain back perspective and to get settled again. In July that year (2017) I moved into an apartment up the road in Paddington – sharing with one other – and finally, six years on, moved my few remaining belongings out of storage.

At the end of November I was offered the role of general manager of a new and soon to be opened boutique hotel in Surry Hills. It was a cool, unconventional project and I was excited about having found what had the potential of becoming my Australian version of the Miramonte. As I soon came to realise, however, the Miramonte was unique and re-creating my experience was not something that could be forced. Always conscious of keeping my options open and not succumbing to the pressures that reality was presenting, I, again, decided that a casual job – or two – would be the go for the time being. This time round I went for the position of event supervisor at the Australian National Maritime Museum, located in Darling Harbour, just down the road from the Sydney Convention, Exhibition and Entertainment Precinct. The setting was very inspiring and the events were varied, ranging from award nights to product or book launches, business events and celebrations of all kinds.

Outside of work I resolved to get my own book finalised and to start looking into publishing options. It had been three and a half years since I had completed the first draft and while I was still waiting for life to write the final chapter (in regards to the conclusion of my legal case), the fact that it could potentially take another couple of years for that point to come around made me re-think its ending. I felt that unless I made the book happen now, my passion for it would dissipate and my years of work might never see the light of day. Working on my manuscript had always put me into a blissful state and this was going to be a good time to revel in that. I needed an exciting project to work on and who knew where it might take me?

* * *

Epilogue

On 17 January 2019 I awoke to an email from my lawyer advising me that the Federal Supreme Court had rejected our complaint regarding the non-admission of our appeal (and with this our request for revision). As for a reason, the judicial decision stated *'Reasoning is omitted, because it would not be suitable to contribute to the clarification of the conditions under which a revision is to be allowed'.*

After nine years, my legal battle had come to an end. And while the outcome was supremely incomprehensible, there was no benefit in further analysing it. It was time to move on. Justice hadn't prevailed but at least I can say with absolute certainty that I had done everything in my power to fight for it, leaving no space for potential future regrets.

Following the initial shock, I was overcome by a surge of energy and yet another 'just you wait!' defining moment. This was not the end of me. It was part of my journey and I was ready for the next chapter.

'You have to take risks. We will only understand the miracle of life fully when we allow the unexpected to happen'
– Paulo Coelho

Printed in Poland
by Amazon Fulfillment
Poland Sp. z o.o., Wrocław

53372857R00171